T0367847

MAKING PEOPLE PAY

The Economic Sociology of Taxation

MAKING PEOPLE PAY

The Economic Sociology of Taxation

Sibichen K. Mathew

PARTRIDGE

Revised Edition 2018

ISBN:	Hardcover	978-1-4828-0150-7
	Softcover	978-1-4828-0149-1
	eBook	978-1-4828-0148-4

Print information available on the last page.

To order additional copies of this book, contact
Partridge India
000 800 10062 62
orders.india@partridgepublishing.com

www.partridgepublishing.com/india

S. S. N. MOORTHY, IRS
Chairman, CBDT &
Ex-Officio Spl. Secy.
to the Govt. of India

GOVERNMENT OF INDIA
MINISTRY OF FINANCE/DEPARTMENT OF REVENUE
CENTRAL BOARD OF DIRECT TAXES
NORTH BLOCK, NEW DELHI - 110001

Foreword to First Edition

Taxation and tax compliance are at crossroads in an age of rapid economic transformation all over the world. Globalization has heightened international mobility of economic activity. Countries need to be competitive not only in creating an environment that promotes entrepreneurship but also in providing an efficient and effective tax administration. Research and planning on reforms in taxation and tax administration are at the top of the agenda of most of the countries and organizations like OECD, World Bank etc for quite some time. India has spearheaded its tax reforms much before many other countries in the world. It is in the process of ensuring the successful implementation of legislative and administrative innovations such as new Direct Tax Code and uniform GST. I find that this book is being released at the most appropriate time, as there are a lot of discussions in the public domain on how to ensure better tax compliance in a globalized world.

It is very interesting to observe that the author has analyzed the entire gamut of taxation and tax compliance with a social sciences perspective. He has analyzed the historical, political, economic and sociological dimensions of tax evasion and tax enforcement in the global context. It is proved that the payment of tax is not just an economic decision but depends on various social, political and psychological factors. He has also conducted two systematic empirical studies to understand the why and how of tax evasion. The study on taxpayers who were searched by the income tax department is a pioneering attempt in the area of tax compliance research. The insights that have emerged from the studies are of great policy significance. The analysis and discussions given in the book are of greater academic and policy relevance not only for developing countries like India but also for several developed countries in a world of transnational economic mobility.

The book is the result of several years of painful research and analysis. I congratulate the author on presenting the results in a simple, systematic and easily comprehensible style. This book not only will be of great interest to all taxpayers but can give better insights into various categories of readers such as policy analysts, tax practitioners, tax officials, social scientists and students.

S. S. N. Moorthy, IRS
Chairman
Central Board of Direct Taxes
New Delhi

MAKING PEOPLE PAY: A 'JUDICIAL' VIEW

M.N. Venkatachaliah
Former Chief Justice of India

Someone made a cynical and uncharitable remark that for one half of us intellectual effort is painful and for the other half, impossible. The eminently readable "Making People Pay" by Sibichen Mathew indicates that great intellectual effort is still enjoyable for men of Mathew's genre. We thank God for such gifted men who think deeply and passionately on the implications of the role of the Government in one of its important departments.

Power of taxation, it is said, is a fundamental attribute of Sovereignty. Constitutional provisions touching the powers of taxation are not grants of the power to tax. They are limitations on the otherwise unlimited and illimitable sovereign power. All modern governments have eschewed the philosophy of unbridled economic individualism. In modern governments, taxation is not a mere means of raising money to meet the expenses of government. It has a social and economic mission. Fiscal tools are part of government's repertoire for securing social and economic change. "I pay my taxes and buy civilization" said the eminent American Judge Oliver Wendell Holmes.

Advancement of science and technology and economic prosperity has made life busier and not necessarily better. Knowledge is power either for good or for evil. If growth of knowledge is not accompanied by a corresponding growth of wisdom, knowledge will turn out to be a power for evil. Amartya Sen writing in his "Idea of Justice" says: *"There is considerable empirical evidence that even as people in many parts of the world have become richer, with much more income to spend in real terms than ever before, they have not felt particularly happier than before. Cogently reasoned and empirically backed doubts have been raised about the implicit premise of no-nonsense advocates of economic growth as an all-purpose remedy of all economic ailments, including misery and unhappiness, by asking the question, to quote from the title of a justly famous essay by Richard Easterlin, 'Will raising the income of all raise the happiness of all?"*

Tax policies and more particularly the way they are administered and the men and women who administer them have incurred the criticism of being an uncivilized regime. Big sharks get away baring their teeth or paving their way-out with gold. It is the small fry, the honest tax payer, who is always at the receiving end. It is there that the dramatic preponderance of the power and might of the state is pitched against the hapless citizen. There is an old story of the eleventh Century of Lady Godiva making a deal with her husband, the Earl of Mercia, that he would lighten the tax-burden on the impoverished subjects of Coventry if she rode naked on a white horse through the town, she did. She became the patron-saint of tax relief. The honest tax-payer needs the metaphor of another Lady Godiva, this time a non-exhibitionist one.

Why do people disobey the law in many countries? The reason perhaps is that the cost and burden of obedience out-weighs the great rewards of disobedience. The Task Force on Direct Taxes in India admitted, that “What induces people to comply with tax-laws is an enigma”. Direct tax collections have gone-up substantially in the past years. But less than three percent of the population is assessed to Income tax in India. Numerically the country is under-assessed. There is a great and thriving parallel economy. Of about three lakh thirty seven thousand crore of direct tax receipts, seven cities of the country alone account for about eighty per cent of the collections.

At the end, I must congratulate Sibichen Mathew for this scholarly work. The work has extensive research back-up of the history of taxes, experience of other countries and data from the field. Some of the anecdotes are really hilarious. I refrain from calling the work 'monumental' for I know the tyranny of superlatives. This work, in a non-trivial sense, gives great credit to the Department that it has and can retain such brilliant and creative minds. I have enjoyed reading this book. It has its own wry humor of the tax-man. The book amply rewards the reader.

DEDICATED TO

Amma,
the source of my energy and enthusiasm;

Rani,
whose love, inspiration and understanding make me confident and optimistic;

Nirmal and **Nilima,**
who had been waiting to throw away my laptop immediately after the delivery of this 'baby'.

PREFACE TO THE CURRENT REVISED EDITION

Taxes are and always will be a bitter pill for people across the world. Governments are yet to find a reservoir of holy oil or a land mass containing precious stones in the laboratory of nature so that they can leave citizens in peace without taxing them anymore. There is no other way other than sugar coating the pill and making people aware of its benefits. Though there is absolutely no scope for reducing its frequency or dosage in an era of economic slowdown and depletion of resources, governments across the globe are reinventing their best strategies to make the process smoother, if not totally hassle free. Every country expects investments from outside, but adopting a consistent and optimum position that ensures overall equity and justice amidst global tax competition is a challenge for many.

Taking clue from the responses, expectations and criticisms of the taxpayers from Generation Y, many tax administrations have rolled out systematic designs that demonstrate to the public that they are equitable, fair, transparent and friendly. However the Generation Y individuals and entities expect much more than this! They demand accountability for every payment made by them. What do I get back? The representative of the individualistic culture asks this in sharp contrast to the fundamental theoretical and pragmatic premise that there cannot be any quid pro quo in tax transactions. Even when the governments emphasise that no amendments are possible or desirable to the conventional but robust tax principles in a highly stratified society, the taxpayers retort forcefully: 'Tell us then, where did it go and how much benefit did the community receive from it?'.

It is true that tax administrations have absolute powers, technology and potential to deploy much more ingenious measures to track every penny earned by a person, establish machineries to capture the due much before it lands on the taxpayer's hands, impose stringent penalties, invade his castle, intrude into his secret world, injure him mentally and physically, and impose restrictions on how he earns income. Will this ensure compliance? Will this alone could instil a commitment to pay taxes? Is the human action of payment of direct taxes, parting with a portion of money that one earned, considered merely a mandatory mechanical process and therefore there is no existence of or significance for any emotions, logic, past experience, expectation, or comparison?

The attempt in this book is to explore the fiscal-sociological dimensions of tax policies, tax compliance and tax enforcement. The theoretical and the empirical analysis done in the book provide answers to some of the questions raised in the foregoing paragraphs. As the revised edition of the book is being published, it is pertinent to acknowledge the wide appreciation received for the earlier edition from various scholars, policy makers, taxpayers, tax practitioners and students. Taxes are here to stay to bring in smiles on all citizens. But how long it would take for all of us to pay our taxes with a smile to a fair, transparent, efficient and friendly taxman?

BEFORE YOU READ

This book is not for everyone. This is for those who want to live in a civilized state. The book is not aimed to proselytize for a tax state. Nor does it advocate a tax haven. And least about a prospective tax-free heaven. It only tries to answer certain mundane but frequently asked questions: Why pay taxes? What prompts people to hate taxes? What happens if not paid? How to make the payment less painful? Is paying taxes, a matter of money or a matter of mind?

Observing people and their behaviour and understanding the patterns that shape their decisions were of immense interest to me since early in my life. I tried to comprehend and appreciate the principles of and practices in natural sciences, where individuals and their environment were dissected to understand their inherent properties, composition and factors of sustenance. Even while engaging in experiments in the chemistry lab, I was puzzled at the rationale of duality created in knowledge as natural sciences and social sciences. Is natural science really 'natural'? Does social science have more to do with nature than 'social'? Natural science had lost its naturalness the moment man started acting on it. I found that the distinction between both the sciences was increasingly getting blurred. As most of the changes happening in the world are due to human interventions, one needs a social science perspective to understand them. It was thus clear to me that, to understand an event or a situation one has to know the people behind it. And in order to understand people, one needs to understand their attitudinal and behavioural patterns as well as the forms relationships take in an interactive environment.

The above paradigm switch in my thought process might be an important factor that propelled me to turn to the study of social sciences. The decade-long training and reading in social sciences were indeed stimulating. The opportunities to learn the finer theoretical and methodological themes that dominated the intelligentsia in different periods of history and different cultural contexts have enriched my understanding. I sincerely wished to be an arm chair academician at that point of time.

Gradually I realized that it is easy to dissect individuals and groups in the cozy libraries, seminar halls, and project reports. It is not that comfortable to face people as they grapple with issues and challenges that emerge day by day. That is what I found when I joined the Indian civil services. My job as a taxman was not without challenges. I was seriously involved in the exercise of deepening of the tax base, presuming that figures scribbled in the returns represented just a portion of the actual. But within a few years I realized that the tax potentiality lies not in the microscopic minority within but the vast majority outside the system. The road to widening the taxpayer base can never be smooth unless there is appropriate policy intervention, infrastructural transformation, and effective service delivery. The efforts of the government in this regard started bearing fruit with every little step in the right direction. But, it was not clear why a country with considerable tax elasticity and tax potentiality found it difficult to attract more people to its tax rolls and gain more money to the direct taxes kitty.

I started my search for the answers several years ago. Slowly I realized the need for a systematic macro analysis of the issues. I was in fact plunging myself into what many call 'research' on the subject. Is tax aversion unique to some countries? My analysis proved not. There are several historical, political, and sociological factors that deter people from paying taxes globally. It is not just economic factors that determine tax compliance as it is widely thought of. The attempt in this book was to analyze those factors. Theoretical analyses given in the book were aimed to provide an understanding of the subject of tax compliance with a global perspective at the macro level. It threw up certain valid questions.

Why people in some countries comply better than in others? Why is tax evasion not frowned upon in some countries and is deemed as disgraceful in some other countries?

Any theoretical analysis on the behaviour of people is incomplete without analysis of primary data. Any statistical analysis based on secondary data cannot translate finer emotional and sociological facts in the realm of individuals and groups. An empirical analysis is imperative if one has to understand the why and how of tax non-compliance. A scientific analysis of the attitudes and perceptions of a sample of taxpayers can provide valuable insights not only into issues such as tax compliance and honesty at the personal level but also about interconnected social traits such as trust, reciprocity, and altruism at the societal level. A sample from a developing country like India which has been in the process of implementing very aggressive and sincere fiscal reforms in the last two decades, can provide valuable data for various other similarly placed countries. I have provided a methodological critique on the study of tax compliance before describing the results of the empirical studies conducted in this book

A unique attempt was also made here to understand tax evasion and tax enforcement through a study of tax evaders (or who were branded so) themselves. As a researcher, I was really surprised at the frank and genuine responses of the sample of taxpayers who were searched by the Indian Income Tax Department. The interviews and case studies with them have, without exception, cumulatively and intellectually enriched me as they helped me to understand the behavioural patterns, attitudes, perceptions, and expectations of taxpayers in general.

It would be bliss if one can get rid of all taxes. But in a world of widespread inequity and inequality, income taxation is an economic-sociological instrument for overall well being of the people. Countries like India and other developing countries need to nurture their increasingly affluent citizenry in their endeavor to plug the inequalities. Globalization demands not only efficient, fair, and transparent tax states, but also increased tax co-operation to tackle tax evasion.

Please take note of this disclaimer. All views expressed in this book are my personal views. The book is not from a taxman or a civil servant but from a social researcher. The sole aim of the book is to provide a new analytical framework in the study of and approach towards tax evasion and tax enforcement.

ACKNOWLEDGEMENTS

What do I have that was not received?

I am grateful to the guidance, inspiration, and support of many near and dear ones in completing this book

My teachers at the respective institutions where I have studied have rekindled the spirit of enquiry and research within me. To name only a few, directly under whom I learnt the steps in scientific method: Rev Dr E J Thomas and (Late) Rev Dr Jose Murickan (Loyola College, Trivandrum), Prof. T K Oommen (Jawaharlal Nehru University, New Delhi), Prof Chiranjib Sen (Indian Institute of Management, Bangalore), Prof Lakshman Singh (Bharathiar University, Coimbatore), Prof Larry Schroeder (Syracuse University, New York State) and Prof. Mukul Asher (Lee Kuan Yew School of Public Policy, National University of Singapore). I fondly remember them and the lessons of life.

I am proud to be part of an organization that has a pool of brilliant officers who happily share their knowledge with utmost humility and sense of devotion. I have immensely gained from each one of them. I was fortunate to have only mentors and not bosses throughout my career. My respectful regards to all of them. I am grateful to my current mentors Shri K Madhavan Nair and Shri G M Belagali, for appreciating my academic endeavors.

My desire to write a book would have remained just a dream, but for the guidance and assistance of a few persons. Mr K P Karunakaran, my first mentor, instilled in me the much needed self-confidence. He took pains to sift the sense and nonsense and gave me very valuable suggestions after examining the draft. I am profoundly grateful to him. Mr Cheri Jacob, Mr Manjunath and Mr Anil Kumar scanned the manuscript to reduce the errors. Sebastian, my dear friend and Mini Jose, my dear sister were with me all along providing ideas and suggestions.

Sajjive Balakrishnan is a divinely gifted cartoonist. He needs only a minute to finish a caricature. I was amazed by the way he comprehended my themes and quickly converted his finest strokes to wonderful images. I am very thankful to him for finding time in spite of his busy schedule as the Public Relations Officer of the Income Tax Department.

My heartfelt gratitude to Marudhachalam for data processing, Balaji for the cover design, and Ramesh, Yashpal and Keshava for the layout. I am also thankful to all those who helped me at various stages of my study. My friend Dr Senu Kurien George took time to go through the manuscript for the second edition and has offered valuable suggestions. I am grateful to him.

I am grateful to the Government of India for providing an environment that encourages scientific temper and rational analysis. I am thankful to the librarians of Jawaharlal Nehru University, New Delhi; Indian Institute of Management, Bangalore; Syracuse University, New York State; National Institute of Public Finance and Policy, New Delhi; Indian Institute of Public Administration, New Delhi; Library of the Ministry of Finance, Government of India; and Nehru Memorial Museum and Library, New Delhi; and also to the web administrators and providers of thousands of valuable data bases in the cyber space.

Dr N K Singh and the Global Vision Publishers brought out the first edition of this book in January 2010 and I express my gratitude to them.

I am grateful to Penguin Books India Pvt Ltd and Partridge Publishing for bringing out the 2013 revised edition. I thank the sincere efforts of Gemma Ramos and Dia Mercado at Partridge for making the revised edition print ready.

I apologize for inadvertent errors and omissions, if any.

CONTENTS

CONTENTS

CONTENTS

Text Boxes

SOME CLARIFICATIONS

Preferred neutral terms are used to avoid sexist terms to the extent possible. However in some places the pronoun 'he' and its derivatives are used. They signify both genders and transgender.

Though the word 'tax' is used repeatedly, the focus in the book is on income tax.

The comments and analyses given on specific instances, trends and tendencies may be construed as descriptive and explanatory in that context and should not be viewed as critical or judgemental.

All decimals in the tables are corrected to the nearest whole numbers. All amounts are given in Indian rupees (₹) unless specified otherwise. In chi-square tables, '*' indicates significance at five per cent level and '**' indicates significance at one percent level.

CHAPTER-1

INTRODUCTION

Paying Taxes: A Matter of Money or Mind?

If English language speakers ever come together to fix the most unpopular English word, the word 'tax' would top the list. The same is the case in most other languages; 'tax' indeed has a deplorable status. The word generates such a dreadful feel that often the most difficult tasks are referred to as 'taxing'. Not only taxes, anything connected to the word 'tax' is widely considered to be an unwelcome stuff - be it a person, an object, or an event. This ominous hate-list does not spare taxmen (tax officials), tax laws, or tax procedures as all of them signify forces that grimly restrict the freedom to keep with oneself all the money one has earned. Throughout history, tax collectors were hated in all cultures; the Bible records instances where people considered tax collectors as outcasts and equated them with sinners. Since time immemorial, legitimate and illegitimate rulers of various nation-states used their might to collect legitimate and illegitimate taxes to fill their personal exchequers. The historic shifts from the feudal to the mercantile social structure ushered in major changes in our ways of life. Yet, when it comes to governance, the 'tax' mechanism has remained the one constant that the state relies on to garner resources for its functioning. Even in our contemporary times, where democracy has become the dominant political institution, tax remains; tax proposals are debated and voted upon in the Houses of people's representatives. But tax enactments are still unpleasantly received by the people.

Man engages in myriad activities to earn his bread and butter. The necessity and the urge to earn an income to satisfy his primary and secondary needs force him to maximize his income earning potential. During the course of the activities, he subjects himself to a network of transactions some of which are voluntary and some others involuntary. For example, a person who is engaged in the business of selling grocery enters into definite transactions with consumers, purchasers, commission agents, transporters, etc. At the same time, he also discharges his liability to the local administration and other service departments for their services. Sellers, purchasers, and consumers all pay for the transaction costs related to such transactions. Taxes on goods and services are considered transaction costs by the people. By and large they are paid for then and there, though there could be instances of unrecorded transactions as well. There are instances where sellers and service providers avoid collecting taxes to please the customers and clients. More shrewd ones collect the necessary taxes but fail to pay the same to the government account. All transactions of this kind end within a specific period of time and the persons involved either make net gain or net loss by the end of the time period. The net gain is translated and understood as income and it is subsequently utilized for various consumption and investment activities. It is only at this stage that the issue of 'income tax' comes into the picture. Such a tax, which in real terms may be understood as the state's share in the profit/gain, is ascertained and valued only after debiting all deductible expenses. In short, the income tax department demands the tax due from a person after he has pocketed the net income, though a part or whole is already deducted as income tax during the transaction stage itself. But the person finds it painful to part with a portion of his hard-earned profit/income as taxes. Thus, unlike in the cases of other transaction taxes, people are wary of income tax. Hence, from a social perspective, people need to take affirmative decisions with respect to the giving of income taxes.

Visible and invisible taxes

By now it must be obvious that the 'pain' of the income tax is a perception problem. Taxes on goods and services are often merged with the total price of such goods and services and the tax burden is less visible to the consumers. The focus of the consumer while finalizing a particular transaction is on many aspects such as the quality of the product or service, the conditions of guarantee and warranty, the competitive advantage, the delivery and installation, and the taxes, etc. In such a scenario, taxes are only one of the many concerns at the time of finalizing a transaction and get divided attention in the decision-making process. In most cases, aspects other than taxation claim priority and the addition on account of taxation gets overlooked.

However, in the case of income tax, the context of payment is rarely merged with any other decision. Even the fact that the income tax is withheld or deducted during the transaction would not make much difference to a person as it is credited to his/her account and there is always a possibility of claiming a refund. And in many cases the assessments do result in tax refunds, some times with interest. Huge amounts are refunded to taxpayers every year as they tend to file the return showing the net income after making various claims. However, the percentage of tax returns subjected to audit (or scrutiny) is very less and thus many of the claims of the taxpayers go unchecked. It is also true that in several cases, particularly where there are contract receipts, tax withholding is seen as receipts due at a later date since refunds are considered as additional revenue received in another year (though not accounted that way). This is very much true in countries were the refund process takes considerable time and taxpayers are burdened with another transaction cost in the form of bribes to tax officials.

But the aggregate income tax payment towards the end (called in some countries self-assessment tax) and after the financial year (during the assessment year) is almost a solitary and exclusive event for the income earner and it is not conditional. The attention is undivided and therefore he needs to take only one decision: How much should I pay? All other decisions like how much one should show as one's expenses, how much tax incentives one should claim, etc are related to the above decision regarding payment. Often, these related decisions are taken much after the professional or business transaction is over. While entering into a transaction a person weighs the payoff as against the immediate advantage consequent to the transaction. However, at the time of payment of income tax the person has nothing much to think about the possible receivable benefit. Rather, one gets worried about the burden relating to the payoff. Thus, income tax becomes a much more visible tax as compared with the taxes on goods and services. Therefore the extent of compliance to income tax is a decision which is taken very consciously.

Visible and invisible benefits

While engaging in an occupation or a transaction, the rational human being weighs the extent of benefits he receives. He is able to observe and experience the benefits accrued either instantly or within a short while. Thus, humans are not only rational in their decision-making but also evaluative about their contributions and efforts and the resultant gains. Thus, if a person makes a pay-off as income tax, even if it is a charge on income rather than a contribution *per se*, he would definitely evaluate the necessity and rationale of such an action. The moral instinct in persons would prompt them to evaluate the benefit received not only by them in return, but also by their immediate community or society at large. While one is forced to pay a cess on higher education along with income tax as a percentage of total tax due, one would invariably desire to see additional opportunities for higher education to the rural and underprivileged masses. Thus, the personal and social reciprocity from the state to which one has credited the income tax is a determinant in tax compliance decisions. This is more evident in countries with high tax rates coupled with shallow tax enforcement in a governance environment of inefficiency and corruption. In such countries where governments and bureaucracy are seen as corrupt and inefficient, public trust on the state is weak. Every action of the state is watched closely with suspicion. It may be that while taxes are more visible, the consequent services from the state are invisible. This apparent imbalance, as perceived by the tax payer, affects the tax compliance to a greater extent. At the same time the inherent presence of moral and social traits prompt some cross-sections of the people to comply with taxes for the sake of 'universal good' in spite of the invisibility of benefits. Another cross-section may act out of fear or may act for prestige and some others prefer to take risks and subsequently fail to comply.

INTRODUCTION

What is income tax compliance?

Simply defined, 'tax compliance' may be said to be the act of disclosing one's entire income (on an annual basis) and then paying the due taxes accurately. In fact, various scholars have defined 'tax compliance' more or less in this manner. Taxpayer compliance has been defined by Roth, Scholz and Witte (1989) as the compliance of the taxpayer with the reporting requirements such as prompt filing of tax returns and accurate reporting of the tax liability as per laws, rules and judicial decisions. Seen from the other end, Kinsey (1984) defines 'non-compliance' as the intentional or unintentional failure of taxpayers to meet their tax obligations. As per the US Internal Revenue Service (IRS) definition, compliance means that the taxpayer files all required returns within the due dates and that such returns accurately report tax liability in accordance with the Internal Revenue Code, regulations, and court decisions applicable at the time the return is filed. In a nutshell, one can state that there are innumerable definitions for tax compliance. Concisely, the following defaults can be grouped under the head 'tax non-compliance':

a. Non-reporting of income
b. Claiming excess deductions from taxable income
c. Claiming excess tax rebates or incentives
d. Wrong claims for exemptions
e. Incorrect calculation and payment of taxes, interests and penalties
f. Non-filing or delay in filing of tax returns
g. Non-compliance with statutory provisions and procedures

Though one can arrive at a simplistic answer to the question, 'what is non-compliance', finding an answer to the related question 'why non-compliance' is very challenging. One can perhaps start with some of the Frequently Asked Questions (FAQs) that taxpayers and citizens constantly pose globally.

Why should I pay?

A person driving down to spend a weekend in the suburbs with his family finds a new broad underpass recently constructed to ease the traffic congestion. Though happy to take the car through the neatly laden underpass, the person may feel upset when he finds a toll gate just as he crossed the underpass. Even when the service is visible then and there, there is a hesitation to pay for it. If that is the general human response, one can possibly predict even worse reactions when there is no visible service at all.

Since taking a decision in respect of the nature of tax compliance has substantial cost-benefit implications, it is but natural that on the individual front, there is a very cognizant effort to analyze the scenario in the 'context involved'; that is, the social, economic and political settings. The decision is taken after a careful analysis of several possible apprehensions: What is the extent of the benefit for the person? How much of the deducted amount reaches the needy? How much do others pay? How 'taxing' the whole process is? How risky it is? The following are some of the questions raised by taxpayers across societies and cultures:

Why should I pay

...if I don't get any benefit?

Basically, tax is a charge on the income of the individual and it has nothing to do with the services the state delivers to society at large by using the capital derived from the individual. Though a *quid-pro-quo* is absent with respect to taxation, 'hot' debates over tax utilization is alive in the public domain. This can affect the decisions of taxpayers when it comes to voluntary compliance. There can be a nagging feeling that the tax one pays has no proportionate benefit. Even in some of the most advanced countries where the national budgets and expenditure are collected and spent in a most transparent manner or even in countries where the bulk of the population possesses essential civic awareness, people protest against higher taxes. In many of the developing countries including India, the tax protests (though not very vociferous but general it may effectively be aimed at specific tax proposals), have also increasingly centered around the feeling that the contributions of taxpayers are not being reciprocated by the state. The question is 'why should I pay if I don't get any benefit out of it.?'

INTRODUCTION

Why should I pay

...if what I pay is siphoned off?

If a country is perceived as very corrupt and inefficient, the taxpayers' perception would be that the taxes collected are being siphoned away by people in the power structure. This doubt would get validated if scams and bribery scandals are reported frequently in the media. Such a report would affect public perception and this would in turn affect the legitimacy of the tax system. In such circumstances taxpayers may feel less committed to paying taxes voluntarily. While taxes tend to be more visible to the public eye and the services are perceived to be poor (or invisible), the taxpayer response would be negative.

Why should I pay

...if what I pay is inefficiently applied?

In some contexts, the perception is that tax funds are not efficiently utilized by the government and the various agencies. In such a scenario, the prevailing sentiment is one of apathy towards the system of tax collection. This will be an important deciding factor for taxpayers, especially in countries where citizens are aware of the various channels through which funds are flowing, the various sectors where funds are required, and also the extent of attention given to deserving sectors. Bureaucratic inefficiency and lackadaisical attitude while performing public service make taxpayers feel that the amount collected from them is not efficiently applied.

Why should I pay

...if it is such a hassle to follow the procedures?

It is a joke among tax practitioners that even tax officers depend on the former to prepare their tax returns. This reveals a lot about the complexity that is perceived regarding tax returns. Perhaps it could be one reason for the thriving profession of tax consultants all over the world. This is in spite of the fact that many countries have introduced simplified e-filing procedures for tax returns. Unlike other laws, tax laws are always in a state of flux and the tax rates and slabs keep on changing year after year. Laws themselves undergo several frequent amendments so as to add, withdraw or change provisions pertaining to incentives, rebates, deductions, exemptions, etc. The fact that there are several such tax incentives built on the ever shifting conditions make tax laws bulkier. Thus, there is an inevitable legal complexity to ensure right tax treatment for different taxpayer categories.

Why should I pay

...if it is so difficult for me to understand the legal intricacies?

It is a truism that acquisition of knowledge and its application by individuals are guided by perception regarding its utility. 'Interest' is also a guiding force in choosing what to learn. Citizens shy away from the 'tax realm' by invoking these very same parameters negatively, i.e. boring and not exactly useful ! Learning about tax laws and its procedures is indeed utilitarian. And one should evoke interest for one's own sake. Although 'ignorance of law is not an excuse' is a widely accepted maxim, citizens make no conscious effort to learn the various nuances of the law. This is all the more true in respect of laws such as tax laws which are perceived as inherently complex and technical. For taxpayers, asking a tax practitioner to take the right decision on their behalf is considered an easy option rather than asking 'the expert' as to what are the possible options in a particular situation. The taxpayer putting options in front of the practitioner for evaluation is a near total impossibility. So one can least expect people to take concerted and sincere steps to read the tax laws by themselves.

The facts that tax laws are perceived as complex and that there is a tendency to depend on the tax practitioners, have made the practitioners and consultants a valuable Commodity in the market. This has affected the elasticity of demand for tax consultants. The cost of engaging a tax consultant has naturally gone up. Thus, the perception of tax laws as incomprehensible and procedures as complicated, and the subsequent experience that tax consultants are either inaccessible or unaffordable or both, could necessitate the choice of non-compliance.

Why should I pay

...if it is so harassing to interact with the tax department?

Down the centuries, the taxpayer-tax collector relationship has never ever been a smooth affair. History has several recorded instances of harassment by tax collectors and reciprocal protests by taxpayers. Tax collectors were a hated lot under various rulers, especially because of the unjust tax policies and enforcement. Though tax administrations have been radically transformed in the wake of democratic governance across the world, there is still a perception that tax administration is 'unfair' and that tax officials are high-handed. To add to this imagined 'woe' taxpayers are generally wary of audits and scrutiny assessments. Even a simple verification notice from the income tax department creates great flutters in taxpayers' minds. All this is because of the perception that it is such a hassle to undergo the procedures of the income tax department which always 'suspects' the taxpayer.

The fact is, the inherent complexity of tax laws and procedures and the natural ignorance of the taxpayers can be a fertile setting for the tax officials to show an upper hand. Lack of proper and easy access to the tax officer, and the near ignorance about the internal procedures make taxpayers naturally uncomfortable. There are general feelings that the tax administration is corrupt and that one has to grease the palm of several officials in the hierarchy to get a clean chit. Even if there is no verification or investigation on the tax return filed, or even if it is just a normal processing of the return and granting of tax refund, the 'affair' is not considered as a smooth one. In these circumstances, (where most of the fear may be out of hearsay, rather than own experience), taxpayers think of keeping as much distance as possible from the tax authorities and decide to comply only if they are compelled. Thus, voluntary compliance eludes a country where the above-said fears exist strongly in the taxpayers' minds. Such tax behaviour continues to be the norm among large sections of income earners in countries where the enforcement mechanism is weak and the tax administration is corrupt and inefficient.

Why should I pay

...if I am unduly audited and investigated into?

Audit (scrutiny) of the income tax returns filed and related investigation by tax authorities are areas of worry for taxpayers. There are countries where investigations are efficiently carried out and punishments are stringently enforced. There is yet another set of countries where enforcement is weak and evaders can get away without any stringent penalties. However in both the cases, what is important are the criteria for selection of the cases for audit or scrutiny and the chances that some categories of returns may fall into the investigation net. The crucial questions would be the following, irrespective of the country and the nature of the tax system: a) Whether a specific person's case is targeted on the basis of any fair analysis? b) Whether others who are similarly placed like that person are also targeted? c) Is a person being regularly targeted (most frequently or year after year)? d) Is the targeting by virtue of a person's income level or the nature of source of that person's income?

Why should I pay

...if it is too costly for me to comply?

Even if one decides to part with one's taxes to the government, one needs to incur many other costs incidental to that. They are called compliance costs. Bluementhal and Slemrod (1992) have defined compliance costs as the value of time spent on tasks related to filing tax returns as well as to any expenditure on goods and services for that same purpose. Apart from the filing expenses, many taxpayers incur costs even after filing returns for rectification procedures, refund procedures, scrutiny or audit proceedings, etc. These are called the 'hidden costs of taxation' by Sandford (1973) and they are difficult to estimate. As the tax laws keep changing almost every year, taxpayers need to update themselves of the changes in the Annual Finance Act and Budget provisions. They need to watch keenly for changes in tax rates, tax withholdings, amendments related to any incentives, exemptions or deductions hitherto claimed by them, procedural changes, and deadlines. Such knowledge updating demands considerable time and money.[1] There are also costs related to filing such as software updation (wherever e-filing of tax returns and tax withholding/tax deduction statements, etc are in vogue), Forms, tax preparation charges if assisted by tax practitioners, audit fee if the income statements are audited prior to filing, travel costs, etc. Further, expenses may be incurred in some cases at the time of summary assessments, detailed scrutiny or audits, refund claims, rectification and appeal proceedings, etc. There might be huge losses on account of delayed refunds which affect the cash flow. There is also a cost involved in maintaining the connected records for a considerable period of time. Apart from these, some taxpayers may also complain of expenditure for greasing the palms of tax officials! Also, considerable time is spent by each taxpayer on tax matters, starting from entering the transactions in the books of accounts and filling up various columns in tax returns.

Why should I pay

...if the people around me don't pay?

Most of the above-mentioned taxpayer responses may invariably translate into definite tax decisions and consequent tax behaviour. This can have a spiralling effect on the overall tax compliance of the population. That in turn influences the tax behaviour of the individuals. Individuals in a society keenly watch the behavioural patterns of others. Though the tax behaviour of a person is not very well exposed to others, people in the immediate social and economic environment would definitely get hints about the tax behaviour of others. Apart from what is observed in the immediate surroundings, the information projected in the media based on various reports about tax evasion would also result in the formation of a public opinion about the general tax non-compliance in society. Such vicarious learning results in the emergence of a particular attitude about tax evasion. In countries where tax evasion is rampant and where it is not considered a serious economic offence, people tend to divulge to others their tax non-compliance behaviour. People may even boast about the extent of tax they saved by not disclosing their true income. Thus the attitude 'why should I pay, if my neighbour doesn't pay' might finally come up as a good motto.

Why should I pay

...if my non-payment does not benefit society but only gives me gains?

This is akin to the story of a village where a king had once asked people to contribute milk to the common storage container so that it can be distributed to the needy. Each villager thought, 'It doesn't matter if I put a bottle of water instead of a bottle of milk in the big container; no one would find it.' Almost everyone thought the same way and ultimately the container had only water and no milk! Similarly, there is an attitude that if the taxes one pays would not make much difference for the national revenue, why should one pay? Such an attitude may emerge out of the strong individualistic orientations which suppress patriotic feelings.

This is more evident in countries where the proportional contribution of income tax to the national revenue is not substantial and where there is a 'soft' tax administration.

Most of these questions are natural posers among the taxpayers of many countries. However the extent and intensity of such questioning depends on the nature of the governments, their tax laws, and the tax administrations. They also depend on the dominant popular attitude in a particular society. If the majority of taxpayers are motivated by the rationality of self-interest, they may be more vociferous in analyzing the costs and benefits. Altruism may prevail in taxpayer attitudes in countries where people recognize taxation as a social policy and tax contributions as a necessary social trade-off. But none of the above extremes (whether completely rational or perfectly altruistic) exist in modern society. Though some countries, by virtue of a historically stable tax administration and efficient redistribution, have compliant taxpayers, it does not necessarily mean that all taxpayers are voluntary contributors. Similarly one cannot expect everyone to pay taxes with missionary zeal, even if the people of that country have internalized its socialistic goals. However, tax behavior can reasonably be predicted to a larger extent based on an analysis of the popular perceptions of nature of the government, its bureaucracy, the fiscal policies and the governance. Analyses of empirical data on attitudes and perceptions of taxpayers are thus relevant in predicting tax behaviour.

Tax evasion - is it a serious offence?

Tax evasion is a worldwide phenomenon. No country can boast of perfect tax compliance. In fact, the proportion of non-compliance is substantial in almost all the countries. Even developed countries with centuries-old tax systems suffer a 'tax gap'[2] of about 25 per cent.[3] Tax offenders, by and large, enjoy a privileged treatment in many countries, for centuries, as compared with other economic offenders. They are basically perceived as crimes against the government. However, these evasions are not seen as a crime affecting the society. The irony is that though almost all countries have elaborate and stringent punishments for various offences pertaining to tax non-compliance, their strict implementation is lacking. As a result, there is widespread criticism against the tax administration and also a general disregard for tax laws and procedures.

INTRODUCTION

Is tax evasion immoral?

Is tax evasion considered an immoral activity even when the taxpayers find a way out through the tax loopholes? All societies have normative orders that comprise of norms and values. All individuals are expected to conform to the norms of the society. Moral values are ingrained in these societal norms. Cheating is considered a deviant behaviour. However how serious is cheating the government on taxes? In a recent interaction, a Roman Catholic nun who is an administrator of a hospital run by her congregation did not hesitate to say that unless she pays her doctors 'under the table', no doctor would stay with the hospital. The Roman Catholic Church issued a revised catechism in 1993 - the first since the year 1566 - that categorizes tax evasion as a sin. Ancient Hindu scriptures also extolled the rationale of taxation. Tax evasion was regarded as anti-social in several ancient cultures. Historically, as we see in the subsequent chapters, the bulk of the tax revenues were utilized for security and war. Asks McGee (1994), if your taxes go to finance unjust wars, is there anything immoral about tax evasion? However, in the recent decades taxes are applied more for the 'social security' of individuals rather than for the 'physical security' of the state. The moral obligation to pay taxes would be undoubtedly linked to the general moral mindset of society. But the issue here is whether the conduct of the tax system and the trajectory of the tax policy of the state invoke feelings of moral responsibility to pay taxes.

Though crimes such as theft, bribery, etc are punishable with similar punishments just like tax evasion, the latter does not have much public disapproval. Though tax evasion amounts to the stealing of public money, the tax evader is never classified as a thief by society. Rather, he is seen as an unfortunate sprinter who was caught for committing a foul in his enthusiasm to forge ahead of others.

In search of answers

The questions asked in the previous sections were many. The discussion highlighted the social , economic, moral, and a host of other factors that an individual considers before deciding to pay taxes, the discussion also touched on the rampant tax evasion even in a modern society where people are conscious of the inevitability of paying taxes. The discussion illustrated the channels through which taxes are evaded with impunity. Some were rooted in the premise of economic rationality and some were the outcome of intense feelings and perceptions at personal levels. At one end of the spectrum, the apprehensions are related to the costs, benefits, revenue leakages, etc. At the other end, the tax attitudes are influenced by issues such as general tax non-compliance in society, fear of harassment, tax system complexity, lack of moral binding, etc. The entire gamut of tax non-compliance can be analyzed under four broad headings: A Matter of Time, A Matter of Money, A Matter of Power, and A Matter of Mind. The attempt now is to analyze what is the significant role played by each in influencing tax attitudes and tax behaviour.

A Matter of Time ?

Traditional wisdom prevails upon many while giving an optimistic answer to the phenomenon of tax evasion. Consequently, there is a thinking that tax compliance increases as the world moves ahead through various historical stages. As Keynes said, 'The economic transition of a society is a thing to be accomplished slowly.' Thus there is a view that as the people become more aware, as society progresses and as the tax system develops further, there will be complete tax compliance. Does it mean that perfect tax compliance can happen only in a perfectly civilized society? Oliver Wendell Holmes, Jr said, 'I like to pay taxes. With them I buy civilization'. The historic dimensions of taxation and the systemic origins of tax compliance and tax evasion are evaluated for a historicized understanding in the second chapter. Indian tax history is also briefly analyzed to understand the nature of taxation and tax compliance in distinguishable periods to gather insights into the social-structural origins of tax apathy in India.

A Matter of Money ?

Down the ages, human beings have been considered as rational beings. However, this rationality is not absolute. Possibly the oft-repeated statement that human beings are rational might have emerged historically as a result of a comparison with the animal kingdom. The thinking human is supposed to be utilitarian, calculative and evaluative. If that is the case, ideally all human beings will, in all probability, take every possible step to evaluate the pros and cons, costs and benefits and gains and losses in life. If so, wouldn't tax decisions also invariably be based on rational analysis and reasoning?

Some of the possible reasons given by taxpayers for not paying the due taxes were enumerated earlier. Each one of them has a utilitarian element in it. When people are worried about what benefits they will get out of tax payment, they are in fact comparing the costs with benefits. The net gain in the exchange between the taxpayer and the state in terms of money that flows out of the individual's pocket and the money that comes out of the state's exchequer for the individual's collective societal benefit is the predominant determinant in tax behaviour. This supports the economic perspective of utilitarianism associated originally with the works of Adam Smith and several other subsequent economists such as Ricardo, J S Mill, and Bentham; When the citizens are worried about the possible siphoning off of funds, their actual worry is that the nation's funds into which they too have pooled in their money are being grabbed and looted by unscrupulous elements, thus creating huge shortages in the economy. They see pilferages of funds as cunning activities of greedy persons at different levels of hierarchy. They also see collection of speed money for the execution of work. The only difference is that some engage in legitimate activities to earn money and the others engage in apparently illegitimate activities for making money. In both cases the ultimate objective is to make money or gain benefit from society. The rage is not precisely over immorality or illegality of the behaviour of the fund eaters but over the fact that someone is cornering public funds for personal, selfish advantages.

The utilitarian approach in understanding tax behaviour is central to research and policy analysis from the perspective of economics. Such economic perspectives on taxation and tax research are elaborated in the third chapter. The attempt is to understand as to what extent economic approaches to taxation and tax behaviour help in providing an understanding of the subject.

A Matter of Power ?

Many a time taxation has been used by the authorities and governments as an instrument to consolidate their power and to sustain it. Then the whole gamut of taxation is rooted in power. Thus power and taxes are inextricably intertwined, as power results in taxes and taxes help in sustaining power. All along, power has taken different forms in history, drawing legitimacy from religious texts, cultural conventions, colonial ideologies, economic principles, and political convictions. In the fourth chapter, taxation is analyzed in the context of power. Analyses of the political dimensions of tax policy provide insights into the influence and interplay of various pressure groups, political forces, vote banks, and cash banks on tax decision making. The aim is to underscore the predominance of non-economic factors in tax policy and consequent tax compliance behaviour.

A Matter of Mind ? Towards an Economic Sociology of Taxation

Though economic theories have tried to explain human behaviour with a utilitarian perspective, sociological theories emerged as a reaction against utilitarianism. With 'organicismic', functionalist, and structuralist perspectives, the effort was to explain human behaviour in the context of a collective philosophy or collective conscience rather than individualistic dimensions which were predominant in the utilitarian perspective. Sociologists like Parsons, Simmel, and later 'exchange theorists' like Blau have given a contrasting perspective where social context, social interaction and exchange play crucial roles in shaping human behaviour even in purely economic contexts. Thus, tax compliance of individuals is strongly influenced by several non-economic factors as well.

It is appropriate to examine the subject of tax compliance and tax enforcement from the angle of economic sociology. The academic potential of economic sociology as a field in social sciences has been identified several decades earlier. In fact, pioneering works of Emile Durkheim, Max Weber, Vilfredo Pareto, Joseph Schumpeter, Thorstein

Veblen, etc contained conceptual and theoretical foundations of economic sociology.[4] It took a few decades for scholars (Eccles, 1981; Granovetter 1985; Granovetter and Swedberg,1992) to think on the lines of a 'New Economic Sociology'[5]. There needs to be a synthetic approach while analyzing subjects such as tax compliance which cannot be answered from the exclusive domains of either economics or sociology. In economics, individuals are presumed to be uninfluenced by others, whereas in sociology they are presumed to be influenced by others. An economic sociological approach recognizes the social contractarian relationship among taxpayer, society and the state which is rooted in social embeddedness.

The theoretical analysis and overview of historic, economic and political perspectives of taxation taken up in chapters 2, 3 and 4 lead to the conclusion that taxation is not just an economic instrument to generate revenue; it has larger sociological and political dimensions, at the policy level as well as the implementation level. In the light of these insights, the fifth chapter attempts to provide a methodological critique to study taxation and tax behaviour. Various methods and tools for data collection are analyzed. The analysis revolves around an economic-sociological orientation coupled with an integrated methodological tool that facilitates collection of both qualitative and quantitative data.

Two empirical studies were conducted in the light of the theoretical and methodological insights that emerge from chapter five. Chapter six is a brief description about the study on tax and governance attitudes and tax behaviour perceptions in a developing country. The study is based on the data gathered through interviews and case studies on random sample of taxpayers from southern India. In chapter seven, the trajectory of income tax enforcement in India is analyzed. The study explores the tax compliance behaviour in India, through an analysis of the sociological causes and consequences of income tax searches as perceived by persons who were searched by the Indian Income Tax Department.

A detailed analysis of the insights that emerged from the theoretical and empirical explorations is given in chapter eight. The last chapter deals with the transitional and transnational challenges of taxation in the globalized world.

CHAPTER-2

PAYING TAXES A MATTER OF TIME?

The History of Taxation

> *"The fiscal history of a people is above all an essential part of its general history. An enormous influence on the fate of nations emanates from the economic bleeding which the needs of the states necessitate, and from the use to which its results are put . . . . The spirit of a people, its cultural level, its social structure . . . all this and more are written in its fiscal history, stripped of all phrases. He who knows how to listen to its message here discerns the thunder of world history more clearly than anyone else."*
>
> (Joseph Schumpeter)

A common optimistic answer one gets while searching for a historic exploration of the tax system and tax compliance across the world, is that tax compliance is just a matter of time. In this chapter, an attempt is made to understand the historical dimensions of taxation and the systemic origins of tax compliance and tax evasion. Indian tax history is also briefly analyzed to understand the nature of taxation and tax compliance in distinguishable periods.

The concept and ideology of taxation is said to be as old as civilization. All civilized societies have had some type of rudimentary norms and conventions relating to the compulsory contribution by the individual to the authority concerned. According to the evolutionary theory of the state advanced by Goldscheid, (Backhaus, 2002) in the beginning, 'the state personified by the prince could seek either revenues or services in kind'. Taxes are one of the oldest phenomena of human society. (Grapperhaus, 1998) Even primitive man was aware that society was more than a sum of individuals and each tribe member contributed to that 'embryonic' taxation system. Alongside, tax evasion is considered as a pervasive phenomenon in all societies and it is often said that taxation and tax evasion always go together and that income tax evasion is as old as income tax itself. (Webley *et al,* 1991) Since there can be no generalization without comparison and no meaningful social comparison without history, historical analysis is indispensable for getting any insight into the structural and systemic origins of taxation and their historical uniqueness in each period in history. A historical overview of the system of taxation and tax evasion in the world and in India clearly indicates that taxation and tax evasion have a long history.

As has already been mentioned, taxation became an inevitable institution in all states over the centuries. The oldest tax system was set up about 6000 years ago at a place called Lagash. Artefacts indicated that heavy taxes were originally imposed to finance a war and continued even after the war as it was considered to be a powerful measure to extract resources from the people. (Kevin, 1999) The system of taxation became more universal and structured with the emergence of the moneyed economy. According to Schumpeter (1953; 1976), wars by states could never have been carried out had the enormous cost been shifted immediately and visibly to an identifiable public through 'expropriative taxes.' Certainly the history of the state is inseparable from the history of taxation. And 'the modern state was able to survive and flourish because it made fiscal sense.' (Paris, 2001 p.2) The nature and objectives of taxation in each country depend on the unique social structure of that country. Likewise the perception and attitude of individuals on taxation and the consequent tax behaviour of individuals of one country depend on the unique historical background and social structure of that country.

In the beginning, tax collection in kind was the most common system of revenue collection in all societies. However, as the economy became monetized, countries started collecting taxes in cash. In addition to the revenue from the land, tax collection on the basis of ownership of immovable properties too gradually came into force in many countries. Further, the changes in economy in the wake of industrialization and the democratization of polity have drastically influenced the tax policies and tax structure. Indirect taxes became the major source of revenue for many nations as both domestic and international trade gave ample scope for excise and customs revenue.

TB - 2.1

Bigger the window, heavier the tax

There was a tax called 'window tax' in Great Britain and neighbouring countries during the 17th and 18th centuries. That was the time when people resisted any introduction of income tax as it was perceived to be an attack by the government on their personal liberty. However, there was no such protest against the window tax. The bigger the house, the more glass windows it was likely to have, the more tax the occupants would have to pay. But people knew the art of evasion even then. The normal method of avoiding the tax was by covering up the windows before the assessor arrived and re-opening them after he had left! Many taxpayers used to avoid the tax by bricking up the windows. This is said to be the reason for the bricked-up windows seen in very old houses in the UK. The rich constructed houses with the maximum possible number of windows to place themselves 'above' less rich people.

Towards the late eighteenth century, several nation-states started tapping the potential of direct taxes from sources such as house property apart from income from professions. There were taxes such as 'window tax' in Great Britain and neighboring countries. It was easy to collect the former than the latter as it could not be concealed. However, as many countries had property ownership as a prerequisite for voting and to be elected to a public office, most of the voters were owners of large property. Thus, a hike in property tax rates became a difficult proposition. However, every tax faced stiff resistance from the citizens. Still, countries settled heavily for income tax as they faced immediate requirement of large funds. The fiscal policies were evolved over a period of time with marked changes in the nature and objectives as a latent result of the dominant factors and characteristics in each period.[1]

Wars and the income tax

It is said that the history of taxation is a fascinating story of rebellion, corruption, presumptive arrogance and civil destruction. (Kevin, 1999) Expenses related to the wars were the immediate trigger for focusing on income tax in most of the countries. Income tax provided the necessary funds to all countries that were directly or indirectly involved or dragged into the World Wars and the regional conflicts. The British government introduced income tax in 1799 to finance the Napoleonic wars. The United States also found income tax as the best source in the 1850s to finance its civil war. According to an estimate, in 1944, 45 per cent of total revenues in the United States, 55 per cent in Canada, and 43 per cent of revenues in the United Kingdom were extracted through the means of income tax. (Peters, 1991, p.233) Here, one could perhaps wonder whether there would be any income tax at all in the world had there been no wars in history. Though started as a means to cater to war-related expenses, taxes continued to stay in all countries in different guises - initially to curb inflation and to tackle the Great Depression and later on as an instrument for welfare and redistribution of wealth.

TB - 2.2

If the war is won, you get back your taxes
Earliest form of tax refunds

In Greece, the Athenians used to impose heavy taxes whenever there was a war. It was called *'eisphora'*. It was a compulsory levy on all people. However, when the war was won, and there was a net gain in resources, the entire tax paid by the people was refunded.[2]

As mentioned earlier, the British government used income tax as a means of financing the Napoleonic wars. The bill was introduced by William Pitt Junior in his budget speech in 1798. It was imposed in 1799 and tax was levied under 5 schedules: a) tax on income from land in the UK, b) tax on commercial occupation of land, c) tax on income from public securities, d) tax on trading income, income from professions and vocations, interest, overseas income and casual income, and e) tax on employment income. Later a sixth Schedule, f) tax on dividend income in the UK, was added. It yielded considerable revenue to the exchequer. However it had to be repealed within seventeen years. After a gap of thirty years it was re-introduced. Many other countries followed suit and drafted their own income tax laws with different tax rates.

In a similar vein, the United States introduced the income tax to fund the civil war. The tax history of the United States is particularly of academic interest because it was quick to evolve a systematic tax code and was fast to make necessary amendments over a period of time with respect to the changing economic circumstances. The tax systems of many countries have drawn largely from the fiscal trajectory followed in the United States. Most of the international economic organizations have based their fiscal guidelines on the basis of a critical examination and evaluation of American tax reforms. Therefore it is relevant to briefly discuss the evolution of income taxation in the United States.

The history of America's tax system can be written largely as a history of America's wars. (Bank, Stark and Thorndike, 2008) One of the first steps taken by America after the bitter War of Independence with Britain was to set up its own system of taxation. In July 1862, President Abraham Lincoln signed the first income tax law put in operation by the Federal Government. Thus in the first stage, the primary purpose of the above taxation was to raise the necessary revenue for the war related expenses. (Nikolaieff, 1968) Started with a rate of 3 per cent, the rate increased to about 15 per cent during the peak of the war. After the war, the tax lingered until several court cases, such as Pollock v. Farmers' Loan and Trust Co. in 1895, ruled it unconstitutional. The second stage started in 1913 with the aim of redistribution of wealth. The 16th Amendment, ratified in 1913, declared that, 'the Congress shall have power to lay and collect taxes on incomes, from whatever source derived.' Though the stated objective was to tackle accumulation of wealth in a few, it became the principal source of revenue for I World War. Income tax rates were hiked to 94 per cent during the peak of the war. By 1930, about 36 per cent of the total population filed income tax returns. In the third stage, the

1960s ('the roaring sixties'), the United States was in a period of 'abundance' and people talked of the 'end of ideology'. The worry was not revenue, but the distribution of the same.

The fourth stage (1970s and 1980s) was characterized by economic slowdown and taxes became more 'visible' to the tax payers. Increased tax sensitivity in a period of perceived corruption, inefficiency and low returns resulted in tax protests. Adams has made a detailed study of the history of US taxation and has stated that American history is replete with tax revolts (Adams, 1998; Sobel, 1979; Laffer and Jan, 1979). Adams' book is organized in loose chronological fashion, beginning with colonial revolts against British taxation and continuing through the tax bill of 1997. The fairness of taxation was a debatable issue in all public discussions. (Vatter and Walker, 1996; Johnston, 2003; Aaron and Slemrod, 2004; Citrin, 1979) The political arena was full of fiscal criticisms and promises. (Hansen, 1983) Elections were fought and votes were cast based on the stands taken on taxation. (Pollack, 2003; Stein, 1988; Zelizer, 1998) A series of tax protests followed resulting in several tax limitation proposals. There were reports of large-scale tax evasion. (Bailey, 1989; Alm, 1990) One of the results was the historic tax cut by the Congress. President Ronald Reagan and US Congress responded with the 1986 Tax Reform Act. Touted as the biggest tax change since World War II, the law cut tax rates, broadened the tax base and simplified some tax forms by eliminating loopholes. In the fifth stage, one could witness the increased sensitivity of the state to the responses of the citizens. In this period the citizens became more concerned about the nature and extent of contribution demanded by the state. (Stein, 1988) They also became more alert about the way the resources had been garnered by the state and the corresponding services rendered.

Wars continue to be the single largest expenditure from the taxes collected. America's war on terror continues to impact the tax policies, though there is no drastic hike in the rates. However, it is said that there is an attempt to shift the burden on the future generations by postponing the war time fiscal sacrifice. (Bank, *et al;* 2008)

Elsewhere, indirect taxes were the major source of revenue for many European and North American countries in the initial period. While countries like France and Belgium continued to have revenue exclusively from traditional taxes like land and inheritance taxes apart from the revenue from international trade, other nations of Europe started tapping the potential of income tax as a small scale. But by the beginning of the twentieth century, countries such as Germany, Netherlands, Norway, etc could muster about fifty per cent of total revenue from income tax. Germany and Austria introduced radical tax reforms much earlier than many industrialized countries. Austria has the credit for having introduced the first corporate tax which paved the way for many other countries immediately thereafter to do like wise.

History and the tax revolts

It is said that ancient Israel split after King Solomon's death because his son refused to cut debilitating taxes. Much later, in the year 60 AD the Queen of East England rebelled against corrupt tax collectors. The Queen succeeded in recruiting 230,000 warriors to fight the war which resulted in the death of thousands of people. Further down, in 1369, the reason for the renewal of the 100 Year War between England and France was the rebellion of the nobility against the tax policy of Prince Edward.

People's protests against taxes, which culminated in Proposition 13 (against property tax in California) had initiated a chain reaction in many parts of the world.[3] The US has had a history of tax resistance even after independence (Sawicki, 1983). From Whiskey tax to income tax, every type of tax introduced in different periods of history faced strong resentment. Along with tax revolts, people tended to evade the taxes considerably as a mark of protest.

Adams (1994) reminds us of a simple historical fact often ignored by politicians and historians: societies cannot and will not tolerate unjust and excessive taxation for long. Starting with the ancient Egyptians and comfortably working his way through ancient Rome, medieval England, the Spanish empire, and early America, Adams clearly demonstrates how burdensome taxation has played a critical role in the demise of some of the world's great civilizations. There were tax revolts in several countries which point to the historic dissent against the taxation in several countries.[4] There may be several reasons for the vociferous protests against tax policies. According to Wilensky (1976) tax protests were more serious in countries where tax visibility was very high (especially high income taxes) as compared with countries where tax visibility was less (may be due to more number of taxes apart from income tax, that too with less rates). However, Peters (1991; p.179-180) has argued that the above conclusion is based on a shaky empirical foundation. Though there might be several reasons for the tax protests, the extent of injustice and unfairness perceived by the taxpayers has had a strong bearing on the nature and intensity of tax protests in various countries.

TB - 2.3

Women and tax protests

One of the earliest tax revolts was in AD 60 when Boadicea, Queen of East Anglia led a revolt against corrupt tax collectors in the British Isles. It was reported that almost all the Roman soldiers, numbering about 80,000, within 100 miles of East Anglia, were killed in the revolt. The Queen's army seized London, but the revolt was later crushed by Emperor Nero.

According to a legend, Lady Godiva an Anglo-Saxon woman who lived in England during the 11th century was instrumental in getting large reduction in tax rates. Her husband Leofric, who was the Earl of Mercia, promised to do that when Lady Godiva 'offered' to ride naked through the streets of the town[2].

Colonialism and Taxation

Taxation was an effective instrument to strengthen and retain the colonial rule over the colonies. This resulted in large scale protests in the colonies. Colonial governments in North America imposed various taxes, a substantial portion of which was channeled to the imperial government in London. The colonists expressed their dissent to the revenue laws by joining in open revolts. There was a major outbreak of political and social violence in the colonies in the late 17th century.[5] Several rebellions such as Bacon's Rebellion in Virginia (1675-76), Culpeper's Rebellion in North Carolina (1677-79), Leisler's Rebellion in New York (1689), and Coode's Rebellion in Maryland in 1688, etc, were said to have emanated from strong resistance to taxation. In India, too, there were strong protests against colonial taxation. Colonial taxation in India was biased in favour of the British Empire; the domestic economy was drained, thus creating great imbalances.

Indian tax history

The tax history of India is characterized by biases that emanated from several social, structural and political factors. Tax attitudes and tax behaviour of the Indian people have to be necessarily studied in this historical background. Kasper and Streit (1999) emphasize that a common culture produces predictability and an orderly evolution of the corresponding institutions. The unique social and political context which prevailed in India in different historical stages has resulted in a unique tax culture in India.

The Indian economy till the time of British colonization was characterized by village centred production units and the realization of revenue through local administrative units. India's exposure to the international markets was limited to the export of handicraft. Indian economy entered a new phase after the British came to India in 1757. Stringent land revenue enforcement and trade policies favouring the British had created imbalances in the economy. Throughout the history of India, tax policies took different dimensions. The attempt here is to analyze the unique nature of the system of taxation as it evolved over a period of time by focusing on the historically specific dominant dimensions in each epoch or distinguishable period of Indian history. The periodization is also indispensable to historical understanding of any kind since without any context to events, they can have no meaning. When one periodizes a long historical phase (running into more than two millenniums), one is treating it descriptively by enumerating its dominant characteristics, and evaluating them comparatively. (Doff; 1971)

The Dominant cultural and religious determinants : the System before the advent of the British

The genesis of the idea of public finance is well expressed in ancient Indian literature. There is enough historical evidence to show that the principles of public finance were expressed from very ancient times, as part of the 'dharma' and are depicted in the texts of the ancient law givers.

TB - 2.4

Dancing the way to taxes

It is not just businessmen and professionals who pay high taxes. Artists of all categories pay substantial taxes all over the world. It is said that during the Mauryan kingdom (324 BC to 232 BC), a substantial portion of tax revenue came from dancers, musicians, actors and dancing girls in India. This is mentioned in detail in the famous work 'Arthasastra' by the ancient Indian political strategist Chanakya (also called as Kautilya alias Indian Machiavelli).

Even today, artists from the entertainment industry are among the top income taxpayers. Indian film actors Akshay Kumar and Shah Rukh Khan were reported to have paid more than 30 crores in taxes for the assessment year 2009-10. The actor family of Amitabh Bachchan has been one of the top income tax paying families in India for several years.

But there are also people in this industry who miss the date with Income tax. Many celebrities were charged by US IRS for tax evasion. In China a leading film actress, once described as a "billionaire", was recently arrested on charges of dodging taxes. In India, income tax searches in the premises of film artists are not infrequent. Though there are many high profile tax evaders in the world, a former US IRS Commissioner who was instrumental in busting several tax evasion cases of celebrities holds the record for being the most ironic of the alleged cheaters. It was alleged that Joseph Nunan (US IRS 1944-47) who won a $1800 bet that Harry Truman would win the election, forgot to disclose the winnings in the tax return!

(Kane, 1968; Altekar, 1962) Being one of the oldest civilizations of the world, India had a well-developed system of taxation from the very early ages. Thus, direct and indirect taxation was not a novelty in India introduced by the British, as is too commonly supposed. Rather, it was a most ancient and well-known institution. (Jayaswal, 1955) According to Manu, the Hindu law maker,[6] a king should make the traders pay duty on their profits which should be fixed with regard to the rates of purchases and sales, the expenses for food and condiments and the cost of transport and other charges for receiving the goods. The king should fix the rates of duties and taxes in such a manner that both he himself and the man who does the work receive the due reward. Thus, a reasonable tax on the profits of traders was an accepted principle of the Hindu law. The Code of Manu, one of the authentic records of the Indian social and economic system during the Vedic period, presents an account of the system of taxation and various sources of revenue of the state.

Studies point out that in the earlier inscriptions such as the inscription of Queen Balasri of the Satavahana family, it is proclaimed that 'her son levied taxes in accordance with the sacred law. (Jayaswal, 1955) The king's authority to levy taxes was also recognized in the 'Smrithis'. (Kane, 1968) The earliest word used for tax is 'bali' and the tax collectors were called the 'balisadhakas.'

The largest share of tax accrued from agricultural produce and from trade and commerce. Those who were in specialized technical jobs were charged taxes in the form of services (for specific days) for the king every year. (Altekar, 1962) By the close of the Vedic period, the burden of taxation fell heavily on the Vaisyas who were engaged in trade, agriculture and cattle rearing. The nature of taxation in the post-vedic period was also on the same lines as in the Vedic period, the details of which are available in Buddhist 'jatakas'. Adhya, (Panda and Venkateswar, 1991) who studied the economic life in this period, has given a detailed description of taxation in the India of this era.

During the Maurya period onwards, taxation was extensively used to meet the expenses of the administration. The 'Arthasastra' by Kautilya gives details of the nature of tax administration and various laws related to taxation in ancient India. (Smith and Spear, 1988) The *Rummindei* inscription is the only Asokan inscription, which makes a precise reference to taxation. We get information regarding the tax exemption granted to the village of Lumbini, the birthplace of the Buddha, from this inscription. (Thapar, 1963) The other sources of information on the system of taxation in the Hindu period are the 'Sukranitisara' and the inscriptions during this period. According to Kautilya, tax was not a compulsory contribution to be made by the subject to the state. On the other hand, it was a relationship based on *Dharma* and it was the King's sacred duty to protect the citizens in lieu of the tax collected; if he failed in this, the subject had the right to stop paying taxes.[7]

It has always been the practice of Indian rulers to exercise strict supervision over the trade; and taxes were levied on sales; the goods being stamped officially to guarantee payment. Manufacturers were also treated in accordance with the same principles and procedures (Smith and Spear, 1988). Both tax evasion and corruption by the tax collectors were considered as serious offences in ancient India. False statements made by the importers or vendors were punishable as theft, that is to say, by fine, mutilation or even death. It has been recorded that during the administration of Chandragupta Maurya, the evasion of tax was made a capital offence. In spite of the drastic penal code and the 'enhanced severities' on the erring officials, the public services still suffered from corruption.

The uniqueness of the system of taxation in ancient India is that it was shaped by and large in the dominant cultural context of the period. Thus, the system of taxation of ancient India was evolved in the context and conduct of *Dharma.* (Narayanan, 1983) *Dharma* was defined as the divinely ordained norm of good conduct varying according to the caste and class. (Basham, 1954) Thus, the system of taxation, which was part of the *Dharma,* had in it, the characteristic features of the social structure that was believed to be divinely ordained. While those destined to be born in a particular stratum of the caste hierarchy had to pay taxes by virtue of their business/trade, some others were exempt from any tax. Though Brahmins were not totally exempt, the provisions were extremely liberal and they were almost spared from contributing anything to the rulers. (Ghoshal, 1976) Thus, the cultural and religious factors played a prominent role in shaping the fiscal structure of ancient India.

TB - 2.5

The pilgrim taxes

Pilgrim taxes in ancient India consisted of a number of imposts.

a. A tax on all pilgrims who visit famous temples, pagodas and shrines
b. A toll on all the offerings brought by the devotees with them
c. Fixed sums to perform various penances
d. License fees for shops, booths and stalls during religious festivals

Even today, temples and shrines continue to attract huge sums from the devotees. Billions of money and valuables flow to places of pilgrimage in India. Generosity of devotees, when it comes to God(s) and Goddesses is unique to India. It is not known how much of those contributions suffered taxation in the hands of givers.

Similarly, during the medieval period, the changes that happened in the socio-political structure of society, predominantly the replacement of Hindu rulers by Muslim rulers had its impact on the nature of fiscal policies and systems of taxation. However, in both the ancient and medieval periods, the cultural/religious dimensions were dominant in shaping the system of taxation, except for the difference of change is the political system mainly led by Hindus to a system mainly controlled by Muslims. As taxation came to appropriate a sizeable part of the peasants' surpluses in countries of the Islamic world, a mechanism had simultaneously to be devised to collect this from the peasantry and distribute it among the members of the ruling group. (Raychaudhari and Habib, 1982) It is noted that the historians and scholars always expressed their amazement about the glaring contrast between the massive wealth of the emperor and his amirs, who formed a paper-thin upper class and the dire longings of the masses who lived on the verge of poverty. (Grapperhaus, 1998)

The rulers of the Delhi Sultanate, particularly during the period of Allauddin Khilji, had used taxation as a tool for discriminating one religion as compared with others. Special exemptions and privileges granted to Brahmins during the Ancient India were taken away and the policy of taxation followed was biased against the Hindus. Most of the subsequent rulers abolished all privileges of revenue officers, like the Khuts and the Muqaddams, since they were all Hindus. Taxation was also used to augment the much-needed finances for strengthening the army to protect the empire from Hindu rulers. (Raychaudhari and Habib, 1982) It may be noted that Mohammed Tughlaq went to the extent of raising the rates of taxation ten to twenty times higher than the existing norm, especially in places like Doab. Consequently, violent attacks on revenue officers were common during the Muslim period by the poor Hindu peasants and traders for enforcing such huge levies. (Smith and Spear, 1988) During the regime of Babur, there was no orderly tax system. 'Plundering was his main source of state income'. (Grapperhaus, 1998) Even then, the Muslim peasants were required to pay only one-tenth of the produce on wet lands and one-seventh from the irrigated land; simultaneously, the Hindu peasants had to pay as tax one-third to a half of the produce.

The rates were slightly reduced during the period of Shershah and Akbar. In fact, during the period of Sher Shah, an effective administrative organization was created and this structure introduced a better tax system. However, there were discriminating taxes against Hindu traders and businessmen as compared with their Muslim counterparts. 'Jizya' was levied on non-Muslims on the contention that, a Zimmi (non-Muslim) had no right to live in the kingdom of a Muslim Sultan unless 'Jizya' was paid. Akbar abolished Jizya in 1564. In order to compensate for the loss of revenue, he with the help of his minister Raja Todar Mal introduced a ten-year settlement in the case of the land tax and substituted money payments for payments in kind. Except Akbar, most of the other rulers pursued the policy of discriminatory taxation during their respective regimes. The last of the Mughal kings, Aurangazeb, laid down in 1671 that henceforth only Muslims were allowed to collect taxes. He re-introduced the Jizya in 1679 in order to resume the tax discrimination against Hindus. It is said that he ordered a number of protesting Hindu businessmen to be trampled upon by his elephants. The Jizya, not the amount of the tax as such, but the method by which it was assessed and collected, was at any rate one of the causes that finally led to the downfall of the Mughal Empire in India. (Pragar,1920)

However, during the Mughal period one witnessed the setting up of a systematic taxation system. There was a definite public finance policy. 'The Mughal administration aimed at realizing about 60 per cent of the total claimed land revenue. With such a large share of the surplus appropriated by the apparatus of the state, its distribution among the ruling class necessarily contributed a major element in the economy of the Mughal India'. (Shireen, 1987) The nature of tax enforcement was such that it was noted that the taxes were collected with an iron hand, with the assistance of the army.

Exclusive colonial-economic orientation: the taxation during the British period

In ancient and medieval India, the taxes were imposed and collected by the state, much for the personal needs of the kings/rulers and for the protection from internal revolts and external aggressions. The objectives of the system of taxation under the British also remained the same, since it was designed to protect and enlarge the interests of the Company and the British Crown. While the cultural and religious dimensions were dominant in the fiscal policy of the ancient and medieval India, the nature of taxation in British India was purely 'economic' and oriented towards the economic and strategic interests of the East India Company (EIC) and the Crown. The system of taxation in British India evolved in the background of the 'Protective Policy' followed by the Great Britain which was always against the interests of the people of India. (Banerjee,

1922) The commercial expansion in the East was the only objective of the EIC. When the EIC assumed ruling powers, it developed its own tariff system. The tax laws were framed and implemented in such a way that it did not affect the export and import trade with Great Britain. The produce and manufactures of India, heavily taxed by the inland systems, were placed in an unquestionably disadvantageous position in coming into competition with free or lightly taxed foreign articles. According to Baneerjee, (1922) these changes resulted in a great loss of public revenue, and caused taxation to operate within an unequal environment, that dried up considerable source of revenue. Cohn (1997) has analysed the nature of law enforcement during the colonial period. According to him, though in the British cultural system, the capacity to assess taxes was inextricably linked with law, the tax management of the British in India was totally unsystematic. They found that, due to mismanagement, their actions had caused a horrendous famine, in which it was estimated that a third of the population of Bengal died.

TB - 2.6

James B Wilson : The man behind the Indian Income Tax?

2010 marks the 150th anniversary of the introduction of income tax in India. To be precise, on 22 February 1860, Sir James B Wilson, who was the financial member of the Council of India introduced what may be called a triple assessment: 1) a tax on income of all kinds; 2) a system of licenses for arts, trades, and professions; and 3) a tobacco tax. The bill received the assent of the Governor General on 24th July 1860. Out of these, the last two were dropped as there were difficulties in levying and also for the reason that they were found unnecessary. It is said that 'for the first time in the history of the world it was demonstrated that India, an oriental country was ready to meet with equanimity and courage the greatest engine of western finance, a modern income tax'. (Pragar, 1920)

Income tax was withdrawn within 5 years. The stated reason was understatement of income. In what were then called the North-Western Provinces, out of every hundred income tax returns, 'only four were acceptable to authorities'. More than one-fifth of the total tax was paid by the public officials and the fund holders, 'this portion being deducted at source, which seems to be the only redeeming feature of the Act'. (Pragar, 1920) The basic exemtion was Rs 200 in 1860 and later raised to Rs 500 in 1862.

A MATTER OF TIME?

During the period from 1858 and up to 1900, India was compelled to follow the principle of free trade, ostensibly on the ground of reformative theories, but, really for the benefit of England and India was not allowed to develop any industrial enterprise if it happened to come in competition, even in a remote and indirect way, with British Industry. After the sepoy mutiny of 1857, the British placed the administration of the British India under the direct political control of the Crown as a branch of the British Empire. Consequently, the Governor-General in the Council was saddled with the sole responsibility of making relevant legislation for the entire country. To overcome the financial difficulties, which followed the mutiny of 1857, Harrington, then a temporary member of the Executive Council, proposed a bill on the 13th August 1859 for imposing a license fee on every person, company, association or body of individuals. This was not, however passed into law. The first tax on traders and professions was proposed by James Wilson, the first Finance Member of India, in his Financial Statement on the 22nd February 1860, and it became operative within a month. He, while introducing the Act, quoted from the authority of Manu, the ancient Indian law giver for levying income tax in the country.

It was thus that the Indian Income Tax Act took a concrete shape; it remained in force till 1865, when there was a total restructuring of the

TB - 2.7

Charles Trevelyan: The man who opposed income tax in India

Sir Charles Trevelyan, the most popular Governor of Madras, officially opposed income tax, the imperial impost in India vehemently. However he had to pay the penalty by being recalled for his opposition. He was Governor of Madras from 1859 to 1869 and Indian Finance Minister from 1862 to 1865. He was reprimanded for openly sending a message suggesting alternate fiscal plans. Sir Charles Wood, the President of Board of Control stated in the recall order that 'Sir Charles Trevelyan is an honest, zealous, upright and independent Civil Servant. He was a loss to India, but there would be danger if he were allowed to remain, after having adopted a course so subversive of all authority, so fearfully tending to endanger our rule, and so likely to provoke the people to insurrection against the central and responsible authority'. (Hansard, 1860)

Income Tax Act, classifying the various sources of income. When World War broke out, there occurred in India, a general dislocation of trade and finance. (Rush Brook, 1985) There was a considerable demand for the remittances of money to London. Accordingly, in the budget of 1916-17, the Government of India strengthened its position by a programme of taxation that included the revision of import tariffs, increased export duties and the direct taxation of income. India was thus able to offer to 'His Majesty's Government' a special capital contribution of 100 million (which is much more than her annual revenue), towards the expenses of war. It is said that 'as the British income tax was a direct outcome of Napoleonic wars, so was the Indian income tax precipitated by the increased military preparedness for the "Russian Menace", and also for the annexation of Burma, in the interest of British capital and enterprise, against the wishes of the intelligent public opinion in India'. (Pragar, 1920) In order to meet the recurring charges, which this offer entailed, additional taxation was imposed. This new taxation took the form of a super-tax on incomes. (Rush Brook,1985)

TB - 2.8

New wine in old bottle?
Manu and income tax

James B Wilson while introducing the income tax in India drew substantially from the ancient Hindu Law Code 'Manu Smriti' (also called as 'manava dharma' , Manu Samhita and Code of Manu) to provide contextual legitimacy to the system of taxation in his attempt to indigenize the same.

As per the Code of Manu, the king is justified in levying direct taxes on land, merchants, artisans, and mechanics. Revenue was collected both in kind and coin in ancient India. On cattle, gold, and other moveables, the state's share mounted to one-fiftieth, which in time of war or invasion might be increased to one-twentieth. On land, one-twelth, one-eighth, and one-sixth of gross produce, according to quality of soil and the labour to cultivate it. As per the Code, the king might also take one-sixth of the clear annual profits of wood-cutters, butchers, dairy-men, potters, perfumers, tanners etc. The mechanics and artisans as well as other manual labourers were required to work for the state one day in each month.[8]

Thus it is very clear that the system of taxation during the British period had taken a purely 'colonial' character, which was exclusively 'economic' but oriented solely to satisfy the interests of Great Britain.

The predominant 'social' dimensions: Taxation in post-independent India

Though the system of taxation in Independent India, in its legislative content, was rooted in the earlier enactment of British India, there were radical changes in the nature and objectives of taxation, with corresponding changes in the ideological structure of the Indian political system. The revenue objective of taxation in independent India is directly linked with national programmes on welfare maximization. Due to the partisan and discriminatory fiscal policies followed in ancient and medieval India and under the British, people in general and the taxpayers in particular had developed total aversion/apathy towards the tax legislators and the tax administration. The above attitude evolved due to the historical-sociological factors discussed earlier. According to Smith and Tylor (1996), the tax compliance would be most likely when the authority in question is included in a superordinate identity, where most people are included in one's self-definition. When the authorities are perceived to behave in a fair manner, they are considered to be representative and their decisions are seen as legitimate. Tax apathy emanates in people when they see the authorities as partisan and biased. Due to the perception that taxing powers of the erstwhile administrations were illegitimate, the people of the country had developed a negative attitude about taxation in general. Therefore, the government of post-independent India had to re-orient the system of taxation to reassure the people of India about the broader objectives of taxation, which were aimed at the total welfare of the people.

Thus, in Independent India, taxation is an instrument not only to augment finances of the Government treasury, but also to fulfill certain 'social' objectives. In fact, the former ultimately leads to the latter. The idea of differential taxation was introduced for the reduction of inequalities of income and wealth so as to secure economic justice. The principle is that equal amount of taxes be paid by the tax payers with equal abilities (horizontal equity) irrespective of their caste, community or religion and that different amounts of taxes be paid by the assessees with different abilities to pay (vertical redistribution). The provisions of taxation and tax exemptions were formulated so as to encourage individuals to save through constructive schemes and to discourage unproductive investments and conspicuous consumption.

In short, a historical analysis of systems of taxation and tax enforcement in India during the ancient, medieval and the British period clearly brings to light the discriminatory and partisan characteristics that dominated each distinguishable period. The fiscal policies are evolved over a period of time with marked changes in the nature and objectives as a latent result of the dominant factors and characteristics in each period. While the system of taxation in ancient and medieval India had predominant cultural and religious moorings, with inherent disparity based on caste, community and religion, the system in Colonial period has taken a purely 'economic' character with an unquestionable bias favouring the interests of the British government. However, in both the periods the ultimate objective of taxation was to satisfy the selfish interests of the ruling class. Thus, there is a historical-sociological reason for the apathy of Indians in general and of taxpayers in particular against taxation and tax enforcement. In sharp contrast to the tax policies before independence, the system of taxation in post-independent India has taken a 'social' character, with emphasis on vertical redistribution and horizontal equity. However, by that time, the historical apathy to taxation was deeply ingrained in the society.

Creating history

This quick analysis of global tax history, especially Indian tax history, has shown the transitions in tax policy under different socio-political regimes. Thus, changes in tax compliance and tax attitudes are not just automatic transitions as time passes, but are results of both economic changes as well tax policy changes. Economic changes and tax policy changes are mutually dependent, but the former exercises comparatively more influence on the latter than the reverse. One has to create a new history of tax compliance, by creating a socio-political and economic environment which creates a positive tax attitude. Only a fiscal policy that is formulated with a clear understanding of the sociological needs and expectations of the taxpayers can bring about such a desired tax compliance culture.

040

MAKING PEOPLE PAY

CHAPTER-3

A MATTER OF MONEY?

The Economics of Taxation

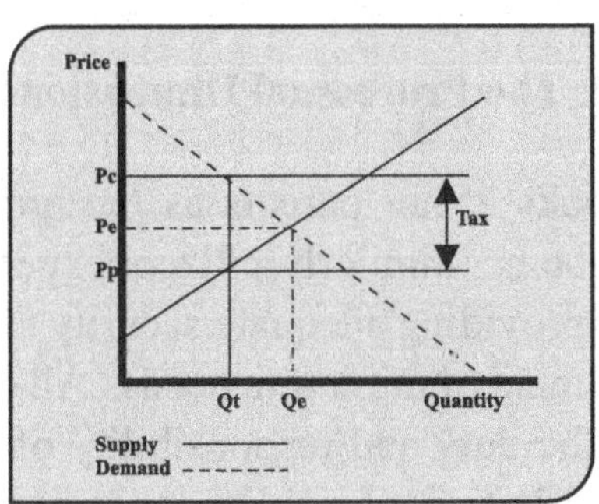

'Now a seriously silly thought. From this focus on open-minded reasoning, there is much that economists too can learn. The subject stands to lose a lot from dogmatic beliefs of one kind or another (for example, we are constantly asked: "Are you against or in favour of the market? Against or in favour of state action? Just answer the question - no qualifications, no 'ifs' and 'buts,' please!"). This is an invitation to replace analysis by slogans - to be guided by grand dogma, either of one kind, or of another. We do need "the clear stream of reason." What Tagore, the poet, and Chandrashekhar, the physicist, demanded, we need in economics too - for much the same reason. That is the last silly thought I inflict on you tonight.'

(Thus did, Amartya Sen end his Nobel Banquet speech)

In this chapter, the subject of economics of taxation is dealt with at two different levels. Firstly, at the processual level, taxation is analyzed in the background of economic theory and policy. Here the system of taxation is analysed as an economic institution for resource mobilization for investments and expenditure and also aimed at redistribution. Secondly at the theoretical level, it is examined as to what extent economic analysis can explain tax policy and tax compliance behaviour. The former would help in providing a descriptive analysis of 'what and how' of taxation and the latter is expected to provide the explanatory analysis of 'why' of taxation and the tax behaviour. In the first case the focus is on economics as a process and in the second case the focus is on economics as a discipline.

I. The Processual Dimensions

A young child looks at her parents as the provider of goods and services for her well-being. Similarly, citizens expect the state to be their guardian not only in providing adequate security and freedom, but also in ensuring the fulfillment of minimum needs. All over the world, it has been recognized as the duty and responsibility of the governments to ensure equitable distribution of public goods and to provide for the needs of the less privileged citizens and groups. An effective mechanism to draw and manage resources is thus necessary for the state. Various economic instruments are in use to gather the much-needed resources to maintain the citizens and the territory.

Mobilizing revenue in a dynamic economy

Governments adopt several methods to raise revenue for the equitable development of the country. Some of the methods other than taxation are: owning business enterprises; administering service charges and user fee; fund raising through lotteries, loans and contributions from financial institutions and individuals, etc. Apart from the above, countries (more often in the recent decades) adopt monetary strategies such as devaluation of the currency. All these methods to raise revenue have several deficiencies and difficulties.

Governments in several countries, despite large-scale transition to capitalistic society and privatization, still own a large number of business enterprises. However, many such public sector concerns have earned an awful reputation of being inefficient, corrupt and of making losses. Revenues from such white elephants are fast depleting in several countries. The current maxim is that 'the government has no business to do the business.' The public opinion echoes the private sector plea that government's role should be that of a facilitator than that of a provider.

The second method of earning revenue is through charging for services. Even in the wake of privatization and globalization it is the responsibility of the national governments to provide services to their people. Providing security (internal as well as external), an environment conducive to raise income, free / concession facilities for education, health, food and shelter, etc are perceived as some of the unfailing responsibilities of governments. Therefore, even after privatizing a host of services, government continues to be the large-scale service provider in several countries. This is more so in highly populated countries and in countries where the per capita income is low. In such a scenario, the introduction of service charges or user fee or a marginal raise in service tariffs would invite hardship to people and that would result in large-scale resentment. Thus, this method is not successful in plugging the resource crunch.

The third method is raising funds from the public. Many governments have tried lotteries to raise revenue, in spite of the criticism that it amounts to state-sponsored gambling. As early as the 16th century, lottery was used by many countries to raise quick revenue. Among many lower income groups, the purchasing of lottery tickets and then expecting a good fortune has got habituated to the level of addiction, leaving the families to suffer further financial crisis. This is worsened with the entry of several private online and paper lotteries in several countries. The frequent frauds in the operation of private lotteries have resulted in their prohibition by many countries. In fact, many affluent figures sometimes use the lottery route to 'clean' their unaccounted wealth by 'purchasing' winning lottery tickets. Of late, the revenue from the state owned lotteries is very meagre and governments tend to discourage this due to the several negative consequences mentioned above.

The fourth method to raise funds by the governments is through borrowings. Countries demand contributions from public in the name of provident funds, welfare funds and insurance schemes. Governments also resort to large-scale loans from international financial institutions like the International Monetary Fund (IMF), the World Bank and from regional financial institutions such as the Asian Development Bank (ADB) to make long-term capital investments. However most of these funds tend to be used to meet revenue expenditure, unproductive capital investments and to reconstruct and maintain loss making public enterprises. Due to misapplication and misutilization of funds, the repayment schedules get disturbed and the interest burden increases by leaps and bounds. India, for example, ended up using more than half of the revenue receipts of the government merely to pay interest on the accumulated debts. Thus, governments rarely earn considerable revenue out of investments made through financial borrowings. In such a grim scenario, an option, though unfortunate but practical, before several governments was to earn quick revenues through the sale of public enterprises and the collection of huge license fee from service providers.

Many governments resort to the more 'easy' method of currency devaluation to uplift the economy. Many countries such as Great Britain, the United States, France, Switzerland, India, Thailand, Mexico, The Czech Republic, etc have devalued their currencies to stabilize the economy and to encourage exports. However, many a time, this becomes counterproductive. The large circulation of money as a result of such devaluation results in inflation and in drastic increase in prices. These affect the low and middle income groups and the value of the money they hold diminishes without any proportionate increase in the capacity to generate an actual increase in income.

Emergence of market economy and issues in public goods delivery

A most simplified definition of market economy would be that it is a market in which supply and demand are either not regulated or least regulated. In a competitive market, it is assumed that there is fair play where efficient players are rewarded and inefficient players are wiped out. However players in this game start at different locations in the track. Many players position themselves much ahead of many others by virtue of their innate capacities resulting in relative deprivation of the latter. It is never possible that competition starts on a clean slate without any carry forward of ascribed gains or ascribed privileges.

Markets in a globalized and liberalized economic environment tolerate and cater to anything big. And small is no longer 'beautiful'[1] and viable as it was thought earlier. Markets are fertile ground for giant firms engaged in wholesale and retail businesses. Those who earned a living setting up small businesses like provisional stores, small-scale industries, provision of various services etc in their native localities had to down their shutters in the wake of stiff competition from big players who spread their net into every possible income-generating activity in society. Most of those erstwhile proprietors of small firms took a wise (which was rather inevitable) decision to join as employees in those big firms and others who had not joined have slipped into extreme poverty and debt. Governments of various countries could not close their eyes to these realities in the aftermath of the emergence of market economy. Service providers with multinational presence, create a consumer base and they believe that it is the consumers who ultimately gain out of the competitive tariffs. However, in the process, a sizable number of potential consumers are kept out of the bargain due to 'un-affordability' even at the least quoted tariff. Those masses look at the government for support in the form of subsidies, waivers and concessions.

In the spirit of the finer principles of market economy, governments by and large relieved themselves of their responsibilities of owning business enterprises, including those which made profits. Revenue from providing services also dwindled due to the entry of multiple players. At the same time, governments have their primary responsibility to provide public goods[2] for all those who cannot otherwise afford them in the competitive market. Thus, governments thought it fit to introduce a new set of regulators in many service areas where private enterprises made inroads. Regulatory bodies in areas such as insurance, power, telecom, banking, etc started playing the roles of watchdogs in many countries to protect the interests of the public. However, most of the private service providers whose sole aim is to earn maximum profits are least interested to step into fields which are less yielding. Therefore the responsibility remains with the governments to provide public goods such as education, health care, subsidized supply of food grains and cooking fuel, housing, etc for the disadvantaged citizens. In order to achieve this, the governments need to create a balance in the economy and plug the inequality created by the market economy. However, that demands huge expenditure for governments especially of countries with large population. Therefore the governments have no other option but to depend heavily on taxation to raise resources.

Taxation as an instrument to resolve the resource crunch

As discussed earlier most of the sources through which governments earned revenue have dwindled over a period of time. Taxation is increasingly recognized as an instrument to generate consistent revenue across the world. Various types of taxes are being introduced in different names in different countries. Though there are various classifications typical to different countries, broadly the taxes can be classified into taxes on goods, services, income and wealth. Some are traditionally labeled as 'direct' taxes (where the burden to pay tax and the primary liability are exclusively on the person against whom it is charged) and others as 'indirect' taxes. (where the burden to pay can be shifted to another person) However, according to several contemporary experts in public finance, the distinction as direct and indirect is incorrect, as the burden is increasingly being shifted among the categories.

Though an examination of the fiscal history of various countries shows hundreds of types of taxes on goods, income, people, assets, services, etc, tax categories in contemporary times are more or less uniform across the world. Income tax, Wealth tax, Corporation tax, Goods and Services Tax, Excise tax, Inheritance tax, Property tax, Value

Added Tax, etc are some of the prominent taxes. The level and structure of taxation are different in different countries, though there are several similarities. This is because the social and economic requirements vary with respect to each country. Economists see taxes as not only a transfer of wealth from public to the state but also as an instrument which can either decrease or increase the overall wealth in the economy. This depends on the utilization of taxes collected to create further resources.

Deadweight costs of taxation and optimal tax theory

Economic analysts find that taxation leads to 'deadweight losses' when goods are supplied in a perfectly competitive market. Tax reduces economic efficiency (the value of lost output) by prompting people to switch from higher valued to lower valued economic activities. The tax revenues utilized by the governments need to be weighed against the deadweight losses incurred at the time of levying. However, no clear quantification of such deadweight loss is done by governments. According to economists most taxes, not only income tax, have a deadweight cost. It is said that by reducing deadweight losses, tax cuts tend to stimulate growth. Countries which significantly cut taxes between 1980 and 2000 enjoyed an average per capita economic growth rate which was nearly three times more than the growth garnered by those nations that did not do so. (Robson, 2005) Optimal tax theory examines questions such as 'what is the type of tax that is most suitable?' and 'how progressive should the tax system be?' Optimal taxation theorists consider how taxes can be structured so that the deadweight costs can be minimized. According to Ramsey (1927), putting the highest tax rates on the goods for which there is most inelastic supply and demand will result in the least overall deadweight costs. However, many scholars have been critical of this[3] and the theory could not provide a proper direction to tax policy. The theory does not recognize the importance of political externalities and social costs. The assumption that consumer behaviour is solely based on rational and prompt decisions may not be always correct. It is imperative to examine various social structural determinants that trigger utilization of money by individuals.

Inability of Laffer Curve to explain tax behaviour

The concept of Laffer Curve, though said to have been originally conceived by a 14th century Islamic scholar Ibn Khaldun, is currently known after Arther Laffer, who strongly advocated the idea more appropriately in the context of taxation. Based on the concept of Taxable Income Elasticity (TIE) from the school of supply-side economics, it advocates that government can maximize tax revenue by setting tax rates at an optimum point. According to this concept, the government collects nil revenue when the tax rate is either 0% or 100%.

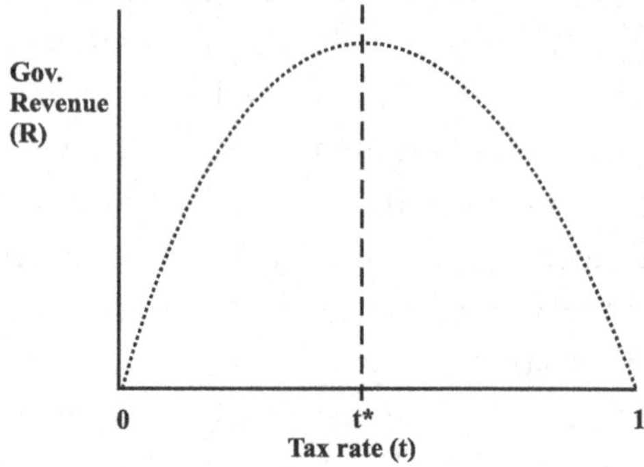

('t' signifies the tax rate at which maximum tax revenue can be realized, which need not necessarily be 50 per cent; 0 is 0 per cent tax rate and 1 is 100 per cent tax rate.)*

Many theorists have attempted to explain the fall in tax revenue by the steeper tax rates and have noted the examples of countries where tax cuts have resulted in increased revenues. The supply-side economists elaborated upon the Laffer Curve and advocated that lowering taxes to the right level can raise revenue by causing faster economic growth. They pointed to the tax cuts of the Kennedy administration and the high rates of the Hoover and Nixon administrations in justification of this explanation.

However, this concept cannot explain the fiscal behaviour in a dynamic economy. It would be impossible to attribute the quantum of tax revenue realized when there is no flat tax rate. Not only in the case of income tax, but most of the contemporary taxes cannot be explained through this concept. In countries where the taxability of income itself is preceded by several conditions, exemptions and incentives, the Laffer Curve has no meaning at all. Tax compliance may increase or decrease based on several other factors apart from the quantum of tax rates. It also depends on the overall economic well-being and purchasing power of the people. The Laffer Curve assumption cannot be applied in tax systems which provide for several categories of exempted income, gradation in rates (slabs), etc. Thus, even when there is a widespread feeling among tax payers that tax rates are very high, that does not necessarily translate in equal proportion to the tax compliance behaviour. In countries where tax evasion has a long history, where tax non-compliance is not frowned upon, where substantial population is outside the tax net and where the tax enforcement is weak, the tax behaviour cannot be explained in such a simplified fashion. Consequently, tax policies cannot be formulated solely based on tax rate as a variable.

Do tax rates have an impact on tax revenue?

It is generally viewed that high marginal tax rates discourage work effort, savings, and investment, and promote tax avoidance and tax evasion. Subsequently, it is perceived that a cut in tax rates will have a reverse impact. That is in fact the objective behind tax cuts in several countries. Most of the developing countries too have followed suit in relaxing the tax policies of their domains; this is mainly to fall in line with the globalization agenda. For them, the aim has not been just increased tax revenue but a sharp economic growth in the liberalized competitive environment.

In many countries across the world there were attempts to reduce the tax rates in the decades after 1980. In the USA, there were two major federal tax reforms, the Economic Recovery Tax Act of 1981 and the Tax Reform Act of 1986. As a result of these reforms, the top marginal tax rate at the federal level fell from 70 per cent in 1980 to 28 per cent by

1988, and the income tax schedule was reduced from 15 brackets to four. Scholars have said that the overall elasticity of taxable income with respect to changes in net-of-tax marginal rates is 0.4.[4] That is, a 10 per cent change in the marginal net-of-tax rate (that is, the difference between 100 per cent and the marginal tax rate) leads to a 4 per cent change in taxable income. It was argued that this elasticity is primarily the result of a greater response by taxpayers with high incomes. The studies showed that after the high marginal tax rates of 1981 were cut, tax payments and the share of the tax burden borne by the top 1 per cent climbed sharply.[5] There is a contrasting view as well that almost all tax hikes have seen dramatic and indisputable growth in tax and that tax cuts increase tax collections is a myth.[6] It was humorously remarked that the claim that the Reagan tax cuts caused the doubling of revenues is like a rooster claiming credit for dawn.[7]

Studies have shown that low-income countries have imposed, on an average, the highest rates of marginal tax despite having the lowest incomes. It was also found that the higher marginal rates of low-income countries fall on a comparatively low level of income. (Pillarisetti, 2003) Allingham and Sandmo (1972) suggested that changes in the marginal rates will result in offsetting effects. According to them, a higher tax rate will reduce after-tax income which, assuming decreasing relative risk aversion would tend to reduce evasion - the income effect. A higher rate would also make it more profitable to evade taxes, resulting in increased evasion - the substitution effect. Using the TCMP data, Clotfelter (1983) examined the effects of marginal tax rates and found that both income and tax rates were positively related to non-compliance. It is said that the expected change in compliance due to a change in the tax rate would be ambiguous. (Allingham and Sandmo, 1972) In a laboratory experiment, Friedland, Maital and Rutenberg (1978) found that penalty rates were positively related to compliance and tax rates were negatively correlated to compliance.

However there are neither clear conclusions nor consensus among economists that lower tax rates have contributed to stronger economic growth. It is extremely difficult to arrive at a clear conclusion on the impact of tax rates on tax revenue, as there are different types of taxes and multiple rates in various countries. It is also important not to neglect the impact of surcharge, cess, changes in tax incentive structure, increase or decrease in tax concessions to select categories, etc. Similarly, non-tax concessions to industries also contribute to overall impact on the economy.

The analysis of data regarding tax revenues of different countries over a period of time has not given any clear indication that reduction in rates have resulted in higher tax revenues. Similarly, there is also no consensus among economists and other scholars about the positive impact of tax cuts on overall economic growth. However, it is quite clear that neither higher marginal rates nor lower marginal rates would lead to more revenue. That need not necessarily accelerate or retard growth considerably. Similarly, no standard rate can be adopted across the countries, in spite of the globalized economic environment. That would squarely depend on an analysis and appreciation of the facts such as per capita income, the extent of population falling in various income slabs, the history of tax compliance behaviour, and the nature of enforcement. Thus, an economic analysis of tax compliance on the basis of a quantitative study of tax rates cannot provide an appropriate explanation for all countries for a considerable period of time. However, such an exercise would be quite insightful when specific tax proposals on specific categories for particular periods are examined.

The tax revenue, the GDP and the per-capita income

The tax burden of a particular country can be measured by analyzing the ratio of tax revenue to GDP. As per the OECD report, the higher tax ratios are a result of stronger economic growth in these countries, and more generally across the OECD. Stronger growth increases both the profitability of companies and the level of personal incomes, leading to an increase in the level of taxes that they pay.[8]

Minh Le, Moreno-Dodson and Rojchaichaninthorn, (2008) after analysing the Gross National Income estimation by the World Bank for 1994, 1998, and 2003, found that higher income countries collected higher tax revenues and the pattern holds for all the three groups of countries of different levels of income per capita. In the high-income countries, the tax-GDP ratio increased dramatically from 21 per cent to approximately 30 per cent over the decade. The levels of collection efforts, however, did not significantly change for the groups of low and middle-income countries. Low-income countries' collections stayed relatively flat, at around 14 per cent, while middle-income countries experienced a modest increase from 20 per cent to 21 per cent. It was found that the average of tax-GDP in all groups of countries rose from approximately 19 per cent in 1994 to 22 per cent in 2003. Their review of the tax-GDP ratios indicated that tax collections tend to be linked positively to a country's level of income.

Though many countries rely on the Tax-GDP data to compare their respective potential and performance with other countries, many scholars tend to disagree with this tendency. Pillarisetti (2003) argued that it is a misleading measure, 'since lower 6.8 per cent for Zambia should still constitute a higher tax burden for low-income Zambia as compared with the high-income UK'. This is true for several other countries as well. (Prest, 1979) The share of taxes is not more than one-fifth of the GDP for many countries in the world.[9] In India, the tax-GDP ratio declined immediately after the liberalization in the early 1990s, and could improve only after about 15 years. It was about 10.1 in 1990-91 and the same declined to 8.2 when liberalization was at its peak and the tax rates where stabilized without any further cut.

A study by World Bank has indicated that taxes tend to rise as the per-capita income rises.[10] It was found that tax ratio rose from about 17 per cent in the low-income group, to 22 per cent in the medium-income group, and 27 per cent in the high-income group. As the per-capita income increases, the revenue from income tax increases much more than from many of the indirect taxes.

Tax reforms across the world

Most of the tax reforms across the world were centred on reduction of taxes, particularly those other than income tax. The first step in this direction was the progressive reduction of export and import tariffs. It is said that 'Rome was not built in one day, nor should a full-fledged modern tax system be set up within a year or two'. (Lief, 1992) The 1980s and the 1990s witnessed a series of tax reforms across several countries. The USA took the lead among the advanced countries and there were radical reforms in countries like New Zealand, Australia, Canada, France, Japan, Sweden, etc. Many countries in Latin America, Asia, Middle East, Africa, etc have spearheaded the reforms among less advanced countries. (Thirsk, 1990) Various countries have continued to scale town the tax tariffs in the recent decades. A few developed countries took the lead and several other countries followed suit. The basic premise is that lower marginal tax rates would boost the economy.

Another trend is to channelize the tax policies in such a way that the share of the direct taxes increases and the indirect taxes decreases. The reason for this shift is because of the increased realization that direct taxes are progressive and the indirect taxes are regressive. Chu, Davoodi, and Gupta (2000) found after reviewing 36 studies of tax systems (all taxes) in 19 developing countries, that 13 studies found the tax system progressive, 7 studies found the tax system regressive and other studies have by and large gave mixed findings. For income tax systems, of the 14 studies, 12 found the same progressive, one study reported the system regressive and the another study gave mixed findings.

In the area of income tax, the reforms were basically oriented to rationalization and simplification. The reforms also aimed at curbing double taxation and to widen the tax net to the sectors of the economy hitherto untaxed. The reforms were also aimed at improving the tax administration through steps for computerization, reduction in collection costs and effective checks to curb corruption. Most of the reform initiatives in developing countries were in line with the structural adjustment programmes prescribed by the international development agencies. (World Bank 1997; 2005) Though all countries aimed at higher tax revenues with least pain for the stake holders, each country needed to follow its own trajectory to achieve the above goal. Therefore, tax policies vary significantly between developing and developed economies.[11] However, an analysis of tax reforms across the world clearly indicates that there have to be country specific policies even among the developing countries, in order to achieve optimum results.

Most of the countries (especially the developing economies) have focused on expanding the income tax base. Income tax is considered as less regressive as compared with goods and services taxes. Income tax inflicts less excess burden on the taxpayer than does a specific tax of equal yield. It is so because it interferes less with the choices of the consumers and the resource allocation.[12] Thus, there is ample scope for expanding the income tax base. The reforms are more oriented towards simplification of laws and procedures and better taxpayer services.

In recent decades, radical tax reforms have been initiated in several countries irrespective of the stage of economic development. Gillis (1985), Harberger (1989), Asher (1997), *et al* have extensively studied the reform trajectory in Indonesia. Indonesian tax reforms were centred on the redesigning of the tax structure and the restructuring of the tax administration. Philippines also attempted radical reforms in taxes in the 1980s. The Tax Reform Program, 1986 of the Philippines adopted measures not only to trim down evasion opportunities but also advocated measures to promote equity, simplicity and efficiency in the hope of steering taxpayer behaviour towards honest tax compliance.

World Bank (1988) has done a detailed study on tax reforms in Columbia, Poland, Belaruz, Canada, Bolivia, etc. Sandford analysed tax reforms in six developed countries and recognized the following factors as contributing towards their success: a) strong political will, b) strong backing from the chief executive, c) radical and comprehensive reform package, d) comparative and measurable gain for people as a whole,

e) total transparency and f) a highly competent team to propagate the proposals among the public.

The Study Group on Asian Tax Administration and Research (SGATAR)-an organization comprising member countries such as Australia, Indonesia, Japan, Korea, Malaysia, New Zealand, Philippines, Singapore and Thailand-has analyzed the problems of tax avoidance and evasion in these countries in the 1980s.[13] The report indicated that substantial extent of income went unreported in these countries and most of the methods of tax evasion were similar in these countries irrespective of the stage of tax reform, though there was increasing compliance reported in countries like New Zealand, Singapore and Australia.

Tax reforms in India

In India revenue deficit continues to be a fiscal challenge. Drastic steps to reduce the revenue deficit have been taken by the Government of India since 2003. Finance ministers considered fiscal stabilization the top priority in achieving macro economic growth. The landmark step in this regard was the unanimous decision by all political parties to vote for the Fiscal Responsibility and Budget Management (FRBM) Act 2003[14] introduced in Parliament. Though the Act was aimed at complete elimination of revenue deficit by 2007-08, this could not materialize that year. Drastic reforms were proposed in the area of fiscal policy, monetary policy and exchange rate policy. One of the key strategies identified in the area of fiscal policy was tax reform. Various fiscal reforms proposed in the FRBM Act are aimed at giving India a world-class tax system by reducing compliance costs, tackling tax evasion and eliminating the distorted behaviour that comes from tax avoidance. The fiscal deficit of the centre, as a proportion of GDP, has come down from 6.2% in 2001-02 to 3.4 per cent in 2006-07. The gross tax-GDP ratio increased to 11.4 per cent in 2006-07[15] and it was further increased to 11.9 per cent of GDP in 2007-08. As per the budget estimates of 2008-09, central direct taxes (gross) to GDP was 6.68[16] per cent. Total direct tax collections (corporation tax and personal income taxes) in the financial year 2009-10 was Rs. 3,78,350 crore.

India has one of the lowest levels of the Tax/GDP ratio in the world. As there are several types of tax exemptions and tax concessions, tax from the total revenue is grossly disproportional. Though several steps have been taken to reform the central excise provisions and procedures, they are still marred by several complexities. Lack of clarity in classification and numerous exemptions which are subject to misuse are the main hurdles in the smooth levy of central excise. As the share of the service sector in the GDP has increased considerably, the Tax Reforms Committee recommended the levy of a tax on services in 1991. The Finance Act, 1994 introduced the service tax of 5 per cent on three services. Service tax rates were hiked since then, and tax was expanded to various other services. As against the larger share of central excise and customs revenue in earlier decades, the post-1990 period witnessed a drastic increase in the share from income tax.

India has only a microscopic minority which pays income tax on a regular basis. As per the statistics as on March 2009 there were more than 3.01 crore individual income tax assessees in India; a mere 3 per cent of the total population. If one considers the fact that lakhs of assessees claim refund of the taxes withheld at source, the effective taxpayers would be much less than the number of income tax return filers. However, India has witnessed radical growth in both the number of taxpayers as well as the tax collections in the last two decades. In the year 2008-09 alone there was an increase of 9.01 lakh new assessees.[17a] This is because of the increased recognition of direct taxes as a potential source of revenue by the Government of India and its effective tax reforms. Still, income tax is a strange subject for a large cross section of people; large quantities of unaccounted income are circulated in the economy. There are no clear statistics on the percentage of tax evaders in the country. There are also no clear estimates of the extent of unaccounted income or wealth in the country. The unaccounted income and the consequent undisclosed wealth multiplied several-fold in the late twentieth century in India. Though there is a plethora of studies on the parallel economy or the illegal wealth in India, none of them give a clear picture. (Kumar, 1999) Thus, we have to be content with only 'guestimates' on the extent of undisclosed income in India. But nobody can deny the fact that a very substantial portion of the money generated by the Indians escape the tax net.

Researchers and Public Finance Analysts have tried to understand the features of the parallel economy. (Kabra, 1982; Kaldor 1956; Acharya,1985) They have explored the diverse ways in which unaccounted money is generated. (Gupta S.B, 1992; Kumar, 1999; Bhattacharya, 1999)

> "In our country, (however), tax evasion and black money have now reached a stage which can only be described as a menace to the economy and a challenge to the fulfillment of the avowed objectives of distributive justice and setting up of an egalitarian society...Today the country is seriously handicapped in its endeavor to march forward, when the resources needed for development are not adequately forthcoming for the reason that business is carried on in "black.""
>
> (Report of the Wanchoo Committee (1971))

The Union Government has constituted several committees at various periods of time to study the system of taxation, the nature of tax evasion and tax administration. The John Mathai Commission 1963, Prof Nicholas Kaldor Committee 1956, Direct Taxes Enquiry Committee 1959, Boothalingam Committee 1967, Wanchoo Committee 1971, Direct Tax Laws Committee 1978, L K Jha Commission 1981, Dr Raja J Chelliah Committee 1991, etc are some of the committees. The Government has considered most of the recommendations made by the committees and appropriate amendments have been made in the tax laws and the administrative machinery has been revamped from time to time. The committee headed by V Kelkar had submitted its report to the Government in 2002. Some of its suggestions are the following: a) better taxpayer service by the income tax department, b) mandatory filing of annual information returns by third parties, c) electronic data exchange with other departments, d) establishment of Tax Information Network, e) establishment of institution of income tax ombudsman, f) income tax on agricultural income, g) elimination of various tax exemptions, and h) rationalization of tax slabs. Some of the recommendations of the Kelkar Task Force have been implemented.

The Direct Taxes Code (DTC) introduced by the Government of India was an attempt to improve the efficiency and equity of the tax system by eliminating distortions in the tax structure. Principles that have gained international acceptance were adopted in the DTC. The best practices in the world were studied and incorporated in this Code. Some of the salient features of the Code, as delineated by the Ministry of Finance are: a) a single code that covers all direct taxes, b) simple language, c) less ambiguity to avoid litigation, d) consolidation of provisions, and e) certainty about tax structure. The definition of 'income' for purposes of DTC include all accruals and receipts of revenue and capital nature unless otherwise specified. Provisions of exemptions are on the basis of positive externalities, equity, encouraging human development, reducing risk, and reducing compliance and administrative burden[17b]. The functional impact of the Code will be known only after a few years of its implementation.

In view of the increasing levels of unaccounted money generation and growing economic disparity in society, the Union Government has recognized the importance of stringent tax enforcement provisions. In order to effectively tackle the problem by detecting tax evasion and appropriating the ill-gotten income/wealth to the government treasury, Parliament had enacted provisions for search and seizure. Though there had been continuous initiatives to reform the income tax laws and procedures, tax evasion continues to plague India. The country thus faces the problems of tax evasion by the existing assessees and the challenge of bringing in millions of affluent people who are outside the tax-net.

Here it may be said that India has both tax capacity as well as tax potentiality. By tax capacity, it is meant that the country needs to expand its tax base (widening the tax net) not only to the top 10 per cent of income earners but also to the affluent middle class which constitutes about 20 per cent of the population. Barring about 30 per cent of people who are below the poverty line or bordering it, all the others need to be brought to the tax net for contributing their bit to the exchequer. Loud thinking is required to extend direct taxes to the heads and types of income that are hitherto not taxed. Tax rates can drop down to much lower levels if more people are brought to the tax net. The second method to exploit the tax capacity of the country is to ensuring that the existing assessees disclose their true income for taxation. Perception of tax potentiality stems from an optimistic evaluation of the prospects of the country as it is on a growth track. Rapid economic growth triggered by domestic investments as well as investments by foreign institutional investors has already given positive signals in this regard. What is important is that concerted tax efforts can bring about enhanced tax collections. (Chelliah *et al.* 1975; Stosky and Wolde Mariam 1997; and Minh Le, Moreno-Dodson and Rojchaichaninthorn 2008

It is very clear from a review of tax reforms across the world that the reforms were mostly centred on tinkering with the tax rates, and the restructuring of tax slabs and tax incentives. Thus, tax reforms were basically oriented to give a quantitative impact on the tax revenues through legislative changes rather than bringing about voluntary tax compliance through systematic socialization. The approach was based on rationalistic perspectives with the fundamental belief that individuals act on the basis of analysis of costs and benefits and perception of sanctions and rewards. This approach is also very evident in most of the studies in the area of taxation as detailed below.

II. Analytical dimensions

Taxation and tax compliance: The economist explanation

Undoubtedly, tax and taxation are terms that directly fall under the purview of any discipline concerned with monetary attributes. And anything concerned with money is often considered the exclusive domain of economics. Taxation as a subject has always been considered an exclusive part of economics for centuries. Now, the fundamental question is whether taxation is just a matter of money or it has any other structural or social linkages. As taxation as a subject comprises several theoretical and pragmatic dimensions such as tax rationale ('why' of taxation), tax policy ('how' of taxation) and tax laws ('what' of taxation), the scope of study goes beyond the boundaries of economics. Similarly areas such as tax administration, tax enforcement, tax compliance, tax evasion, and tax attitudes, take the subject to the realms of other social and behavioural disciplines. However, in spite of all such possible macro dimensions, economists do believe that their discipline can explain the phenomena independently. The reasoning is apparently quite convincing, became the basic view is that taxation and tax compliance are things concerned with money and are basically rooted in the utilitarian dimensions of human action.

It is not that the economists reject the non-economic dimensions of taxation. They tend to agree with the social, political and psychological dimensions of the whole gamut of taxation. However, their position is that all those linkages come under 'economics', since it is an inclusive discipline concerned with all utilitarian decisions. It is said that there is a continued process of 'economic imperialism' so as to extend the scope of the discipline.[18] Therefore, it was the economists who were the first to evince interest in the study of taxation and tax compliance in different parts of the world.

The primary attention of economists was centered on the nature and extent of underground economy and the growing non-compliance of the individuals. They have also made several studies on the optimum levels of taxation and public expenditure. The belief was that the economic theory plays an important role in providing a better understanding of the workings of the 'black economy'.[19] (Cowel, 1990, p 27) However, it is often commented that though the economists are the ones who are technically competent to give estimates of the extent of tax evasion and the sectorwise evasion, they have failed to give even rough estimates which are acceptable. It may be due to the diverse ways in which undisclosed money is generated and the frequent changes in the mode and channels of such transactions. As Cowell (1990, p. 196) points out, because of the inevitable problems of getting accurate data, there is a tendency to spend more time writing about how to measure the evasion activity rather than about the actual estimates. Estimating the unaccounted income in any country is extremely difficult because those individuals engaged in such income generating activities wish not to be identified and also because of their very dubious nature, such activities usually go unrecorded.

One of the studies by The Fraser Institute of Canada, contained a detailed analysis of the underground economies in several countries. Mirus and Smith estimated the under ground economy of Canada to be as large as 20 per cent of the measured Gross Domestic Product. It is estimated that the underground economy of the UK is about 7.5 per cent of its GDP.[20] The IRS estimated the amount of tax lost through evasion to be $US 127 billion in 1996 (Warsham, 1996) and $US 310 billion in 2004. (Stratton, 2004) A TCMP study by the US IRS in 1988 showed that 40 per cent of the US households had underpaid their taxes for that year. (Feinstein, 1999) According to estimates by the Centre for Economic Studies of the Private Sector, the informal economy in Mexico represents, depending on the method employed, between 25 per cent and 35 per cent of the formal gross domestic product.[21] As per the figures based on a Berkeley-Duke survey of emigrants from the USSR, about one third of the urban population's income was derived from the second economy.[22] (Grossman,1987) According to Feige (1990) China's underground economy has the features of being illegal, unreported, unrecorded, and informal, though specific figures are not estimated.

Webley, after reviewing the major studies on evaded income, provided a summary listing of all the main studies conducted by various persons and agencies using diverse methods. He has concluded that there is a 'consensus' that the underground economy is about 2 to 10 per cent of GNP in western economies; with 7 to10 per cent being a reasonable estimate for the US. (Webley and others,1991) Several such country-wise studies are mentioned by the above scholars. In India, several studies have been conducted to estimate the unaccounted income.

(Kabra (1982); Narayanan S (1983); Gupta and Gupta (1983); Monga and Sanctis (1983), *et al*) Kumar, (1999) has given a detailed review of all such studies. He has examined the standard explanations for the causes and consequences of unaccounted income generation and the methods suggested for curbing it. He has emphasized the adverse effects of unaccounted income on the macro economy and the need for structural remedial measures. Schneider, Chaudhuri and Chatterjee (2003) have done an empirical investigation on the size and development of the 'Indian Shadow Economy', and a comparison with 18 other Asian countries. They found that the size of the hidden economy in India has shown an increasing trend over the years, but it is still lower than that of several other Asian countries.

Economists have recognized the growing imbalances created by the drastic and widespread increase in tax evasion and have attempted to search for reasons within the economic framework. They have concentrated on factors like tax rates, audit frequency, cost-benefit analysis, and tax buoyancy, in their analysis. Tax evasion is classified by scholars and public administrators as 'white collar crime', a concept coined and developed by E H Sutherland. (1940) According to Cowell, economic theory plays a particularly important role in helping us to understand the workings of the black economy. (Cowell, 1990 p. 27) However, Cowell himself says that the economic analysis of evasion entails a specific difficulty - 'by the very nature of the subject, factual evidence is neither plentiful nor of good quality'. (Cowell, 1990 p. 48)

It is very clear from analyses of the studies done exclusively within an economic framework, that the issue of tax evasion needs a much wider perspective. Caroll (1992) while commenting on the approaches of economists have stated that the economists had relied most heavily on indices of costs and benefits of tax paying embodied in income levels, marginal tax rates, audit rates, etc. It is argued that these studies rarely gave insights on why the taxpayer acted in a particular way. Economists were of the view that many elements of the phenomenon of crime are recognizably economic in nature and can be better analyzed with standard economic models. This fact was recognized by several economists themselves and spurred a proliferation of studies by economists approaching the issue from the angle of crime or criminal behaviour. Economists like Kantona (1971), Schmolders, (1960; 1970), *et al* have stressed the need to look at tax evasion beyond the confines of economics. The economic deterrence theorists tend to analyze the tax compliance by attempting an objective measurement of compliance, sanctions, etc. However, they have ignored various other factors which either triggers deviant behaviour or encourage people to conform. The cost-benefit analysis by the taxpayer need not be exclusively monetary but can also be based on a sociological analysis.

Economic- criminological approach

One of the pioneering efforts in this direction was made by Allingham and Sandmo (1972) in what is commonly called the 'The classic model'. In this model they have pointed out the influences of tax rates and penalties and the probability of detection in the tax evasion behaviour. The model presented by Allingham and Sandmo, views compliance as an example of the economics of crime. Allingham and Sandmo incorporate the non-monetary variable 'reputation' and the notion of 'risk aversion' into their model. They have applied the 'economics of crime' approach of Becker (1968) in the study of tax compliance. (Hessing and others, 1992) The prediction of the classic model that both the probability of detection and the severity of penalties will affect evasion (Webley, 1991 and Hessing and others, 1992) has been viewed widely as a presentation of the problem in a simpler way. 'Given the somewhat mixed nature of the evidence it is perhaps surprising that the classic model has been so widely used. Our guess is that it is its simplicity that is appealing'. (Webley *et al,* 1991, p. 9) According to Hessing and others (1992) the classic model by Allingham and Sandmo is not quite as simple as has sometimes been claimed.

The traditional model suggests, as given in the formula below, that taxpayers try to maximize the utility.[23]

$$E(u)+(1-p)\,U(w-tx)+p\,U(w-tx-P(w-x))$$

Where p = probability of detection, constant across x; w = true income; x = reported income; t = tax rate and P = penalty rate.

Such a scientific calculation simply cannot be expected from an average taxpayer. In many countries like India, the taxpayers have very poor awareness about taxable income, tax rates, penalty rates, enforcement strategies, etc. Therefore, it is extremely difficult to presume that they can estimate the costs and benefits involved in tax compliance and tax evasion in order to arrive at a considered decision. With the assumption that taxpayers have perfect knowledge, these studies ignore differences in the actual audit and penalty parameters and those actually perceived by the taxpayers. (Birnbaum, 1973 ; Cuccia, 1994)

Even the proponents of the standard model have reportedly said that, 'even a model as simple as the present one does not generate any simple result concerning the relationship between income and tax evasion'. (Allingham and Sandmo, 1972:329) Several scholars have pointed out the limitations of this framework. (Sheffrin and Robert, 1992) It is pointed out that the model substantially 'unpredicts' the number of honest taxpayers. It also does not provide strong predictions about the socio-economic determinants of evasion. Individuals have a choice of how much income to declare and may report none, some, or all of it. Thus, tax evasion is seen as a rational act by the economic analysts (Witte and Woodbury, 1985) even as they approach it from the angle of the economics of crime. The assumption is that people will commit any offence if they maximize their utility by doing so. (Webley and others, 1991)

Becker (1968) argues that people become criminals not because their motivations are different from that of the others but because their costs and benefits differ. In the above approach it is assumed that individuals essentially engage in a cost-benefit analysis while responding to tax laws. The behaviour of the taxpayers is considered to be utilitarian and it depends on their beliefs about the probability of detection and punishment. (Fischer *et al,* 1992; Beck and Jung, 1989) Applied in the context of taxation, this treats people as rational amoral decision makers whose aim, in this as in all the other areas, is simply to maximize utility. It was mentioned by Caroll (1992) that although economic model can be extended to include social consequences, at some point it stops resembling the economic model. On the one hand, the components of the consequent calculation become subjective and socially constructed rather than objective aspects of marginal tax rates and audit rates.

Economic-behavioural approach

The economic behavioural approach by the economists is the recognition of the relevance of non-economic factors in the behaviour of individuals. This has resulted in an understanding that the decisions of the individuals are influenced not only by their rationality but also their perception of the economic opportunities within society. As Cowell (1990:3) puts it, this widening of approach by the economists has come out of a 'nagging feeling that the economic approach to law breaking and law enforcement neglects some important issues that are bound to have a bearing upon criminal activity and therefore upon the way in which it might be prevented or counteracted.' The standard economic models of crime and the control of crime are incomplete in two important respects. First, in economic terms evasion is not an ordinary crime. Second, no careful attention is given to the way in which individuals' motivations are incorporated into a model of the collective response to the system of taxation and tax enforcement. (Cowel, 1990) Thus, individuals make their decisions and choices based on several other factors. Before looking at the decisions and choices and consequent behavioural pattern of the individuals, it is pertinent to explore the nature of the system of ideas, norms and beliefs underlying these decisions and behaviour. Weigel *et al* (1987) and Alm (1991) have argued that a classical economic perspective with strong roots in utility theory cannot explain tax compliance behaviour.

Deterrence factors

Researchers have attempted to examine the reasons of non-compliance by individuals using different methods and hypotheses. Schwarts and Orleans (1967) examined the comparative effectiveness of the threat about penalty and prosecution and appeals to conscience. They obtained tax compliance figures for three groups of taxpayers, a threat group, an appeal to conscience group and a control group. However, the results of the study did not support the assumption that appeal to conscience is a better way of reducing evasion than threats of punishments.[24] The deterrence value of civil and criminal penalties remains uncertain. In another study Kinsey suggests that for criminal behaviour in general, penalties are less of a deterrent than the probability of being caught. (Kinsey, 1984) Some researchers have argued that above a certain threshold of probability of detection, a mild penalty is as effective a deterrent as a heavy one. (Friedland, 1982; Jackson and Jones, 1985) Studies which showed no impact for penalty rates are Yancey (1988), Webley, Morrris and Amstutz (1985), Webley and Halstead (1986), Webley (1987), Giese and Hoffman (2000), etc. In short, there is no clear evidence to show the extent of the impact that different degrees of punishment have on tax compliance.[25]

There are several other studies examining the deterrence factors in non-compliance by individuals.[26] In most of the countries, audit (similar to the scrutiny in India) is an important tax enforcement strategy. In some of the western countries like the UK and the US, taxpayers are scared of the audits as these exercises often lead to strong penal actions if non-compliance is detected. Thus the audit is considered a strong enforcement strategy in these countries. Therefore several researchers have studied the role of audit as a deterrent measure. Let us briefly review a few such studies.

In most of the advanced countries data regarding compliance by the individuals are well recorded and the data bank is updated with information collected from various sources. Historical records of the income returned by the assessee, details of sources, allowances claimed, etc are available systematically with the Enforcement Agency. Therefore, most of the researchers could largely depend on the official data for analysis. In a few countries, in the US particularly, the governments themselves monitor the data systematically with an academic or research interest (Taxpayer Compliance Measurement Programme of the United States is an example). Using the official data, Dubin and Wilde (1988) have found that audits had had a deterrent effect. Mason and Calvin (1978) report that in their survey study the highest correlation with admitted evasion was the perceived probability of not being caught (by the audit). Webley and others (1991) have quoted several studies which had shown that those who evaded had strongly felt that there was less probability for the audit.

However, Spicer and Hero and Webley (1987) have concluded that the probability of an audit appeared to be more effective a deterrent for those who had already been audited than for the others. Kurt J Beron and others (1992) have done empirical studies on the effect of Audits and socio-economic variables on compliance. They have found that higher levels of education had typically reduced compliance. Brian Erard (1992) has studied the influence of tax audits on reporting behaviour. It was found that a substantial proportion of taxpayers had demonstrated improvements in compliance following a large number of audit assessments. However, it is criticized that government compliance measures are largely inappropriate for ensuring taxpayer compliance. (Long, 1992) Experimental studies have confirmed the importance of the audit probability. However, Webley and others (1991) have quoted a contrasting result, which came out of a study based on TCMP (Taxpayer Compliance Measurement Program) data in 1987, which showed little specific deterrent effect in the wake of audit.

Thus, there are contrasting findings on the effect of audit on tax compliance. While scholars like Beck, Davis and Jung (1991), Mason and Calvin (1978), Alm, Jackson and Mckee (1992), Brian (1992), Cronshaw and Mckee (1993), *et al* found that a higher audit rate leads to better compliance, scholars like Friedland, Maital and Rutenberg (1978), Spicer and Thomas (1982), Benjamini and Maital (1985), Jackson and Jones (1985), *et al* have found that audits have little effect on compliance. Strumpel has studied the impact of enforcement techniques and argues that the techniques which end up emphasizing detection and punishment have two opposing effects on tax compliance. (Kinsey, 1992) The first is 'the expected deterrence effect: the fear of getting caught and the severity of sanctions motivate taxpayers to comply with the law. However the retroactive, confrontational, and coercive aspects of a deterrence approach to law enforcement also have an indirect,

TB - 3.1

I Confess .....
My fault, my fault, my most grievous fault........

The Tax Amnesties

To err is human. But to forgive is divine. Tax departments in many parts of the world believed in this maxim quite literally. This is evident in the series of taxpayer (tax evader?) immunity schemes launched widely to encourage disclosures of unaccounted income or wealth. Most of these schemes had promises to the payers that no questions will be asked about the source of the income and the method by which it was earned and no penal action will be taken.

The success of amnesty schemes globally shows that tax evasion is ubiquitous, irrespective of developed or developing countries. In the last few decades, many countries had tax amnesty schemes, including India, Pakistan, Sri Lanka, Malaysia, Belgium, France, Italy, Ireland, Australia, Indonesia, New Zealand, Philippines, Chile, Argentina, Russian Federation etc. In the last twenty years, about forty states in the United States have enacted some form of tax amnesty, sometimes more than once. IRS in the US came up with an amnesty program in October 2009 for taxpayers that have used undisclosed foreign accounts and undisclosed foreign entities to avoid or evade tax.[27] Tax amnesty launched during October-December 2009 in Italy surpassed $150 billion within a month of announcement. The amnesty was aimed to encourage citizens to bring back the parked funds in so-called offshore banks, which has had a longstanding policy towards banking secrecy.[28]

A MATTER OF MONEY?

Germany had a history of tax amnesty schemes, that goes back to 1913. It was reported that tax amnesty scheme 2005 in Germany helped to collect amounts secretly transferred by thousands of Germans into low tax havens.[29] Australian Tax Office recently gave business owners a one-off opportunity to correct past mistakes (for the period 2001-02 to 2006-07) regarding payments and loans from their private companies.

The tax amnesty scheme launched by general Parvez Musharraf in Pakistan in 2000 reportedly yielded about Rs. 125 billion in tax as about 88,000 persons made declarations. It was stated in a study that only 'less than ten per cent of the untaxed concealed money was declared despite being the lowest ever cost of whitening of black money'.[30] Pakistan had amnesty schemes in 1958, 1969, 1976, 1997 and 2000. India had a successful amnesty scheme in the year 1997 called 'Voluntary Disclosure of Income Scheme (VDIS) 1997'. It was reported that income of Rs 33,000 crore was disclosed and about Rs 10,050 crore tax was collected.

Do tax amnesty schemes result in demotivating the ordinary taxpayers' compliance in the long run? Do frequent amnesty schemes send a message to taxpayers that the tax authority is unable to enforce the tax laws? It is imperative to have systematic empirical studies in various countries to answer the above questions.

negative effect by alienating tax payers and lowering their willingness to comply with the law'. Kinsey has mentioned several studies, which emphasize the difficulty of adequately articulating, and applying uniform legal standards to the multiplicity of fact situations experienced by those subject to regulation. It is reported that these studies emphasize the limits of enforceability in the face of organized resistance to legal authority. A few studies emphasize the importance of law enforcers as being seen as reasonable bargaining partners, capable and willing to moderate or renegotiate government expectations when citizens face excessively high costs of compliance.

Studies on the influence of penalty rates have also given varying results. While scholars like Maclejovsky, Kircher and Schwarzenberger (2001), Friedland, Maital and Rutenberg (1978) and Alm, Mclelland and Schulze (1992) found a positive relationship, Webley (1987), Geise and Hoffmann (2000), *et al* found no effect of penalty in gaining a clear understanding of the link between tax enforcement and tax evasion. Researchers have often used the term 'non compliance' to characterize the intentional or unintentional failure of taxpayers to pay their taxes correctly. In the empirical study on taxation and tax enforcement in Indian society, explained in detail in chapter 6 and chapter 7, the focus is more on the term 'non-compliance' instead of 'tax evasion.' The reason for this is the comparatively mild connotation of the word 'non-compliance', which includes an unintentional act. This may be appropriate in the explanation of the tax behaviour of a part of the population who are unaware of tax provisions. 'Non-compliance' is more a neutral term than 'evasion' since it does not assume that an inaccurate tax return is necessarily the result of an intention to defraud the authorities and it recognizes that inaccuracy may actually result in over payment of taxes. (Webley and others, 1991)

The tax-compliance game: The agency models and general equilibrium models

The above models are in the context of the information absorption of the taxpayers about the tax authority and *vice versa.* (Cuccia, 1994) In the agency model, the tax authority formulates the enforcement strategies to ensure maximum compliance irrespective of the tax behaviour of the people. This may be very true in societies where tax potentiality is very high and the tax-GDP ratio is comparatively low. In general equilibrium models, the tax authority formulates and re-formulates enforcement strategies based on the nature and extent of tax compliance over a period of time. Here, both the taxpayer and the taxing authority may possibly play a game where they direct their actions in response to the action of the other party. Thus, if the enforcement is such that it would detect the evasion, then the taxpayer tends to comply. Similarly, the tax authority also acts based on the information received about the tax behaviour. (Graetz, Reinganum and Wilde, 1986) However, such a game is feasible only if the actions of both the parties are known to each other. This can happen only if there are effective channels of communication, formal or informal, through the media and the official agencies.

Economic analysis of taxation - an appraisal

As we saw in the review of approaches for many centuries to taxation and tax compliance after the introduction of income taxation, the path followed was quite linear. Scientific analysis of taxation and tax compliance was originally within the boundaries of economics, and more particularly the utilitarian school. Economic-criminological approaches, econometric approaches and economic-psychological approaches were evident in subsequent studies. Still later, many scholars started recognizing the importance of social, psychological and sociological factors. However, one can observe a fundamental shift in the approaches to taxation back to its economic roots in the recent years, especially in the wake of globalization and tax competition across and among countries.

The current approaches for many countries, with no exception for developing countries, is centred around four perspectives: 1) an increased emphasis on the tax-GDP ratio without realizing the tax capacity, 2) a tax structure which facilitates transnational trade to make countries tax competitive, 3) an increased recognition of taxation as an exclusive revenue mobilizing institution without appreciating its social objectives such as equity and redistribution and 4) an elimination of tax incentives and concessions, which were originally aimed at promoting disadvantaged sections of the society, calling then irrational or distortionary.

Thus, the current approach to the subject is akin to the centuries old 'economic' analysis of taxation and tax compliance. This approach which is triggered by the forces of economic globalization is detrimental to the specific countries, unless the tax capacity, sociological contexts and structural uniqueness of each country are incorporated. Therefore countries and more particularly developing countries like India need to understand these factors while analyzing tax compliance and framing tax policies.

There is an increased recognition of factors such as tax-GDP ratio and transnational tax rates. Economic analysts spend considerable time in examining the impact of global fiscal policies on the overall economic growth. However, scant attention is paid to the regional and local imbalances and uneven growth across sectors of the population. Though there should be a global uniformity in tax structure and tax provisions, it should not be at the cost of inflicting damage on substantial cross sections of people in particular countries. Tax rates need to be competitive and comparable to facilitate optimum levels of inter-country business transactions. However the same should also recognize the fact of intra-country inequities. For example, a country with a stable mechanism of social security and institutionalized welfare schemes can take bold initiatives to broaden the tax base, eliminate tax concessions and reduce the tax slabs. The same would be detrimental in an unstable economy, with low per capita income and with no social security worth the name. Tax analysts need to recognize the non-economic factors such as the relative tax awareness of the people, the discriminatory and inequitable social and cultural environment and the historical and structural contexts. Quantitative analysis of data such as tax rates, audit rates, penalty rates, reported income, concealed income, etc alone would not explain the tax compliance behaviour. Any policy initiative that is squarely based on such economic indicators and that does not recognize non-economic factors with due consideration would be a disappointment.

MAKING PEOPLE PAY

CHAPTER-4

A MATTER OF POWER?

The Politics of Taxation

> *"When a man spends his own money to buy something for himself, he is very careful about how much he spends and how he spends it. When a man spends his own money to buy something for someone else, he is still very careful about how much he spends, but somewhat less what he spends it on. When a man spends someone else's money to buy something for himself, he is very careful about what he buys, but doesn't care at all how much he spends. And when a man spends someone else's money on someone else, he doesn't care how much he spends or what he spends it on. And that's government for you."*
>
> Milton Friedman

Taxation is not just about money, costs and benefits. Ideas, interests, and institutions play a central role in shaping tax policy.[1] Scholars have argued that taxation and tax compliance have deep political significance as there are different degrees of compliance under different political systems.[2] As against the personification of the state as a 'benevolent dictator' by scholars of public economy, many political scientists are of the view that tax policy evolves as a result of the ideology of particular political parties in power as well as the views of the dominant pressure groups. As no one likes taxes, no political party likes to impose them on people. However, they are forced to do that, as taxes are necessary for the public service. As the system of taxation has emerged as an important part of the economic structure of any society, governments all over the world have recognized its crucial role in the stability of the state. Naturally, politicians and administrators are interested in a balanced tax structure expecting maximum yield with least resistance from the citizens.

Ideologies of taxation

Every society possesses a political culture that triggers a particular type of tax attitude and tax behaviour. And the political culture is determined by the dominant ideological predispositions. The ideology about taxation revolves around ideas such as economic liberty, individual freedom, *laissez faire,* equity, etc. Ideology also emanates from the various types of perceptions about society: rationalist, ethical, subjective, objective, etc. The ideological context of taxation has been a fascinating area for several scholars and political theorists.

Though there are several ideologies related to taxation, one which is very basic and historically relevant in all societies is the organic ideology that the state represents society and that it has superior foresight as to what is required for the people. Here, the state and society are perceived to be inseparable. The legitimacy of the income earned or the wealth possessed by an individual and the freedom to use it largely depends on the normative structure of society. Thus, individual freedom is restricted for the purpose of common good and all individuals are expected to act in conformity with the societal norms and within the legal framework of the state. According to Adam Smith, 'the subjects of every state ought to contribute towards the support of the government as nearly as possible in proportion to their respective abilities; that is in proportion to the revenue which they respectively enjoy under the protection of the state'. (Smith, 1776) In order to achieve the goal of total welfare and to make society egalitarian, various governments have incorporated tax laws in the respective legal systems. Here too, the income earned and the wealth possessed within the framework of economic laws and taxation only are considered as legitimate, and any infringement of this norm is considered illegal and anti-social. Any income earned by a person which has not suffered taxation is considered as illegitimate.

Eisenstein (1961) has made a detailed analysis of the ideologies of taxation. According to him, there are three primary ideologies of taxation: the ideology of ability, the ideology of barriers and deterrents, and the ideology of equity. The ideology of ability declares that taxes should be fixed according to the ability to pay and the ability to pay should be properly measured based on the income or wealth. Therefore, it is suggested that the ideal levy is progressive income tax. However, the ideology of barriers and deterrents take a different view. This view embraces three related precepts: progressive rates dangerously reduce the motivation to work, discourage the incentive to invest and they impair the source of the capital. The ideology of equity is closely concerned with the eloquent theme of equality among equals. It maintains that those who are similarly situated should be treated similarly and those who are differently situated should be differently treated. (horizontal and vertical equity)[3] Eisenstein's identification of a set of ideologies is very relevant when one discusses the politics of taxation. He has identified three categories of ideologists: those who believe through interest, those who believe through compensation, and those who believe through principle.

The first group consists of those who directly gain from the application of their ideology. They speak as taxpayers. In almost all countries, organized taxpayers bargain for better tax deals and incentives to them. In many countries merchants' association and industry groups lobby for tax cuts. In India, it is observed that various organized groups like the chamber of commerce, trade associations, manufacturers associations, export groups, etc. play a vital role in budget formulation. One can clearly observe their solidarity, strategies and lobbying during the pre-budget exercises. The second group consists of those who are devoted because they are paid for their exertions. They are the lawyers, the chartered accountants and the other consultants. Their role is crucial in countries where tax awareness is comparatively low and procedures are complicated. The third group consists of those who believe regardless of any pecuniary benefits. They are the statesmen, the scholars and the professional experts.

An analysis of the three sets of ideologies and ideologists clearly points to the fact that such a distinction is not universally applicable. Also, considering the frequent changes in the perceptions and the multiple roles played by individuals, there is enough scope for overlapping among the categories. Moreover, the third categorization of ideologists who are supposed to be doing social service with dedication without any pecuniary advantage may be too idealistic. In the same way, ideologists of the first two categories can also work without any self-interest. However he has later admitted that 'these are modest efforts to classify belief and behaviour in the universe of taxation.' Since belief and behaviour are flexible, discrepancies should be expected. Adherents of one ideology may borrow the language of the other to be more persuasive. And each group invokes the ideology of equity as the occasion warrants.

TB - 4.1

Mark Twain's Dilemma

In 1871, the famous author Mark Twain wrote a story. Once he had a mysterious visitor whose occupation was unknown. During the chat with him Twain boasted that he had earned a huge income of 2,14,000 dollars in the previous year. Immediately the stranger revealed his true identity and declared that Twain owed 5 per cent of his income to the government. The person was a tax collector! Annoyed by this, Twain frantically searched for loopholes but couldn't find any. He approached a wealthy businessman in the neighbourhood for guidance. He replied, 'Men of moral weight, of commercial integrity, of unimpeachable social spotlessness' followed the course of tax evasion. The neighbour continued, 'Had he not falsified his deductions he would have got beggared every year to support this hateful, wicked, extortionate and tyrannical government.'[4]

Another important group, which Eisenstein possibly ignored, was the media. May be this group did not carry strong ideological positions some years back as they do today. The present media not only disseminates the ideology of others but also propagates its interest couched in the form of an ideology. This is very prominent as there are large numbers of specialized news channels either influenced by the business groups or fully or partially supported by competing industries. The media interpret and analyze the fiscal scenario and tax policies in their own way and this may not necessarily be a fair view.

Political decisions can never be independent of dominant public opinion. And public opinion often revolves around various political groups. It can vary on the basis of different affiliations *viz*. left, right, democrat, socialist, republican, conservative, liberal, etc. According to Michael and Oldman (1975), as political factors have a decisive role in successful planning and implementation of the tax policy, the tax reforms need to be sensitive to the political environment. However, the same can be smoothly designed and administered in political conformity if the policy is designed scientifically within a stable institutional structure. Thus, not only a strong political mandate but also deep ideological convictions and unwavering administrative will are necessary for a stable tax system.

Politics, equity and taxation

The principle of equity is the hallmark of any democratic country. Even in countries that are not categorized as democratic, social and economic, equity is considered to be a political ideal. It is significant to note the relevance of the concept of equity in the discussion of the system of taxation. The first canon of taxation by Adam Smith was about the equity in taxation. The equity theory is considered as one of the pioneering models in the ideology of distributive justice.[5] This is closely connected to the theme of exchange. Both are relevant at the level of the individual and at the level of the system. 'Feelings of inequity may arise from a person paying far more in taxes than he receives in benefits or from a comparison of one person's treatment with that of another'.[6] The common typology of horizontal and vertical equity, which was mentioned earlier, is reported as significant in many countries irrespective of the status of development. Slemrod and Bakija (1996) have given a detailed discussion of horizontal and vertical equity in the United States. They argue that there is a 'kind of unanimous schizophrenia by which people will pursue their own private interests to the neglect of the public purse, even though they would actually benefit from the public purse'. (Caroll, 1989:47)

However, the behaviour of the individuals cannot be compartmentalised in terms of monetary gains. The feeling of equity or inequity carries in itself several non-monetary factors such as status, prestige, feeling of equal consideration, loyalty to state and society, etc. It also affects the inter-personal relationships in society. But the perception of the individuals need not be uniform. Rather, it may be influenced by the external environment. Caroll has studied the concepts of equity and the effect of what he calls 'externality.' According to him, if someone induces a favourable externality, everybody feels better off and evades more; if the externality is unfavourable the reverse happens. This analysis shows clearly that one has to specify fairly carefully what one means by the inequity or injustice that is often cited as a motive for evading taxes. He rightly argues that what is important is how the person perceives his own role in modifying that externality.

While focussing on equity and taxation, Eisenstein (1961) quotes three typical declarations on the nature of equity. One states that 'individuals in like economic circumstance should be treated alike.' The second states that 'two persons whose relevant circumstances are the same should pay the same tax.' The third states, 'equity is achieved when persons and businesses in a similar economic position are taxed the same.' However, Cowell reports on certain experimental evidence that does not establish any association between perceived inequities in the system and non-compliance. As reviewed by Sheffrin and Robert, (1992) researchers have found that beliefs about tax morality were more important than beliefs about fairness of the tax system. In a similar vein, it is reported that perceptions of honesty of others were directly related to the individuals' own tax ethics. (Song and Yarbrough, 1992) Thus, there emerged a viewpoint among several researchers that, ' a good deal of tax evasion appears related more to perceived inequities in the tax system than to the simple desire to retain more money from the receipts. (Peters Guy, 1991)

Another important political concern would be how far income taxation will reduce the inequality in society. Taking a slice from the rich will not automatically and proportionately add to the share of the poor. There is no direct transfer of funds from the wealthy to the needy. Only a part of the tax revenue is channeled to uplift the low income groups. Scholars have pointed out that taxes have had only moderate success in reducing income inequality in developed countries and appear to have had even less success in reducing income inequality in developing countries. (Bird and Zolt, (2003)

Contractarian perspectives in taxation

Why do citizens adhere to the rules of the state? Is it because the constitution demands so? The element of rationality in human behaviour is a determining factor in this regard. However, the citizens' response to the state may be based on their extent of recognition of the relevance of the state as a provider and protector. The relationship between the citizens and state is built on an unwritten social contract. Thinkers like Hobbes, Locke, Rousseau and Rawls have in various contexts used this idea and the concept of social contract. Contractarian theory is one of the key foundations of 'welfare economics' as propounded by Buchanan. (1959, 1977) Musgrave has also recognized the importance of social contract when he stated that 'it is not for the economist to stipulate rules for good taxation *ad hoc,* and without reference to the underlying social contract'. (Musgrave, 1996)

It is pertinent to analyse tax evasion in the context of a psychology of social contract. According to Vihanto (2003), people will follow the rule of honesty in so far as they see taxation conforming to a conceptual social contract to which they give their tacit consent. According to this view the government can enhance tax compliance by enacting only specific tax laws that are in harmony with constitutional rules that meet with the unanimous approval of the people. A vital element in the policy is to assure that the tax laws are diligently and consistently implemented, within reasonable costs of enforcement, so that the compliant taxpayers do not feel cheated. In a study conducted by Torgler (2005) on the tax morale in Latin America, it was found that if a taxpayer feels that he is in a sort of unfair contract he would probably be less likely to comply. Countries like New Zealand have given great emphasis to ensure tax system fairness, considering it as an important factor in generating tax compliance. (Tan, 1998) However, getting unanimous approval for all tax laws is too idealistic. Similarly, taxpayers cannot be expected to be well aware of the nature of taxation and its fairness or unfairness. Therefore, the existence of social contract needs to be seen in the context of the perception of taxpayers about the fair exchange of resources and services rather than perception of fairness of the tax laws. The Scenarios can be different under various regimes as given below. (Figure F 4.1)

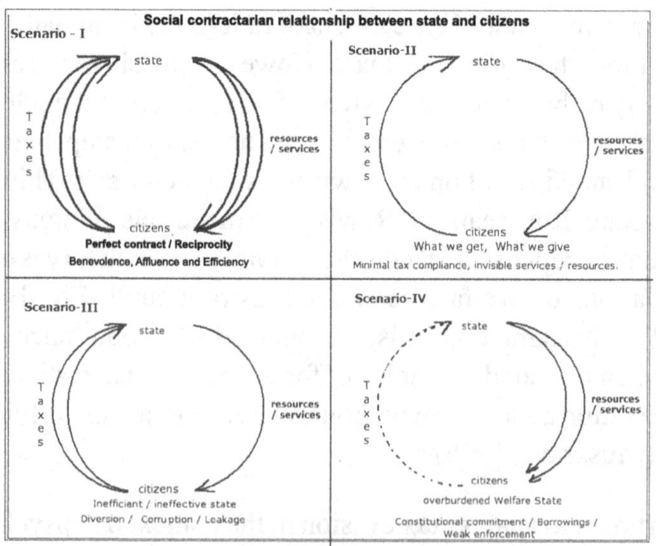

Figure F 4.1

In Scenario-I, citizens contribute voluntarily and benevolently to the state. The state in turn willingly and generously caters to all the needs of the citizens. This is a situation of perfect contract and reciprocity. This can happen in a system where affluent citizens and effective state coexist. However, this may be viewed as an idealistic scenario. Scenario-II depicts a system where there is minimal tax compliance by citizens and invisible services by state. This is typical of an economically underprivileged state. In Scenario-III, one can see that though the citizens contribute substantially to the state, there is no proportionate response from the state in terms of resource allocation and service delivery. The state and tax administration are characterized by inefficiency, ineffectiveness and corruption. Scenario-IV shows a system where citizens are tax evaders for various historical or economic-sociological reasons. However, the state, may due to certain constitutional commitments attempt to do its best in distributing the resources and providing services. This is typical of an overburdened welfare state which survives on borrowings. Data and research are inadequate at this stage to identify perfect examples of states that fit in any of these four scenarios.

As shown in the study by Fehr and Gachter (2000), reciprocity has powerful implications, as it is an important determinant in the enforcement of contracts and social norms; it enhances the possibilities of collective action greatly. As against the self-interest model often propounded by the economists, the concept of reciprocity exists even in a condition where there is no direct material benefit. There are a substantial number of studies recognizing reciprocity as a factor in compliance. (Fehr and Schmidt (2000); Falk and Fishbacher (2001))

However, a few scholars have criticized the concept of social contract and its legitimacy in explaining the compliance behaviour of citizens. One extreme is that of Tim Starr who has stated that “social contract” is doubly one-sided: the only party to agree to it is the state, and the only party that is obliged by it is the people. 'The state agrees to collect taxes and enforce its rules upon the people, and the people are obliged to pay those taxes and abide by those rules. There is neither mutuality of agreement nor any mutuality of obligation between the state and the people, and, therefore, there can be no contract.' (Starr, 2001) Tim has made an extreme argument rejecting the existence of any social contract stating that there is no concrete agreement between the individual and the state. There is no disagreement to his view. But it needs to be clear that the social contractarian relationship needs to be understood and examined in the context of mutual social responsibility in two directions which are complementary. They are the contract towards the state and the contract towards society. The obligation is voluntary in nature and should be enforced by the normative structure of the society than merely by the system of taxation of that state. However, the contract takes roots in the legislative structure of the state, which is formulated by the consent of a reasonably represented group in democratic states. Thus, there is ample scope for incorporating the elements of social contract in the structure of taxation itself.

Performance of the state and the tax compliance

If there is a social contract between the state and the citizens regarding their mutual commitment and responsibility, it is expected that the same is influenced by an evaluation of the performance. (See Figure F 4-1) That is to say, the state needs to watch out for a proportionate contribution from the affluent citizens for the huge expenditure to fulfill its duties. Similarly, taxpayers are equally, if not with greater intensity, worried about the contribution of the state to repay them in terms of service and resources. Therefore, it is expected that the state would not tolerate tax evasion by its citizens. Similarly, taxpayers would definitely frown upon any laxity by the state in ensuring proper service delivery. Any perception that the state squanders the payments made out of hard earned income would definitely make the taxpayers rebellious. That would result in negative tax behaviour.

There are several studies focusing on corruption in government while explaining the citizen's compliance. (Tanzi, 2000; Wei, 1997) Tanzi

(1998) has identified factors such as complexity of tax systems, discretionary powers of the government employees, financing for political parties, etc as contributing to corruption. (Wagner, 1999) The attitudes of the taxpayers about the state and taxation too have been studied by several scholars. (Vogel 1974; Lewis 1985, Devos 2005) Taxpayers tend to form attitudes about taxation based on their perception of the performance of the state. However, it is understood that the attitudes and behaviour would not correspond always. In many cases, the taxpayers who express a particular type of attitude may not behave in the same way in real life decision situations. But there could be varied responses in different countries.

Nature of political system and country specific tax behaviour

Several country studies on tax behaviour have pointed out the unique traits of those countries. In a study conducted by Cummings, Martinez-Vazquez, Mckee and Torgler (2004), it was found that tax behaviour in the US, Botswana and South Africa are different. According to them the tax behaviour in each country is different based on the tax administration fairness, perceived equity of fiscal exchange and overall attitude towards respective governments. Alm, Sanchez and De Juan (1995) and Alm and Togler (2004) have found that there are vast differences between US and Spain in the level of tax compliance. Torgler, Schaltegger and Schaffer (2003) have found that Switzerland and Costa Rica have contrasting traits in respect of tax behaviour. Even in countries which share similar cultural and political background one can observe contrasting tax behaviour. Ockenfels and Weimann (1999) and Torgler (2003) have found that there are differences in the nature of tax compliance in erstwhile East Germany as compared with that of West Germany. Thus, various country studies have given interesting results, which also indicate the uniqueness of tax behaviour in different countries. Thus it would not be quite appropriate to generalize specific country studies to derive conclusions for other countries.

Tax compliance behaviour can vary not only between countries, but also within a particular country over a period of time. These variations can be identified in countries where governments with sharply contrasting ideologies ruled at different periods. India is one example. As has been described in detail previously, the tax policies and consequent tax behaviour have taken different characteristic traits during different historic periods *viz.* the ancient period (Vedic and post-vedic period), the medieval period (under Indian and foreign kingdoms), the colonial period (under the British empire) and the present post-independent democratic polity. The tax policy and consequent tax behaviour underwent different phases with different predominant orientations (such as religious, cultural, colonial-economic and sociological) during these respective regimes. Thus, historically, the political context of tax policy was a determining factor for the type of tax behaviour in many countries. Therefore, one cannot ignore the political context of tax policy even today, as people in general and taxpayers in particular are more politically conscious and are very well aware of their political rights. This taxpayer consciousness is conspicuous not only in democratic countries but also under several other political systems, though the degree of influence may vary.

Political context of tax policy

It is generally perceived that tax policy and its formulation are too technical for common people to understand. However, it is not really so. The most important reason for the perception that it is very complex is its legal language and the jugglery with numbers. Barring a few academicians and policy experts, no one is really interested in going through the budget documents, which run into several pages. The reason for perceiving the tax statutes as complex is the use of long sentences couched in legal phrases. Another reason for the apparent complexity in tax laws is something of its own making. As law gets amended year after year bringing new sections and sub-sections and provisos, there is no proportionate attempt to get rid of the redundant enactments. The fact that fiscal enactments proposing changes in tax laws, tax rates, incentives, etc are preceded by a technical analysis of the economic status of the country (the economic survey, as it is called in some countries) and related analysis of deficits and revenues, citizens feel intellectually at a loss to evaluate the policies. Because of the above perception of complexity, many citizens do not venture to air their opinions fearing ridicule.

This complexity perception has invariably ended up as a strategic gain for governments and politicians, though it was never intended to be so. No one in the political power structure would pleasantly welcome a public dissent on a tax hike. As taxes constitute sizeable revenue for any government, those at the helm of affairs tend to ensure that the state coffers get a steady inflow of resources. Though every election is fought over price rise and high taxes, nothing much could be done to give away substantial tax relief by the winning parties across the world. Even large historic tax cuts were followed either by incremental increases in rates or by new set of taxes. That is why ministers and secretaries in charge of the tax or the finance portfolio face large-scale criticism from the people within the government and outside. Thus, those who are in charge of taxes have to put on a bold face justifying their fiscal decisions in spite of strong opposition from within and outside.

In countries with a federal structure, taxation and the devolution of taxes to states is an area of conflict and protests. States demand a larger share of the tax cake from the centre. In India, central income tax is distributed among the states on the basis of a uniform criterion. However, many a time, the states accuse the centre of being unfair in devolving the taxes. Recently, the chief minister of Gujarat, one of the industrially advanced states in India, openly challenged the centre during a public meeting that his state will not pay any income tax if the centre does not increase its share.[7]

Political popularity

One of the decisive factors in the elections in every country is the tax views and tax promises of the contesting political parties. Citizens closely watch what the parties are up to. The more diligent ones will read the election manifestos. The fear of being targetted by the voters would force political parties to take very soft positions on tax policy. Voters in many countries decide on their choice based on their expectations of a soft-tax regime by a particular political party or a coalition. Parties compete to make many promises to the voters before the elections. Thus, the politics of taxation is critically important in revenue reforms in all countries at vastly different levels of development. (Minh Le, Moreno-Dodson and Rojchaichaninthorn (2008)) Voters take decisions in the elections not only based on the promises but also based on a careful evaluation of the tax policy record of the parties. Voters tend to favor or oppose a particular political party based on their evaluation of the tax strategies followed by the party earlier. (called 'retrospective voting' by Fiorina) The public choice school theorists argue that after a certain level, average voters will express their dissent against the political party or the leader who is responsible for the undesirable tax policy. This is evident both in countries with highly educated citizens and also in countries where a substantial number of the population is illiterate.

Tax incentives and pressure groups

In spite of several virtues claimed by countries such as stable democracy, fool-proof elections, adequate reservations and representations for various communities and groups in the governance structure, the fact remains that various pressure groups try to influence the decisions. There is widespread feeling that money power still rules the world and it is perceived to be the most effective influencing force in many decisions. Thus, tax policies may also be perceived to favour the rich and considered to be affecting the people in the lower economic strata.[8] Often, the ideals of horizontal and vertical equity are compromised and more regressive taxes are introduced. As in other areas of life, people who wield more power will exercise greater control over tax policy decisions. Hence, various taxpayer categories bargain for a fair and better deal for themselves from the government. In order to make the government receptive to them, they rally themselves around the political parties who can influence the tax decisions of the government. Dominant pressure groups will try to gain benefits such as tax rate cuts, tax incentives and rebates. It is argued by scholars that countries like India have their tax policies riddled with overly complex structures and multiple, largely ad-hoc, incentives that narrow the already limited tax base, create more loopholes for tax avoidance and evasion, intensify the public perception of unfairness of taxes, and generate opportunity for corruption. (Minh Le, Moreno-Dodson and Rojchaichaninthorn (2008))

Ideological conflict: Political ideology and economic necessity

We have seen how pressure groups influence the tax policy decision making. These pressure groups work through two channels. One is political parties in power and the other is the bureaucracy. In most societies, and more importantly in democratic polities, political parties are the powerful organizations through which pressure groups operate. Political parties represent particular social, economic, linguistic, regional or ideological groups in society. Various collectivities rally around particular political parties to reap the benefits of power enjoyed by the latter. Individual parties compete to get the support of different collectivities either *in toto* or in part. Once support is garnered from a group, it would be obligatory for the political parties not to displease them with financial burden. Thus, it would be a tough task for the parties to take a strong stand on tax hikes or even on fresh tax proposals. The situation becomes tougher in coalition politics. In many countries, governments are run by multiple political parties, each having their own particular collectivities and manifestoes. Fiscal decision making is never a smooth process in such systems and the bigger parties (usually holding the finance portfolio in the ministries) will find it extremely difficult to muster the support of minor coalition partners.

Vote banks and cash banks

The vote bank for the ruling parties in most of the countries comprises the middle and lower income groups of the population. Considering the socio-economic background of the large voter population, it would be extremely difficult to push through tax proposals to widen the tax base or to hike rates of taxes at the lower slabs. The election manifestoes, mostly stemming from the party ideology would have promised lesser tax burdens. However, once in power, parties realize the necessity of tax revenue to run the government. Thus the economic necessity compels the political parties in power to rely more and more on the tax revenues for resource mobilization.

Apart from the vote bank, most of the political parties nurture 'cash banks' for their survival and sustenance in the power game. Political parties require large funds for fighting elections and to maintain their positions in the power structure. This is irrespective of the ideological lineage *viz.* leftist, rightist or centrist; liberal or conservative; democrats or republicans. Even the so called 'green' parties are not excluded from this type of resource mobilization. Parties depend on large business houses and corporates for liberal donations. Apart from various business entities, they get liberal monetary support from different sectors of the trade and industry. For many businessmen, such contributions are not expenditure but investment. Most of the fund providers expect favourable support and decisions from the political parties. Lora emphasized that taxation is highly path-dependent due to the resistance of the elites. (Minh Le *et al* 2008) The most appropriate time for such elite entities to encash the financial support extended by them is at the time of the budget exercise. Though it cannot be said that business groups and industry associations force political parties to take unfair tax decisions, they can indeed exercise their influence as there are several tax choices before the government.

Institutionalization of political financing by corporate and non-corporate taxpayers

Political parties all over the world require funds for their sustenance. Parties used to manage their financial requirements through subscriptions and small donations from its members. However, in recent times, most of the parties find it difficult to have a strong membership base. Even the parties, who are known for their mass base, are worried over the dwindling cadre strength. This trend has affected the fund positions of the political parties. Therefore, politicians depend substantially on big business houses for large-scale funding for the political objectives and related expenditure.

The most important expenditure for any political party is the election expenditure. The election game requires massive investment. It is said that there is a sort of 'arms-race' approach to election spending. It is estimated that over 50 million pounds each are spent by the leading political parties in the UK in general elections. Political Parties Elections and Referendum Act (PPERA) 2000 of the UK has been only partially successful in curbing unlimited spending by political parties. Huge amounts are spent by political parties in every country on advertisements, media space, travel, meetings, and many covert incentives to woo the voters. Such massive expenditure is met by all major parties through funding from large taxpayers.

The most sophisticated way of sourcing the money from large corporates is through 'commercial loans.' In many developed countries, such loans are sought from large corporate business houses. However, it is not done without any criticism. The 'loans for peerages' affair in the UK has raised several issues related to the integrity of political parties and the corporates as well as the need for transparency and disclosure. What is actually happening in many countries is the large-scale transfer of funds as donations from the big business houses directly or through charitable and educational trusts under the same umbrella. In many countries, industry and trade associations are approached by the fund and campaign managers to mobilize funds from their members.

In India, there are six major parties and more than 200 regional and state parties. Apart from this, there are hundreds of unrecognized political groups who are active during election times. The Confederation of Indian Industry claimed to have insisted that it would not directly collect money to fund political parties, but had asked its 4800 members to make donations to political parties through banks. The major Indian corporate group Tata has emulated many such groups in developed countries and created an electoral 'Trust' to distribute donations to various political parties according to their strength in the Lok Sabha. According to them, the main aim of establishing the Trust is to create an environment for donating money to political parties in a transparent, non-discriminatory and non-discretionary manner.[9] Thus, political financing is getting increasingly institutionalized in many countries. However, its link to underground economy is quite discernible not only in developing countries but also in developed countries.

It is alleged that political donations are not properly accounted for either by the donors or by the recipients . This is an important reason for the growth of undisclosed income and wealth in many countries. Though strict election laws are in place in many countries on election funding and expenditure, they are rarely followed. Limits on spending by individual candidates have existed since 1883 in the UK. The Political Parties, Elections and Referendums Act (PPERA) introduced limits for the national parties regarding overall expenditure since 2000. However such measures had only limited impact.[10] Similar legislations have been introduced in many countries and regions. Amendments were made to the Commonwealth Electoral Act to incorporate rules on election expenditure. Australian Election Commission (AEC) has strict disclosure rules for political parties to provide details of donations and gifts received by them and the expenditure. Political parties need to file annual returns to the AEC. Public Funding of Represented Political Parties Act, 103 of 1997, governs the eligibility of parties and the allocations they receive from the Represented Political Parties' Fund in South Africa. Many countries have framed rules for the state funding of elections aimed at what they call 'clean elections.' However, voters in most countries might not agree to spend these government funds for the sake of political parties. The donations collected from people and groups are subjected to scrutiny in many countries.

The impact of large scale funding of political parties by large taxpayers is at two levels. First, it considerably influences the tax policy positions taken by political parties. Second, receiving unaccounted money from business houses encourages growth of parallel economy in the countries.

In India, an estimated Rs 7000 crore are spent on elections to Parliament and Assemblies in a cycle of five years.[11] More than Rs 1000 crore was spent by the government for the conduct of each general election in the last few years. Unaccounted expenditure of the individual candidates would be much more than the official estimates. Thus, untaxed income is a necessity both for the income earners as well as for the political sustenance of many. It is with this reality in mind that the Election Commission of India appoints Election Expenditure Observers in each constituency to keep a vigil on the expenditure incurred by candidates.

TB - 4.2

Mogens Gilstrup

Mogens Gilstrup led the Anti-tax Party called the Progress Party in Denmark. The party sought virtual elimination of all taxes in Denmark. It wanted to privatize almost all activities of the Government. The party even advocated that the defence budget should be reduced to only enough money to pay for an answering machine that would tell any caller 'We capitulate'. It contested elections for the Folketing (Danish Parliament) in 1973 and received a sizable support of 15.9 per cent of the total votes polled and was then second largest party in the country. It managed to get about 13 per cent of votes in two subsequent elections also. Later, when the ruling government reduced the income tax rates considerably, the significance of the anti-tax party also got reduced. Meanwhile, its leader Gilstrup was jailed for tax evasion. Probably he may be one of the very few persons who evaded taxes openly (declared by him in a television interview) and faced punishment. However, the Progress Party continues to mobilize citizens against high taxes.

Anti-tax political parties

Though tax is a sensitive issue for many political parties in power, it is a necessary evil for running the state. No one can ignore the structural necessity of taxation in the social and economic realm. However, in different parts of the world, there have been exceptions in this regard. There are a few political parties who have boldly advocated a no-tax regime, though none of them are mainstream political parties.

As tax is considered as a burden by many citizens, political parties and groups which have taken positions against taxation have been the favourites of many. Several political groupings gained strong support through their anti-tax ideology and tax protests. The progress parties led by Mogens Gilstrup in Denmark and by Carl Hagen in Norway are among the few successful anti-tax parties in Europe. Small Farmers' Party in Finland also gained substantial support since the 1970s for its anti-tax movement. Similarly, the Alabama Republican Party took strong positions on tax issues. In countries like France, Italy, Scandinavia, etc, political parties have a history of taking tax burdens as important election issues. In India too the Janata Party, led by a former Union minister Subramanian Swamy, demanded the abolition of income tax.

India - The budget and the tax proposals

The preparation of the budget is a long systematic process undertaken by the government of India. It starts with an estimation of revenue receipts and capital receipts for the next financial year. Estimates of central taxes and duties administered by the Central Board of Direct Taxes (CBDT) and the Central Board of Excise and Customs (CBEC) will be furnished by these bodies to the budget division, giving commodity-wise estimates of manufacture and imports. Duty rates and foreign exchange rate assumptions form the basis of these estimates. Likewise other taxes, interest receipts, etc are also estimated. Estimates of receipts by way of loan repayments are also taken into consideration.

While receipts from central taxes are estimated, the revenue authorities have to examine the anticipated tax revenue increase or decrease consequent to change in tax laws, business situation, trends in the economy, etc. Estimates of expenditure are furnished to the budget division in various stages. The estimates are finalized after Secretary (Expenditure) completes discussions with the financial advisers. There is a lot of decision making involved in this stage.[12] Activities and schemes are examined to prioritize those which are important and eliminate, reduce or merge other schemes appropriately. The social orientation of the budget is apparent, as it gives special attention to backward regions and disadvantaged sections of the population. The attention given to gender budgeting is an example in this regard.

The government conducts consultations at different levels on various tax proposals and also on priority areas of expenditure. This stage is marred by bargaining and lobbying by various interest groups. Organized sectors of the business and economy present their claims and demands with well-drafted proposals supported by 'favourable' figures. However, the government may accept or reject the proposals after analyzing them. What is important here is the fact that several unorganized sectors fail to project their needs before the finalization of the budget.

Usually, on the last day of February the Minister of Finance presents the Union Budget before Indian Parliament. Members from both the houses of the Parliament (namely Lok Sabha and Rajya Sabha) are present during the presentation of the budget. Union Budget in India is accompanied by the tabling of various documents such as annual financial statement, demand for grants, appropriation bill, finance bill, memorandum explaining the finance bill, fiscal policy statement for the financial year, expenditure budget, receipts budget, medium term fiscal policy statement, etc. The annual financial statement is considered as the core budget document. It shows the estimated receipts and disbursements by the government for the next financial year in relation to the estimates of the earlier financial year.[13] The finance bill contains

TB - 4.3

The plight of the Finance Ministers[15]

John Mathai, Finance Minister of India spoke as follows while ending his budget speech for the year on February 28, 1949

"Sir, I have come to the end of my story. It is not pleasant for a Finance Minister to appear before the House with a record of deficits and proposals for additional taxation but a Finance Minister is as much the creature of circumstances as any one else..."

Shri C D Deshmukh, Finance Minister introduced the budget on February 28, 1951 and spoke as follows

'I have been greatly heartened (in this task) by a recent communication which I have received from an ordinary villager, who is neither in business or in service, which I would venture to mention to the House. It is from one who at present pays no tax to any authority, central, state or local. He says that he has a burning desire to help the Government of India in some way or the other. He has remitted a sum of five rupees to me and has promised to remit a similar sum every year. It is not the small amount that he has offered but the spirit behind the offer that matters and, so long as...(the country)can produce men and women with this spirit, this country can face the future, however difficult it may be, with confidence'

Morarji Desai, Finance Minister of India in 1967, started his tax proposals in the budget speech as follows:

"I now come to the much awaited and perhaps much dreaded part of my budget speech. I trust the honorable members will not take me to task if the proposals I unfold do not fulfill the expectations of dread..... A deficit of this kind is usually an invitation to a finance minister to sharpen his knife.....On this occasion, I propose to engage myself essentially in a minor operation in the nature of plastic surgery- taking a little flesh out here and adding a little bit there."

the tax proposals and tax law amendments. It also gives the details of imposition, abolition, remission, alteration and regulation of taxes proposed in the budget. This is in accordance with the Article 110 (1) (a) of the Constitution of India.

The finance bill is debated in Parliament for several days till it is passed by both houses to become part of the statute after assent from the President. However, during this period, there will be extensive arguments and representations by affected parties. Some parliamentarians face difficulty in understanding the legal complexities involved in the tax law proposals. However, most of them make concerted efforts to study the impact of specific amendments. Often, politicians including those from the ruling government would find that some of the tax proposals are contradictory to what were mentioned in their election manifestoes. In an era of coalition governments, the finance minister who is from one of the parties, would not have taken into consideration the fiscal promises made by various other parties at the time of elections. This results in strong dissent and disruptions in the parliament. Political parties are pressurized by interest groups to take a favourable position in the Parliament. The finalization of statutes becomes a complex exercise. This obviously results in the accepting of suggestions which are apparently counter-productive in the context of fiscal reforms and economic prudence. Thus, the government has a tough time in finalizing tax law amendments which satisfy different cross-sections of people, taxpayer categories and business groups.

The political context of taxation

It is evident here that political factors play an important role in taxation. It is not 'economics' which influences the tax policy, but several non-economic factors. The interplay of the various political factors discussed so far has a strong bearing on the trajectory of tax policies in most countries. Those who are instrumental in heralding new initiatives and reforms in taxation need to understand the politics of taxation. This is true for both developed and developing countries, though more for the latter. It has been rightly argued by Pillarisetti (2003) in his study that the tax reforms in low-income countries should be viewed in their political context if they are to be successful. However, one needs to ensure that such approaches should not compromise on the objectivity and fairness required in public policy. In plural societies, inter-group competition, comparison and bargaining are very much prevalent. That could end up being more intense and may lead to vociferous protests in countries with huge populations and limited resources. The number of deductions and exemptions will be very comprehensive in a pluralistic system and the most dominant groups would get the maximum benefit.[14] The challenge of the state and the tax administration would be to ensure equity and justice while formulating and implementing tax policies in such pluralistic societies.

CHAPTER-5

A MATTER OF APPROACH?

The Sociology of Taxation

> *Neither the life of an individual nor the history of a society can be understood without understanding both. Yet men do not usually define the troubles they endure in terms of historical change and institutional contradiction. ... The sociological imagination enables its possessor to understand the larger historical scene in terms of its meaning for the inner life and the external career of a variety of individuals. ... The first fruit of this imagination--and the first lesson of the social science that embodies it-is the idea that the individual can understand his own experience and gauge his own fate only by locating himself within this period, that he can know his own chances in life only by becoming aware of those of all individuals in his circumstances. ...We have come to know that every individual lives, from one generation to the next, in some society; that he lives out a biography, and that he lives it out within some historical sequence*
>
> (C. Wright Mills)

In this chapter, let us move on to provide a methodological critique on the study of tax compliance. Analyses made earlier make it amply clear that the system of income taxation and tax compliance behaviour need to be approached with an inter-disciplinary perspective. Taxation is not merely an economic instrument to generate revenue; it does have larger sociological and political dimensions at the policy level as well as at the implementation level. Similarly, the compliance to income tax law is not just a rational decision that evaluates the cost and the benefits, but it is an act governed by historical background, behavioural dimensions and sociological orientations. Therefore, any study in the above area should necessarily involve an understanding of the conceptual and theoretical framework that encapsulates the multi-dimensional status of the subject. Likewise, the methodological strategy to collect data should be comprehensive enough so that the historic, social, economic, political, sociological and behavioural aspects are captured in the researcher's canvas. For this, one has to devise suitable tools and methods of data collection.

Sociological and social psychological orientations

Before describing the possible methodological strategies, the currently existing research orientations in the above area are briefly reviewed below. Scholars have focused on various dimensions of the topic by adopting different methodologies. Some have focused on the moral dimensions. Some others have focused on the role of ethical beliefs. Scholars have also examined the issue by applying the theory of reciprocity and exchange. A few scholars have analysed taxation and tax compliance from the angle of socially shared ideas, opinions and attitudes, which they call social representations.

Studies have been conducted on the link between morality and tax evasion. Baldry (1986) has concluded that some individuals choose not to evade, apparently on moral grounds. In a study conducted by Philip M J Reckers, Debra L Sanders and Stephen J Roark (Reckers MJ 1994), where they examined the influence of ethical beliefs on tax compliance decisions, the research empirically tested whether an individual's ethical beliefs about tax compliance mediate withholding effects (over withheld or tax due) and tax rate effects (low or high) in tax evasion decisions. The results indicate that tax ethics are highly significant in tax evasion decisions and may be a 'missing variable' in decision-making models. Several studies have pointed out the relatively important role played by the ethical beliefs and moral values of taxpayers in influencing the tax behaviour.[1]

The interactive model presented by Benjamini and Maital (1985), recognizes the importance of the social interaction of the individual and his consequent perception of the tax behaviour of others. In the US, Song and Yarbrough (1978) have found that although their respondents did accept that tax evasion was a crime, they did not regard it as a serious one. The large-scale study of tax payer compliance conducted in part by the IRS in 1984 in the US had found that one third of all respondents did not see anything morally wrong with cheating on taxes, another third were somewhat ambiguous. It is said that the prevailing attitude about tax evasion in industrialized countries appears to be 'catch me if you can', rather than any obligation related to the commitment for the common good. Some studies indicate that the high level of tax compliance cannot be explained entirely by the level of tax enforcement. (Graetz and Wilde, 1985)

There are also a few studies conducted from social psychological perspectives. First in this line of research are those studies which focused on the situational (social environment) characteristics as determinants of tax evasion. The study conducted by Groenland and Van Veldhoven (1983) showed that the individual differences and situational characteristics interact to affect the attitude towards and the understanding of the tax system, which in turn affect the disposition to evade. Three different kinds of situational characteristics are discussed: opportunity, socio-economic factors and tax system. These are all seen as having the potential to directly and indirectly affect tax evasion. According to them the particular configuration of the tax system will provide opportunities for evasion for certain groups.[2] Torgler (2001) found a significant correlation between tax morale and the size of the shadow economy based on data from more than 30 countries. Scholars have also found that norms and social values also influence the tax compliance.[3]

Gouldner (1960) has examined at length the nature of reciprocity in the behaviour of individuals in society. As Smith (1992) points out, one of the strongest social psychological reasons for expecting that positive behaviour by administrators toward tax payers will increase the likelihood of compliance is the strong tendency for humans to reciprocate, in kind, behaviour directed towards them. After mentioning a number of studies which have experimented with the concept of reciprocity, Smith (1992) has given two cautions about extending this social psychological research to the relationship between the tax administration system and the individual taxpayer. First, much of the research on reciprocity has involved the inducement of quite specific and simple behaviours, such as the purchase of an item or returning a favour. This method may not apply to "such ongoing, complex and burdensome" behaviour as paying tax. Second, most of the research and examples of effective inducements of reciprocity have focused on the behaviour among the individuals or other more or less equal entities. The picture is less clear for the interaction among individuals and such large, impersonal entities as the state.[4] The theory of reciprocity is akin to the theory of exchange. Falkinger (1988) finds that evasion decreases when the taxpayer is aware of the benefits received in return for tax payments.

Reviews show that though there are several studies which have analyzed the subject with a social psychological approach, many failed to recognize the importance of the social context in understanding the tax behaviour. Most of the orientations are either biased towards individual or to society (or state or country) as a whole, but ignore the intermediate groupings. However, it is imperative that we examine the role and influence of various social and occupational groups in tax compliance behaviour. As Smith and Kinsey have rightly pointed out, many analyses of evasion focus on the preferences and intentions of taxpayers and largely ignore the social context. They have also pointed out that most of the studies have assumed that non-compliance is the result of a conscious and deliberate decision by the taxpayers. (Smith and Kinsey, 1987) As Webley (1991) points out, Smith and Kinsey differentiate between the process and the content of decision-making. According to them most of the studies deal with the content (i.e. the decision to evade) than the process (the process of decision: various factors responsible for arriving at the decision).

Caroll (1992) has also hinted at the relevance of a sociological approach in the study of tax evasion and tax enforcement. He has stated that the economic model can be expanded to include non-monetary consequences of compliance and non-compliance. He has studied various dimensions of the issue, which are predominantly non-economic in character. The process of scrutiny and investigation are by themselves unpleasant, including the invasion of privacy, the time to gather every bit of financial records, the anxiety about the outcome, and having to answer to a comparatively junior level officer. The objective of the two studies described later in this book is to analyse some of these aspects in detail.

There are a few studies on the enforcement contact in the form of audits in the United States and the UK. These studies tried to understand the change in the perception and compliance after the audit. Kinsey (1992) has studied the comparative difference in the compliance behaviour of those who came into contact with the IRS enforcement and those who did not. Previously, non-compliant respondents who had to pay additional taxes as a consequence of an IRS enforcement contact not only perceived a greater certainty for detection, but were also more likely to comply on future returns. But previously non-compliant taxpayers who were not assessed for additional taxes lowered their perception of certainty.[5]

A few scholars have analysed taxation and tax compliance from the angle of socially shared ideas, opinions and attitudes, which they call social representations (See Kirchler, Maciejovsky, Schneider, 2001). In a study conducted by Trivedi, Shehata and Lynn (2003), it was found that both personal factors such as risk preference, moral reasoning and value orientation and situational factors such as audits, tax inequity, and peer reporting behaviour would equally influence tax compliance. They have suggested that standard enforcement policies based on punishment alone should be supplemented by an information system that would acquaint taxpayers with the compliance level of other taxpayers (Trivedi, Shehata and Lynn, 2003). Some scholars have also come to the conclusion that a tax system that combines both punishments and rewards is more effective in ensuring compliance than systems that exclusively rely on punishments.[6]

In a study conducted in Germany and France, it was found that positive rewards lead to a significantly higher rate of tax compliance. (Bazart and Pickhardt, 2009) It is true that there is no such thing as perfect compliance or one hundred per cent compliance in any country. Compliance to tax laws and procedures 'must be created, cultivated, monitored, and enforced in all countries'. (Bird, 2003)

Towards an appropriate research focus

What is given above is a brief review of studies on tax evasion and tax enforcement which have used various theoretical models and approaches with predominant social science perspectives. The list is not intended to be exhaustive. A critique of these studies and some others which are not mentioned here, has given valuable insights into understanding various dimensions of the problem and about the theoretical and methodological views on different aspects of the subject matter from the point of view of diverse social science disciplines. Though none of the above approaches can be reckoned as one which would exclusively explain the attitudes and perceptions of tax payers and their influence on tax compliance, they can guide a researcher in exploring diverse aspects of the problem at hand and undoubtedly offer explanations for some of them, either partly or wholly. Without compromising the basic tenets of inductive strategies, one should perhaps also study the subject with a holistic view, identifying the contextual relevance and interconnectedness of the various themes and concepts that are pertinent in such an exploratory study.

There are several areas which need attention while searching for facts about tax compliance behaviour. First of all, one should understand the unique traits ingrained in particular cultures and societies which have considerable influence on the behaviour of people belonging to that culture or society. Decisions are made on the basis of internalization of what is happening in the immediate circle. Objective relativism[7] very much exists and that would influence the tax behaviour. That would demand studies focusing on people who share uniform historical, cultural and political background. Secondly, even while analyzing a large population which have uniform historicity and social and political culture, one need to identify various groups within that society. The researcher needs to assess various categories of groupings, sub-groupings, and groups within the sub-groups. For example, there can be an urban businessman who is a first generation taxpayer with poor educational background engaged in an export business along with partners who are his relatives. Here one has to narrow down to the utmost inner layer of the population, if it is to be relevant for the study. Obviously in a study that measures tax attitudes, tax behaviour and impact of tax policies and enforcement, one cannot ignore such permutations and combinations. The symbolic-interactionist perspective, shared by John Dewey and George H Mead and fine tuned by Blumer, is very much relevant in this context. (Blumer,1969;1975)

Tax behaviour cannot be studied in isolation. The study should invariably focus on the social and systemic environment that influences tax behaviour in order to study the tax behaviour. That is to say, analyses of the social structure, the economic system, the fiscal system, the tax procedures, the methods of enforcement, the conduct of the enforcers, etc are equally relevant in the analysis of perception of the taxpayers about their own tax behaviour as well as that of others'. Unless the researcher recognizes the interplay of various factors, he cannot get a comprehensive understanding of the subject.

The nature of citizens' responses to taxation depends largely on several historical and social structural factors, which can be called as the social structural determinants. The nature of evolution of taxation in society and the social perception of its operation greatly influence the tax behaviour of the citizens. It is worthwhile to examine whether the perception and attitude of taxpayer and their consequent behaviour are influenced by (a) historical and cultural background (Historicity of tax policy and tax behaviour, by and large common for a country), (b) past experiences with the system of taxation, (c) perception of the behaviour of others closely known to the person and (d) perception of the state as a resource or service provider.

It is a fact that an individual's behaviour is influenced totally by what he experiences and perceives in society. A person's perception of others' attitudes and behaviour in turn influences his own attitude and behaviour. This takes us to Cooley's 'Looking-glass Self'[8] and the concept of 'significant others' by Mead. In Mead's view (Schwartz, 1979) the 'self' emerges from social interaction in which human beings, in taking the role of the other, internalises the attitudes of real and imagined others. Social action takes other people into account by incorporating an imaginative view of their interests and reactions in the original plan of such actions. According to this view, social structures are made as a result of groups of "interacting selves" mutually adjusting their conduct with respect to one another in the light of whom and what they know one another to be. Here comes the relevance of the Symbolic Interactionist Perspective in understanding tax attitudes and behaviour. (Blumer 1969, 1975) It is based on the premise that human beings act, based on the meanings they derive out of their social interaction. In order to understand the process of social action, one has to explore the attitudes and perceptions of individuals in the light of their social experiences and behaviour with reference to others what Blumer calls the reality construction business. (Berger and Luckmann, 1967) In the same way, society as a whole attaches meanings to the 'behaviour of the state.' Consequently, the behaviour of the state influences the behaviour of the individuals.

A certain kind of symbolic communication emerges from the pattern of tax behaviour in the group. Individuals tend to follow the representations available in the social domain on matters related to all transactions including financial transactions and related norms and conduct governing such transactions. It would be interesting to note how new terminologies and symbolic representations evolve in the social domain once a pattern emerges. For example, in a 'cash economy', people tend to formalize certain representations which are easily comprehensible such as 'black', 'number two money', 'under hand', 'outside books', etc to describe unaccounted money, and people tend to communicate in symbols unique to the area or group. People are actors or active agents and create a social world of their own. If the legal system or the enforcement system is weak, the social world tends to control the individual conduct, giving an institutional legitimacy to the patterns of behaviour. In such cases, one can see a general acceptance for deviant behaviour. Therefore, it would be quite natural to find groups and societies which view tax evasion as a smart practice than as a crime. Non-compliance with tax laws can be studied by going deeper into the social structure of groups and particular societies and the symbolic interactions therein. Individual selves emerge from what they see each other as and how the others respond to issues and then develops one's own responses to this.

Applying the above perspective, in a society where large-scale tax evasion is prevalent, individuals tend to conform to the general behavioural pattern in society. If the country has more taxpaying citizens and tax evasion is tackled with stringent enforcement measures, then the tax compliance would be better. However that does not necessarily ensure positive tax attitudes. Favourable tax attitudes are the direct byproducts of the perception by the citizens of the state as a fair resource allocator and service provider. In a country where tax paying citizens are a minority (with many without taxable income) and tax evasion is widespread, and the citizens perceive the state as an inefficient 're-distributor', then the result is large-scale negative tax attitudes. In both cases (more so in the latter case), pure economist or utilitarian approaches in tax policy would not ensure positive tax attitudes and tax compliance. Thus, the negative attitudes emerging from the unique historical experiences and social structural factors can be dealt with through a fiscal sociological approach rooted in an exchange relationship based on a social contract between the state and the citizens.

It is therefore necessary to examine the citizens' response to taxation in the context of the social exchange between the state and the individual. The taxpayer-government relationship can be seen as involving an exchange: the taxpayer pays his taxes and government supplies various benefits. If the exchange is unfair, individuals will take steps to redress the balance. As Caroll (1992) says, the sense of fairness is very important for maintaining the legitimacy of tax paying. 'When people think taxes are unfair, they spend less time reporting carefully and may be motivated to produce what they perceive to be a fair outcome even when this does not conform to the law.'

Tax attitudes and behavioural patterns are largely influenced by the strategies and conduct of the law enforcers. It would be fruitful to examine the nature of tax behaviour by focusing on a group of persons who were searched by the income tax department. By going deep into their lives, one would understand the causes and consequences of tax evasion and tax enforcement as perceived by the respondents. The methodological approach detailed above warrants unique methods for data collection. The study requires careful observation and an ability to pay attention to detail, since data needs to be gathered on several sensitive issues. The methods and tools of data collection for such an empirical study should be such that the same are unaffected by the prejudice and bias of the researcher even remotely. It is also necessary to devise the tools in such a way that the respondents divulge the facts which are generally considered as confidential or hidden from the public domain, including their close associates.

Various research methods

Scholars have used different methodologies to study tax compliance. Many relied on secondary sources to analyse tax compliance. There are also studies conducted after collecting primary data. Methods followed by various researchers include surveys through questionnaires, interviews, and experimental studies.

Disadvantages of using secondary data

Many studies on large population and countries have used secondary data for analysis. They have attempted to compare and analyze data from the official records in order to arrive at the trends in tax collection, increase in compliance by particular taxpayer categories, claim of exemptions and other tax incentives. Studies have been conducted analyzing the data on audits to find out the trends in under-reporting and false claims. Such studies are comprehensive enough to the extent that they can cover a large data base. If the records are available digitally, they can be subjected to statistical techniques without much difficulty. As the data are from official records, these are considered to be authentic. Many governments have set up their own tax research units to study the tax compliance on the basis of the data available in tax returns. In the US many studies of tax evasion are based on Taxpayer Compliance Measurement Program (TCMP) data. Many countries engage research institutions to analyze the data after providing them with official statistics. For example, in Australia, the tax department engages research centres like ATAX for conducting the analysis. In India, National Institute of Public Finance and Policy (NIPFP), National Council of Applied Economic Research (NCAER), etc are often given the task.

However, the use of secondary data sources has lots of disadvantages. First, original secondary data on tax compliance are available only with government bodies or with government-funded research institutions. It would be extremely difficult for an independent researcher to get access to official data from government sources. Though one can obtain macro-level data on trends in collections, expansion of tax base, tax effect of audits and investigations, etc, gathering data on particular categories of taxpayers would be difficult. Such data will ordinarily be forthcoming only when governments themselves charter agencies to do research for them. Second, the inferences one can draw from secondary sources are very limited and it can give only a description of facts or at the most a conclusion about the pattern. It cannot assist in providing an appropriate explanation for the pattern. Third, though official records are authentic, that does not mean that they are true reflections of actual tax compliance. They fail to provide an understanding, even remotely of the tax attitudes and behaviour of the taxpayers. One can get little out of the secondary data if the objective is to understand the taxpayers' perceptions and tax behaviour.

Shortcomings of surveys and questionnaires

If secondary data cannot provide sufficient reasoning for the patterns found, surveys through questionnaires aim at gathering the attitudes and opinions of the taxpayers. Attitude surveys and opinion polls are very widely used in different parts of the world to study tax compliance and tax behaviour. Many researchers distribute questionnaires to taxpayers at random or in groups and collect back the same immediately or after a few days. Most of the studies in developed countries are through questionnaires mailed electronically or otherwise to large number of taxpayers. This method has been found to be cheaper, time saving and has the cover of anonymity. Data can be collected from a large sample and respondents can fill up the same at their own free time. E-mail surveys are easy for further data processing. Telephonic interviews are also conducted by many researchers who will transmit questionnaires over phone.

The above method of data collection through questionnaires (distributed personally, telephonically, through e-mail or post) is not devoid of disadvantages. The response rates in mailed surveys are very poor. Even in cases where responses are received, there are chances that a substantial number is incomplete. Even when the researcher gets sizable responses, the fundamental question would be how far such data throw light on the issues being explored. Even when the questionnaire is open-ended, it cannot capture the actual emotional status of the respondent and the nature and extent of involvement of the respondent to the questions posed.

If the objective of the study is to understand the attitudes, perceptions and experiences of the taxpayers on particular issues and if one needs to draw conclusions about their tax behaviour, it is necessary to devise an appropriate data collection strategy. Studies that explore the sociological and social psychological dimensions of individuals need to move away from stereotyped questionnaires and remote-controlled data gathering techniques. It is necessary to have a one-to-one sitting with the respondent. That will facilitate the right emotional setting for a frank sharing of opinion, experience and information. However, it needs to be attempted before one can tell whether similar results would be forthcoming in an interview with the help of webcam.

Experimental studies

Several scholars have done what are called experimental studies to understand tax evasion and compliance.[9] In many such studies, subjects are given a certain amount of money per period and they must decide how much of it to report. Another type of experimental study is to comparatively analyze the responses of more than one group on separate simulations.[10] There are studies on students, unemployed youth, etc (all of them without any prior tax experience) on their tax attitudes to arrive at conclusions on the perceptions of taxpayers in general. Similarly, tax compliance studies have been conducted by many researchers comparing a control group and an experimental group. Experimental studies are aimed at getting concrete and quick results on selected indicators.

Notwithstanding the theoretical and methodological debate on the utility of attempting experimental methods in social research, it is not clear whether tax researchers have obtained results which have provided valid generalizations and conclusions. Certainly, studies aimed at gathering data on the attitudes, perceptions and enforcement experiences related to taxation cannot merely rely on experimental data. Such a study cannot be done either in artificial settings or through any kind of simulated environment.

Other methods

Feinstein (1990) developed an econometric model called detection controlled estimation to address the issue of non-detection. According to him, though it has several advantages, one of the key weaknesses of the method relates to the fact that it is statistical in nature and not based on detailed information. Another method that is followed is through the analysis of specific data such as taxpayers who have come under amnesty scheme (voluntary disclosure or admission) or taxpayers who have been penalized or prosecuted.

Semi-structured interview and case study

Researches on and about human beings are always challenging and the same cannot be done like usual laboratory experiments or through remote controlled surveys. Humans are not passive beings. They may not be easily willing to become a subject for any study whatever be the great cause the study is aimed at. It will be more difficult when a researcher asks questions on personal experiences and behavioural patterns. He needs to understand the 'self'[11] of the subject in order to draw inferences on what his thoughts are. The challenge of the researcher is to understand and distinguish the two phases of the self process: the inner 'I', which is supposed to be spontaneous and subjective and the outer 'Me', which is the organized attitudes of others. Through an analysis of a group of such 'selves', one can possibly understand the 'generalized other', which is nothing but the organized attitudes of the whole community or group. The interview by the researcher with the subject (respondent) is aimed at gathering as many details about the former within a limited period of time.

In a tax compliance study or any other related study exploring tax attitudes, tax behaviour, etc, one requires the respondent to divulge his thoughts, opinions, experiences and conduct on select topics. As mentioned earlier any such study tends to be comprehensive due to the fact that several social, political, economic and cultural factors interplay in shaping the tax attitudes and behaviour. The researcher needs to gather sensitive data on financial activities, reporting of income, undisclosed income, claims of exemptions and other tax incentives, procedural compliance, audits, enforcement experiences, and penalty. He also needs to touch upon the relationship structure of the respondent with family members, relatives, partners, close associates, government officials and several others. All this requires an appropriate methodological tool which can capture qualitative and quantitative data.

A MATTER OF APPROACH?

If one has to understand the attitudes and perceptions of individuals and to know about their intimate life experiences to draw conclusions about the behavioural pattern and the world-view, the facts need to be gathered by collecting primary data. Primary data needs to be gathered not just by administering a questionnaire to the subject, but through a comprehensive data collection strategy which includes an in-depth interview with the aid of a semi-structured and open-ended schedule. The setting up of a right environment for free and frank sharing is imperative to gather data from the respondents. The objective is not only to gather facts but also to probe the reasons for the same and to provide an understanding of the issues in question. The ultimate objective is to draw conclusions which aid in predicting the behaviour. In a study to explore the attitudes of the taxpayers about the state, tax evasion and tax enforcement and their perception of the tax behaviour, the researcher needs to engage in an in-depth investigation through a comprehensive data gathering tool. Similarly, if one aims at gathering data on the tax evasion behaviour of taxpayers, it is necessary that the data is gathered through intelligent interviews and case studies wherever possible. A semi-structured conversation with the respondent is required for an in-depth understanding of issues under exploration. The following are some of the ingredients of such a conversational interview.

a) Prior appointment should be taken for the conversation as it may take about two to five hours, depending upon the data to be gathered.
b) Should be done in a place where the respondent is most comfortable.
c) As far as possible, the data collection should be completed in one sitting.
d) It should not be in a place or time where the respondent is frequently interrupted by people or calls.
e) Researcher should personally converse with the respondent and record the data rather than delegating the work to untrained data collectors.

f) Questions should be loosely structured, capturing both qualitative and quantitative data. Questions should slowly surface during the conversation rather than conversations following each question.
g) Audio-video recorders should be used if the respondent does not object.
h) The researcher should prepare a conversation diary immediately after the conversation.

The skills of the interviewer are very important in gathering the data without giving an impression to the respondent that he is being probed too much. Respondents who are in a tax compliance study would not wish to reveal the details easily. They neither wish nor expect any solutions or suggestions, unlike many other sociological studies which make people share their intimate experiences on various social issues or personal problems. In many cases, interviews, though do not provide any solutions, are instrumental in providing a relief to them as they share their problems and experiences to the interviewer. However, such a relieving experience is neither desired nor expected by a respondent in a tax compliance study. Thus, it is solely the efficiency of the interviewer which is most important for the success of a tax compliance study.

Two empirical studies

No theoretical analysis is complete without observation of events in the real world. Facts as narrated by the actors themselves speak volumes about the unique experiences faced by them. Therefore attempts were made to gather data in the form of opinions, attitudes and sharing of experiences for two empirical studies. Separate sets of randomly picked up samples from the same geographical area were used for the two studies.

The first study (which is given in chapter 6) is aimed at understanding the tax attitudes and tax behaviour perceptions in a developing economy. The second study (described in chapter 7) is aimed at understanding tax compliance and taxpayer perceptions through an analysis of the sociological causes and consequences of tax enforcement in a developing country. Both studies are conducted through interviews of the sample of taxpayers. However, the method followed in the second study is of conversational interview and a case study of longer duration with each person in the sample of persons who faced an income tax search.

The region covering four districts in the state of Tamil Nadu located in Southern India was selected for both the studies. All these districts fall under a common Chief Commissionerate. This region was selected basically because of the researcher's physical proximity to the area and also due to the availability of various resources connected to the study.The Indian Income Tax Act is uniform in its laws, rules and procedures all over the country and this region is no exception. Even non-statutory procedures are followed in a uniform manner all over the country by the income tax department. Thus, there is absolute uniformity in respect of the nature of income tax administration and enforcement all over India.

Assessees in the region are from heterogeneous categories. It is said that there is an extensive intermingling of gene pools. From the beginning of the 19th century, the traditional as well as the market-oriented economic system have continued side by side. (Singh, 1997) Substantial numbers of businessmen in all the above places were basically from the states of Gujarat, Punjab, Rajasthan, Andhra Pradesh, Karnataka and Kerala. Many assessees who have migrated to this area from northern India, still maintain their accounts in Hindi or Marwari, which is an indication of their continuing bond with their ancestral roots. Likewise many of them who migrated from the states of Karnataka and Andhra Pradesh, generations before, still speak only their mother tongues *viz.* Kannada and Telugu respectively in the family and business settings. It is also observed that they prefer persons from their own linguistic or ethnic community as their business associates or key employees in order to retain their cultural character to some extent. However, there are strong networks among the people in this region in spite of their heterogeneous origins, as evidenced by their combined representations in various social, business and religious organizations. Thus, this is a very unique region with strong representation of national character, considering the geographic, demographic and economic characteristics of this belt as compared with any other region in India. This region is also heterogeneous in respect of various other characteristics: types of businesses, nature of trading, manufacturing and service activities, diversity of professions and proper mix of agricultural and non-agricultural occupations. The area is neither politically over-sensitive nor under-sensitive.

CHAPTER-6

A MATTER OF MIND?

Tax Attitudes and Perceptions of Tax behaviour in a Developing Country

Porfiry, the Detective : *'There is one thing, however, to be said. All these psychological means of defense, these excuses and evasions, are very insubstantial, and they cut both ways.'*

Raskolnikov : *'...I don't contend that extraordinary people are always bound to commit breaches of morals, as you call it....I simply hinted that an extraordinary man has the right...that is not an official right, but an inner right to decide in his own conscience to overstep...certain obstacles, and only in case it is essential for the practical fulfillment of his idea....'*

('Crime and Punishment' by Fyodor Dostoyevsky)

All of us have views on life and society. But many of us choose not to express them publicly. There are also possibilities to have diametrically opposite views on a subject, one when expressed publicly and the other when shared privately. Views get converted into attitudes in the course of time as we observe, experiment with and experience things. Some of those attitudes tend to have strong bearings on our behaviour. In this chapter, the focus is on analyzing the views of people that have shaped particular attitudes towards the state and taxation, and their bearing on tax behaviour.

Certain truths are known to all. Tax evasion is one such fact in all societies. Hardly can we see any society either in history or in contemporary times which has to its credit one hundred percent voluntary tax compliance. Governments and tax administrations across the world have to grapple with the problem of tax evasion. Many a time, the nature and source of tax evasion is very much known to the taxmen, yet they fail to tackle the menace. The reason is the sudden transitions taking place in the area of tax evasion as people tend to invent thousands of new ways and means to generate unaccounted money and conceal undisclosed income. Thus, the cat and mouse game continues between the tax evader and the tax gatherer.

Everyone knows that some part of the income always goes unreported. But no one would state this fact with certainty and clarity about oneself or others to a third person apart from his close family members or associates. Occasional revelations to friends over drinks in a club or during a party cannot be ruled out. Normally, no person would disclose the extent of tax evasion he indulges in to a stranger. Thus, such information is not readily available with the media or any research agency or any government department. Gathering such information is a challenge even in individual cases and estimating the nature and extent of tax evasion for a country as a whole is an impossibility. Therefore, systematic empirical studies are necessary to find out the tax behaviour of the people. Though there are several studies as mentioned earlier, most of them are based on survey data, distribution of questionnaires, internet surveys, simulation studies, etc. Rarely have attempts been made to collect data directly through systematic interviews. Scholars have developed several attitude scales but this too has the serious problem of cross cultural validity.

There is a need to understand the attitudes of person in a given cultural context. In the present study, the attitudes and perceptions of the taxpayers and their perceived tax behaviour and past tax experiences (their exposure to enforcement measures) are examined in order to understand the social structural determinants in the tax compliance in society.

Attitudes and its relation to behaviour

Attitude is broadly defined as an orientation towards a person, a situation, an institution, or a social process, which is indicative of an underlying value or belief. (Marshall, 1998) Scholars have analyzed the attitudes of people in order to understand their behaviour. Attitudinal studies are considered important by both sociologists and psychologists as it is assumed that attitudes and behavior are directly related. It is inferred that attitudes predict behaviour and a person's behaviour can be judged by gathering data on the nature of attitudes of that person. Both Ajzen and Fishbein (1980) and Eiser (1986) have said that attitudes are one of the indicators of human behaviour and the relation between behavior and attitude needs to be studied on the basis of analysis of particular contexts.

Attitudes emerge from both the cognitive and affective realms of an individual. At the cognitive level, the individual's reasoning and logic provide the necessary trigger in the formation of attitudes. At the affective level, the ideas, values, norms, etc have a bearing on the attitudes. Apart from these two levels the situational realm influences the formation of attitudes. Here the experience and the surrounding environment (both past and current) of the individuals are determining factors in the formation of attitudes. This can be better explained through a diagram. (See D 6.1)

Hence, attitudes originate from a synthesis of multiple factors. However, behaviour can be in either consonance or dissonance with the attitudes. This depends on the factors which are dominant as well as the influence of situational factors emanating from the immediate environment. This implies that a person who has strong cognitive rationale for a particular issue may behave differently due to the influence of a stronger affective component. This results in cognitive dissonance. Similarly, a person with an attitude formed consequent to the synthesis of cognitive and affective components can also behave very differently due to various situational factors. Here there will be a behavioural inconsistency which can be called as situation-induced dissonance. In our context of study it would mean that a person who has an attitude to comply with a law based on his rational analysis and the imbibed value system can tend to disobey the law due to situational compulsions.

Tax attitudes

One of the pioneering contributions to the psychological approach in understanding the attitudes of taxpayers was of Lewis. (1982) He adopted the theory of reasoned action of Ajzen and Fishbein (1980) which predicts that attitudes are indicators of actual human behaviour. Peters (1991) analyzed a good deal of evidence about the attitudes of taxing and spending from a variety of sources to compare attitudinal influences in tax policies in Scandinavian and Mediterranean countries.

Empirical analysis of tax attitudes and behaviour of particular taxpayers would throw light on the general trends among the taxpaying community. The problem of tax evasion needs to be analyzed with a micro perspective by going deeper into the causative factors at the individual level. The perception, attitude and behaviour of individual taxpayers need to be analyzed within the socio-cultural settings in which the taxpayers' actions take shape.

Therefore, the subject needs to be approached with a sociological perspective recognizing the situational (social environment) characteristics and the individual differences. It is also necessary to understand the comparative influence of tax policies, tax procedures and tax administration on the tax attitudes and behaviour. Particular configurations of the tax system would provide opportunities for evasion for certain groups. Thus, the overall tax behaviour of taxpayers in a country is the result of multiple factors. One has to recognize the

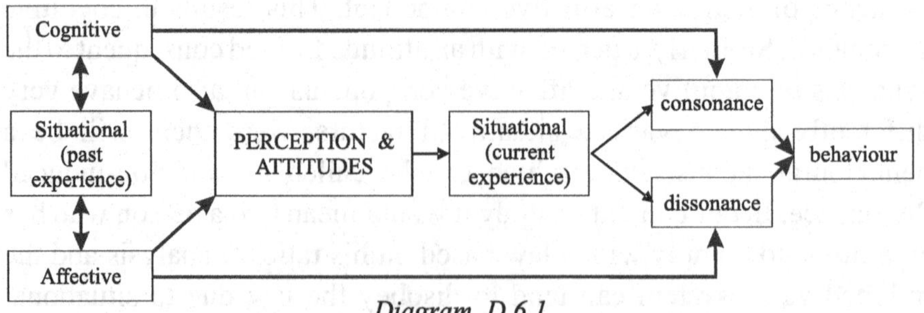

Diagram D 6.1

Factors shaping attitudes and the resulting consonance and dissonance

importance of the interpretative understanding of social action (Weber, 1922; 1968) 'by virtue of the subjective meaning attached to it' by the acting individual. (or individuals) That is to say, the attitude, the perception and the behaviour of taxpayers and the overall tax compliance in a society can be effectively studied by the researcher only with a sociological understanding. Specifically, the methodological perspective of Symbolic Interactionism[1] is of relevance in analyzing this issue. The following are the three basic premises in such a perspective: a) Human beings act towards things on the basis of the meanings that things have for them, b) these meanings arise out of social interaction, and c) social action results from a fitting together of individual lines of action. (Blumer, 1969) The tax attitudes and perceptions are based on the meanings taxpayers give to a particular type of tax system and its overall relevance for the taxpayers themselves. Every system projects an identity for itself, based on its founding objectives or based on the revised objectives amended over a period of time. Its identity is also based on its role and relevance in the social, economic and political context. However, the perception of the system by the people is based on their experiences as well as the public opinion about that system. Here, the proclaimed identity or the label inscribed has no influence if the public find a different meaning for the system. For example, a civic corporation which has an objective of maintaining hygiene in a particular place can be designated as an anti-social corporation which eats away the public funds if it fails to perform for the fulfillment of its objectives. And the entity gets an altogether new meaning in the public domain. Thus, the meaning that the individuals give in a particular context to a particular system determines the popular attitudes and consequent behaviour.

The response of the taxpayers is influenced by what they perceive in society. Apart from the meaning given by the taxpayer himself to the system of taxation, the public perception of the tax system also has an influence on him. Social interaction plays a vital role in forming opinions and attitudes. Such public opinions and popular attitudes can be analyzed only at the individual level. So, the starting point of any analysis about the perception of tax system needs to be the individual taxpayer and his opinions, attitudes, perceptions and tax behaviour as narrated by him.

Therefore, an empirical study (study-1) was carried out on a random sample[2] of taxpayers to understand their tax attitudes and their perception of the tax behaviour. The objectives of the study were: a) to understand the nature of attitudes of taxpayers about taxation and tax compliance, b) to examine the attitudes of taxpayers about tax evasion, c) to understand the attitudes and perceptions of taxpayers about the state in the context of 'exchange' relationship, d) to understand the tax behaviour of taxpayers in the context of the tax attitudes and on the basis of self-reporting, and e) to explore how their tax attitudes and tax behaviour are shaped by their perception of attitudes and behaviour of others closely known to them.

Considering the exploratory nature of the study, though it was advisable not to have any preconceived hypotheses, a few assumptions emerged from the review of literature. These were framed as hypotheses and tested in the study for methodological convenience. The hypotheses were: a) tax attitudes and perceptions of taxpayers are not independent of their attitudes and perceptions about the state and governance, b) tax attitudes and perceptions of taxpayers are not independent of their perceptions of tax attitudes and behaviours of significant others, c) own perceived tax behaviour is not independent of their attitudes and perception of the state and governance, d) own perceived tax behaviour is not independent of the perception of others' tax behaviour, e) current tax attitudes and behaviour are not independent of past tax experiences, and f) tax attitudes and perceptions of taxpayers are not independent of age, level of education, level of tax awareness, nature of occupation, generational background as taxpayer, and level of income.

Background profile of the respondents

The sample contained a number of respondents falling under various age groups. 76 per cent of the respondents were males and 85 per cent of the respondents were married. Also, the respondents were from diverse educational and income backgrounds and were separately grouped based on levels of education and income. There were equal numbers of respondents belonging to salaried, professional and business groups. As the study was in the context of the tax experiences, perceptions and attitudes, it was necessary to ensure that the respondents had enough exposure to income taxation. Therefore, the sample frame was designed to include only those respondents who were assessees at least for the last three years prior to the interview. In the present sample 21 per cent of the respondents were taxpayers for ten to fifteen years. 13 per cent of respondents were taxpayers for more than fifteen years. 39 per cent of the respondents were taxpayers for less than ten years but for more than five years.

As mentioned earlier, generational background of the respondents as taxpayers may influence their attitudes and perceptions. Therefore, data were gathered regarding the number of taxpayers whose parents or grandparents were not income tax assessees (39 per cent) (first generation taxpayers), those whose parents were income tax assessees (44 per cent) (second generation tax payers) and those respondents whose grandparents were income tax assessees (17 per cent) (third generation taxpayers). Interestingly, it was found that those respondents who stated that their grandparents were income tax assessees also mentioned that their parents were also assessees.

Statement specific responses indicating attitudes

A major part of the interview with each subject (respondent) was devoted to examine the tax attitude. In analyzing the tax attitude, the attempt was to understand those attitudes of respondents on taxation, tax evasion and tax enforcement that represent the beliefs, ideas, values, emotions and predispositions of the respondents in the given context. The responses indicate the orientations of respondents towards the system of taxation. This would help us to have an understanding of the problem under study and also it is assumed that they predict behaviour, though partly.

Basically, attitudes are measured by gathering opinion whether individuals agree or disagree about certain statements. Attitudes are also measured using different types of scales *viz.* Likert scale, Thurstone scale, Semantic differential scale of Osgood, Social distance scale by Bogardus, Guttman scale, etc. Many standard scales are developed by psychologists for use in a variety of studies. There are also standard statements to examine tax attitudes devised mostly in developed countries. But there is a serious problem of cross cultural validity if those are used in the given context. Statements have been selected on the basis of the pilot study. The same were later shown to experts for their comments to keep only those statements which were relevant, contextual and which were unambiguous and not misleading. The final selection was made after the pre-test.

Also, the attitudes were measured as simple as possible, with less sophistication, but without compromising the validity of the scale. Similar to the widely used Likert scale, the respondents were presented with a series of statements, some positively phrased and some negatively phrased, which have been found to discriminate between contrasting views on the subject of study. However, it was extremely difficult to allot specific scores to the negative and positive statements, as the concept of both 'negative' statement and 'positive' statement is very 'relative'. Therefore, assuming a particular position to gauge the responses under a particular category was found to be inappropriate in the given context. So, the analysis was made based on the response to individual statements without attempting a re-classification or categorization or summation. However, the statements on common topics have been grouped for the purpose of description.

Respondents were given a set of statements to give their responses on various topics like role of the state, role performance of the state, tax system, tax policy, tax administration, etc. Their responses were marked on a five-point scale and then analysed. The data in tables given below gives a preliminary description of the responses by the respondents to each statement.

Perceptions on the role of the state and the role performance of the state

The statements S-1 and S-2 (Table T 6.1) denote the role performance of the governments in independent India. As a country with a low per capita income and with substantial number of people below the poverty line, the basic mission of the country is to ensure welfare for the masses and to achieve equity. The respondents were asked to give their opinion on the above statements. From Table T 6.1, it is clear that a majority of the respondents were of the opinion that the state was committed to uplift those who are below the poverty line and that it had implemented several policies for the welfare of the masses. One can see here that the respondents have a positive attitude towards the state as far as the state's welfare role is concerned. However, about one-fourth of the respondents did not agree or were indifferent with the above two statements.

Statements S-3, S-4, and S-5 convey a contra viewpoint as compared

	%	Strongly Agree	Agree	Indifferent	Disagree	Strongly Disagree	TOTAL
S-1 Successive governments since independence have implemented several policies for the welfare of the masses	%	8	69	2	20	1	100
S-2 The government is committed to uplift those who are below the poverty line	%	6	63	5	25	1	100
S-3 Government has failed in its role as a service provider for the people	%	9	31	10	46	4	100
S-4 Government is not an efficient allocator of resources	%	6	37	9	42	6	100
S-5 It is better to do charity directly or through charitable organizations than through government by way of taxes	%	13	29	20	34	4	100

Table T 6.1

Perceptions about the role of state and role performance of state

to statements S-1 and S-2. Here the implied meaning is that the state has failed in its role as a service provider. However, 50 % of the respondents disagreed with the statement (S-3) and a significant number of respondents (10 per cent) chose to be indifferent. Only 39 per cent of the respondents agreed with the above statement. A similar trend in attitudes can be seen in the other two statements (S-4 and S-5) too. Only 49 per cent of the respondents felt that the government was not an efficient allocator of resources. The statement S-5 can be seen as a corollary to the above three statements by suggesting an alternative for the welfare of the poor through a non-governmental route. 42 per cent of the respondents agreed with the statement that it is better to do charity directly or through charitable organizations than through government by way of taxes. A significant number of respondents (20 per cent) chose to be indifferent to the above statement.

Perception of the rationale of taxation and perceived fairness of the state

While the above statements (S-1 to S-5) were aimed at gathering the opinion of the respondents on the role of the state and its role performance, statements S-6 to S-8 focused on the attitude about taxation as an institution to collect revenue for the welfare of the country (Table T 6.2). It is interesting to find that almost everyone (92 per cent agreed, 3 per cent were indifferent) felt that taxation was necessary for the overall development of the country. And 72 per cent of the respondents were of the opinion that the taxation of income was an appropriate measure to raise revenue for the nation. Only 18 per cent of the respondents disagreed with the statement. Thus taxation whether one personally likes it or not, is considered as a necessary 'burden' by the majority of the respondents. In order to get a contra view, the respondents were asked whether they felt that the government should not have the power to tax. 63 per cent of the respondents disagreed with the statement and 14 per cent indicated their indifference. Here, it is clear from the responses to statements S-1 to S-8 that the majority of the respondents felt that taxation by the state is necessary for the development of the country and for the welfare of the masses and that the role of state is crucial.

		%	Strongly Agree	Agree	Indifferent	Disagree	Strongly Disagree	TOTAL
S-6	Taxation is necessary for overall development of the country	%	19	73	3	5	0	100
S-7	Taxation of income is an appropriate measure to raise revenue for the nation	%	19	53	9	18	1	100
S-8	Government should not have the power to tax	%	1	22	14	53	10	100
S-9	Taxation of goods and services are enough to raise the revenue for the country and income tax is not necessary	%	11	40	8	39	2	100
S-10	Income tax does not contribute much for the economic welfare of the people	%	8	43	8	39	2	100
S-11	Income taxation has resulted in achieving redistribution from the rich for the welfare of the society	%	5	53	12	27	3	100
S-12	Income taxation is a disincentive in using one's full potential to earn income	%	5	42	13	38	2	100

Table T 6.2

Perception of the rationale of taxation and perceived fairness of the State

While the responses to the above statements indicated a positive attitude towards taxation by the state, the statements S-9 to S-12 were aimed at gathering the opinion of the respondents on their preferences in terms of the nature and type of revenue collection. It is necessary to understand the rationale of income taxation as perceived by the respondents. While responding to statement-9, 51 per cent of the respondents agreed with the proposition that the taxation of goods and services are enough to raise the revenue for the nation and that the taxation of income was not necessary. Income tax, being a direct tax, is perceived generally as more burdensome as compared with the indirect taxes like sales tax and excise duties. The impact of the latter is the same for all people who consume the goods and services. That may be one reason for the preference for indirect taxes to income tax. This is evident in the responses to statement S-12 as well.

As detailed in chapter 4, the perception of utilization of taxes is one of the influential factors for tax compliance. Therefore, it is important to analyze the responses of the taxpayers to statements in this regard. To statement (S-10) that income tax does not contribute much for the economic welfare of the people, 51 per cent have agreed and 40 per cent have disagreed. However, 58 per cent of the respondents felt that income taxation has resulted in achieving redistribution of income from the rich for the welfare of the society (S-11). Only 30 per cent of the respondents believed that income taxation had not achieved this redistribution. It is interesting to observe the responses for statement S-12 that income taxation is a disincentive in using one's potential to earn income. Almost 50 per cent of the respondents agreed with the statement. This is an indication of the wide perception that taxation is a determining factor in the propensity to work and earn income. The feeling is that if the extra effort does not give substantial returns due to the tax burden, then it is better not to work harder.

The changing role of the state in the globalized world

In this era of liberalization, deregulation, and privatization, there is widespread thinking that there should be more and more roles for the private sector and a reduced role for the government in the production of goods and services. In this background, statement S-13 was posed to the respondents to get their response. (Table T 6.3) 57 per cent of the respondents agreed that the government need not involve in the production of goods and services and that these should be left to the private sector. A similar viewpoint is evident in the responses to statement (S-15) where 83 per cent of the respondents felt that there should be competitive production and distribution of goods and services by both public sector and private sector. This can be seen as a desire for quality and competitive costs for goods and services. However, it is significant to see the responses of the majority of the respondents (72 per cent) where they agreed to the statement that only the government can ensure equitable treatment to the people and that the government should continue in its roles as producer and provider. This indicates an apparent ambiguity in the attitude of respondents. Here it is clear that though the respondents had felt the necessity of giving more sectors into the private hands, they were also apprehensive about the equitable distribution of the outputs if things were left to the control of the private sector. There is a feeling that there would be more fair treatment by the government than by any other agency. Only 53 per cent of the respondents felt that, in a competitive system of production and distribution, the needs of the disadvantaged sections of the people would be taken care of (S-16).

		%	Strongly Agree	Agree	Indifferent	Disagree	Strongly Disagree	TOTAL
S-13	The government need not involve in the production of goods and services (except law and order) and these should be left to the private sector.	%	15	42	10	31	2	100
S-14	Only government can ensure equitable treatment to the people and government should continue in its role as producer and provider	%	6	66	10	18	0	100
S-15	There should be competitive production and distribution of goods and services by both public sector and private sector	%	13	70	5	10	2	100
S-16	In a competitive system of production and distribution, the needs of the disadvantaged sections of the people would be taken care of	%	4	49	17	30	0	100

Table T 6.3
Perception of changing role of the state in the globalized world

Analyses of responses to the above statements indicate that the respondents have felt a strong need for taxation for the development of the country and public welfare. They felt that the state can continue to play a major role in ensuring equitable treatment to all. However, it is a fact that tax compliance is poor and revenue from the income tax is still not substantial in the country.

Attitudes about tax compliance and evasion

The statements (S-17 to S-22) were presented to the respondents to get their views on tax evasion and tax compliance in society. (Table T 6.4) Though most of these statements are about general tax behaviour, the opinions expressed by the respondents have bearings on their own tax attitudes and tax behaviour. The responses given by these taxpayers would help in understanding the reasons for low tax compliance in the society.

To the statement (S-17) that the tax rates are very high and therefore it is very difficult to comply, 84 per cent of the respondents had agreed. Though there is a drastic reduction in tax rates in the last few years, the respondents still felt that the rates were very high. They also felt that there was very high degree of tax non-compliance among the taxpayers.

	%	Strongly Agree	Agree	Indifferent	Disagree	Strongly Disagree	TOTAL
S-17 Tax rates are very high and therefore difficult to comply with	%	27	57	5	11	0	100
S-18 Most of the people are dishonest in paying the correct taxes	%	27	54	5	14	0	100
S-22 Most of the people I know evade their taxes	%	19	47	12	21	1	100
S-19 There is better voluntary compliance to income tax in recent years	%	14	63	9	14	0	100

Table T 6.4
Attitudes about tax compliance and evasion

Let us reiterate here that every individual observes the actions and behavioural patterns of the other individuals closely known to him. One would be continuously evaluating and judging the decisions and movements of others on matters of general concern. This may also influence one's own attitudes and behaviour. The knowledge of tax evasion of others is recognized as an important factor in tax decisions. (Webley and others, 1991) 81 per cent of the respondents felt that most of the people were dishonest in paying their taxes. A similar response can be seen for the statement (S-22) that a great many acquaintances of the respondent evade their taxes. 67 per cent of the respondents stated that most of the people known to them were tax evaders. Only 14 per cent of the respondents disagreed with the statement (S-18) that most of the people were dishonest in paying the taxes, though the majority felt that there has been better voluntary compliance of income tax in the recent years. (S-19)

Some scholars like Laurin[3], and also a study by Internal Revenue Service (1984) indicated that those who believe their associates are evaders are themselves likely to be tax evaders. (Internal Revenue Service, 1984) Similarly, those respondents who perceived tax evasion as a less severe crime are themselves more likely to be evaders. (Song and Yarborough, 1978; Listhanug and Miller, 1985, Peters, 1991)

As we saw in the review of the interactive model presented by Benjamin and Maital (1985) in chapter 5, there is a strong relevance for the understanding of the social interaction of the individual and his consequent perception of the tax behaviour of others. It is assumed that the decision of the taxpayers is very much influenced by the behaviour of others. This is because any behaviour, including the tax behaviour of individuals, is influenced by the behaviour of others and every action of the individual has a social orientation. In Mead's (1934) view, the 'self' emerges from social interactions in which human beings, in taking the role of the other, internalises the attitudes of real and imagined others. That is to say, social action takes other people into account by incorporating an imaginative view of their interests and reactions in the original plan of such actions. From this observation, it may be inferred that those who report compliance believe that other taxpayers comply, whereas those who report cheating believe that others also cheat.

It is very interesting to analyze the responses given regarding the penal provisions for non-compliance and the respondents' perception of tax evasion as a crime. One of the reasons for low tax compliance in many countries is the general view that tax evasion is not a serious crime. Many theorists (Klepper and Nagin, 1989; Song and Yarbrough, 1978) have found that people see tax fraud as a less serious crime than many other crimes including property crimes. If tax evasion is not considered as a serious economic offence, that is not because of their support for law violations. On the other hand, it emanates from the perception of general non-compliance around them and also their perception that either violators are not caught or that those who are caught are never properly punished. This does not mean that the people respect the tax evaders. As reported in a study by the US IRS, a majority of the respondents had stated that their opinion of some one would be lowered if that person bragged about cheating on his taxes. (Eicher, 2001)

In the current sample, while about 75 per cent of the respondents agreed that the penal provisions for tax evasion should be strictly enforced (S-20), about 53 per cent of the respondents felt that tax evasion is not to be considered a serious economic offence. (S-21) Apparently one may conclude that there is incoherence in the responses of the respondents. However, it can be inferred that a majority of the

	%	Strongly Agree	Agree	Indifferent	Disagree	Strongly Disagree	TOTAL
S-20 Penal provisions for tax evasion should be strictly enforced	%	17	58	4	18	3	100
S-21 Tax evasion is not to be considered as a serious economic offence	%	14	39	14	24	9	100

Table T 6.5
Perception of tax evasion as a crime

respondents are of the view that the incidence of tax evasion should be tackled with less stringent punishments, but it should be strictly enforced. The respondents might be pointing towards a tax regime imposing lower penalties for tax evasion but which is stern on all the evaders.

Analyses of statements S-1 to S-21 indicate that the majority of the respondents have a moderately positive attitude about the role and the role performance of the state and are of the view that taxation is an important instrument for development and welfare. It is also clear that the taxpayers perceive widespread tax non-compliance in society. They also argue for strict enforcement of the penal provisions, though they still do not wish to view tax evasion as a very serious economic offence. The reason may be their own perception of the universal existence of tax evasion and the tax non-compliance of most of the people known to them. Thus, there is an absence of negative attitude towards the concept of taxation as such among the respondents, though they are not happy with the higher tax rates. In this context, let us examine the attitudes of the respondents about the tax laws and rules and tax administration.

Attitudes and perceptions regarding tax laws and tax administration fairness

One of the key areas of dissent for a majority of the respondents was regarding tax laws and rules. Only about 30 per cent of the respondents felt that the tax laws and rules were not complicated. (Table T 6.6) 45 per cent of the respondents disagreed with the statement (S-27) and a substantial number of respondents (26 per cent) were indifferent. The indifference of more than one-fourth of the respondents is also indicative of their own ignorance about the tax laws and rules.

The tax behaviour of the people not only depends on their perceived fairness of the taxation and the consequent redistribution and utilization of tax so collected, but also the fairness and efficiency of the tax administration. This is quite evident from the data gathered related to the questions posed in this regard. 56 per cent of the respondents were of the view that the income tax department takes action against all types of tax evaders. (S-23) However, 35 per cent of the respondents disagreed with the statement and 9 per cent chose to be indifferent.

	%	Strongly Agree	Agree	Indifferent	Disagree	Strongly Disagree	TOTAL
S-27 Tax laws and rules are not very complicated	%	7	23	26	39	5	100
S-23 Income tax department takes action against all types of tax evaders	%	7	49	9	30	5	100
S-24 Departmental officials often succumb to political pressures to let off evaders	%	19	46	18	17		100
S-25 If there is proper recommendation from political or bureaucratic higher-ups, any assessee who was caught for tax evasion can get away	%	25	40	25	10		100
S-26 Income tax department is well equipped to detect tax evasion	%	8	45	18	25	4	100

Table T 6.6
Attitudes and perception regarding tax laws and tax administration fairness

Taxpayers in general have a feeling that income tax administration is not very fair. This is a natural response to a system which demands a portion of the money one saves. However, it is the endeavor of the governments and the tax administrations all over the world to make citizens feel that tax laws and their enforcement are fair. It is vital to compare the responses of citizens on tax system fairness in other countries, though these studies might not be thoroughly contemporary. In Spain, during 1985-87, about 70 per cent of the citizens thought that tax system was not fair. In Australia, a study conducted in 1982 indicated that 61 per cent of the citizens considered the tax system as unfair. Similarly in Japan, 77 per cent of the citizens found it to be unfair. (Peters, 1991, pp.173-176)

A MATTER OF MIND?

TB - 6.1

Look! He is my man!!

It is often said that the politicians influence government officials and they in turn act unlawfully to satisfy the wishes of the former. The public also believe, perhaps based on what is depicted in the mass media, that enforcement officers allow the accused to go scot-free, heeding requests from politicians even after booking the wrong-doer. A statement was put to the respondents in this regard. 65 per cent of the respondents agreed to the statement (S-24) that the departmental officials often succumbed to political pressure to let off evaders. Only 17 per cent of the respondents felt that tax officials would not succumb to political pressures. A similar trend can be seen in the responses to a similar question where the respondents were given the statement that (S-25) ' if there is proper recommendation from political or bureaucratic higher-ups, any assessee who was caught for tax evasion can get away.' 65 per cent of the respondents felt that the recommendations would work to get the evader away from the adverse action of the tax administration. A significant number of respondents admitted ignorance in this regard by being indifferent (25 per cent), and only 10 per cent of the respondents disagreed with the statement. Here it is clear that the majority of the respondents felt that the tax administration was not fair.

However, a very contrasting response had come from study-2, where respondents were persons who faced income tax searches in their premises and underwent detailed investigation by the Department (see Chapter 7). In that study only 36 per cent of the respondents (as against 65 per cent of respondents from the sample that never faced any income tax enforcement) agreed with the statement that recommendations would work in favour of evaders to get away from the adverse action of the tax administration. Coming from their own experiences, the responses need to be taken very seriously. This indicates how attitudes are formed based on hearsay and general social perception. Thus, attitudes significantly change, based on personal experiences which are very different from what were thought earlier.

53 per cent of the respondents also felt that the tax administration was ill-equipped to tackle tax evasion. What emerges from this data is that there is a strong negative attitude about tax administration in the minds of most of the respondents.

Perception of reasons for low tax compliance

As discussed in the description of the responses to statements S-1 to S-27, there is a strong perception of tax non-compliance in society and in the immediate environment of the respondents. The responses to statements S-21 and S-22 clearly indicated the respondents' perception of widespread tax evasion in society. It is pertinent therefore to analyse the reasons perceived by the respondents for the widespread tax non-compliance. The respondents were asked to rank the reasons according to the weightage they gave. Following were the alternatives given to them a) Shortcoming of the income tax laws and rules, b) Inefficiency of the tax administration, c) Corruption and inefficiency in government, d) Ingenious tax evasion practices followed by income earners, e) Low degree of compliance by the tax payers, e) Legal disputes, f) Too many exemptions and tax incentives, and g) Income tax collections are adequate. They were also allowed to suggest any other reasons which were not in the list. Table T 6.7 lists the top 5 reasons given by the respondents based on the weightages for the first three rankings of the respondents.[4]

Rank	Perceived reasons for non-compliance	Score
1	Corruption and inefficiency in government	173
2	Shortcomings of income tax laws and rules	139
3	Ingenious tax evasion practices followed by the taxpayers	127
4	Inefficiency of the tax administration	125
5	Due to legal disputes	121

Table T 6.7
Low tax compliance: Top ranked reasons

Taxpayers perceived corruption and inefficiency in government as the most important reason for low tax compliance. They are of the view that shortcomings in the tax laws and the inefficiency of tax administration have also resulted in low tax compliance. The shortcomings in the law and the administrative inefficiency might have helped people to follow ingenious tax evasion practices. It is also a fact that huge amounts are locked up in disputes before the appellate forums.

Respondents' ranking for the strategies to increase tax compliance

As the respondents have given their perceptions of tax non-compliance in society and the reasons for the same, it is important to gather their opinions and suggestions regarding the strategies to increase the tax compliance among the people. They were given a set of suggestions (prepared based on the pilot study) giving scope for making alternate suggestions. The choices were: a) Reforming income tax law and rules to plug loopholes, b) Stricter enforcement measures, c) Better infrastructure for and competence of tax administration, d) The administration can be entrusted to private sector, and e) Strict vigilance to tackle corrupt and inefficient officials. Table T 6.8 gives the top 5 suggestions given by the respondents based on the weightages for their first three rankings.

Rank	Perception of strategies to increase tax compliance	Score
1	Reforming income tax laws and rules to plug loopholes	238
2	Stricter enforcement measures	211
3	Strict vigilance to tackle corrupt and inefficient officials	165
4	Better infrastructure and competence for the tax administration	156
5	The tax administration can be entrusted to private sector	104

Table T 6.8
Top 5 suggestions to improve tax compliance

The respondents clearly identified that plugging the loopholes in tax laws and rules and stricter enforcement were the need of the hour for increasing the tax compliance. They also suggested that there should be strict vigilance to tackle corrupt and inefficient officials.

Perception of self tax behaviour

The initial part of the interview with the respondents was centered on their attitudes and perceptions about the state, tax policy, tax administration, general tax behaviour in society, etc. Subsequently, after setting the right environment to get frank responses, more personalized questions were asked to understand the tax behaviour of the respondents. The questions were framed in a very neutral way and the sentences were phrased in such a way that genuine sharing took place during the interview. The table (Table T 6.9) shows their responses regarding the promptness in filing their tax returns.

		%
Do you file your income tax returns regularly	Very regular	27
	Regular	43
	Don't know	8
	Not regular	19
	Rarely filed	3
TOTAL		**100**

Table T 6.9
Respondents' perception of their return filing

27 per cent of the respondents stated that they had filed their returns very regularly indicating very prompt filing in the last several years. 43 per cent of the respondents stated that they were regular and 19 per cent admitted that they were not regular in filing tax returns. Since a mere filing of returns does not indicate full tax compliance, questions were asked to the respondents about the nature of disclosure of income in the tax returns. Table T 6.10 gives the data related to the question regarding the extent of disclosure.

Were you able to disclose all your taxable income?	%*
It was impossible to disclose entire earnings in the income tax returns	72
There might be minor omissions in the disclosure in a few years	66
I disclose all the income I receive through accounted sources	73
I disclose substantial portion of all income	59
I have recorded every rupee of my income for all the years.	34

(Each statement was given separately the option YES/NO)

Table T 6.10

Respondents' perception of their disclosure

The responses in Table T 6.10 give a clear indication that the majority of the respondents have evaded part of their income from taxation. Only 34 per cent of the respondents stated that they recorded every rupee of their income for the purpose of taxation. However, a majority of the respondents clearly stated that they had indulged in tax evasion. (Responses to a similar question posed to searched respondents (study-2) can be seen in chapter 7, where they have narrated their extent of tax compliance after the search)

Since the majority of the respondents admitted to have concealed part of their income, it was important to gather the data related to the reasons for their incomplete disclosure. Respondents were given the option to choose from a set of reasons listed (based on the pilot study) and they were also given the option to give any other reason not listed. Table T 6.11 shows the data in this regard.

Occasionally I tend to omit disclosing	%
The person who gives does not account it properly	66
I have incurred substantial amount as business expenditure which is not deductible	61
Though I had earned income there was no money to pay taxes	65
Absence of right tax advice	68
Since many others in my profession suppress their income	61

(Each statement was given separately the option YES/NO)

Table T 6.11

The reasons for tax evasion

Table T 6.11 indicates that the respondents concealed their income because of so many reasons and compulsions such as general tax non-compliance of others, business expenditure which were not otherwise deductible, absence of right tax advice (indicating low tax awareness), inadequacy of funds (indicating high tax rates), etc. Another question was posed to the respondents regarding the way or method followed by them to suppress their income and to evade taxes. Table T 6.12 contains the data in this regard. Respondents were given the option to choose from a set of methods listed (based on the pilot study) and they were also given the option to give any other reason not listed.

Occasionally I tried to reduce my tax burden	%
I have occasionally understated my tax burden	62
I have claimed some excess exemptions	43
I have claimed excess deduction from taxable income	32
I have shown some non-deductible expenditure	37
I used to account some of my income in others' names	53

Table T 6.12
The methods of income suppression

Table T 6.12 indicates that a substantial number of respondents (62 per cent) admitted that they had suppressed their taxable income and had understated the tax burden. About 53 per cent of the respondents had stated that they used to account their income in the names of others (for example, close relatives), to evade taxes. A substantial number of respondents had admitted to have indulged in tax evasion practices such as wrong or excess claim of tax deductions or exemptions, etc.

Past experience with the Income Tax Department

From statements (S-23 to S-26), it is clear that the respondents felt that the tax department was not very fair and also not efficient in tackling tax evasion. A majority of the respondents felt that the rules and procedures were complicated. In the following tables (T 6.13 to T 6.15), the data gathered regarding the past experiences of the respondents with the tax department are analyzed. The aim was to understand whether there was any impact of such experiences on the tax attitudes and behaviour.

The impact of scrutiny

Table T 6.13 shows the data regarding the scrutiny and assessment experiences of the respondents. Scrutiny is a process of detailed audit of the returns filed by the assessees selected at random or on the basis of specific information or set criteria. Scrutiny is aimed at detecting the concealment of income, wrong claims, etc through detailed investigation of records and documents and cross-verification of transactions by the Assessing Officer. The additional income detected will be subjected to tax, interest, and penalty. From the present data, it can be seen that the returns of 16 per cent of the respondents were scrutinized by the tax department once and the returns of 12 per cent of the respondents were scrutinized twice. It is significant to note that 26 per cent of the respondents were not aware whether their returns have been scrutinized and 40 per cent of the respondents stated that their returns were never subjected to scrutiny.

It is also clear from the table that only in a very few cases has additional income been detected and assessed by the tax department. The audit and assessment functions of the tax department have very minimal impact on the assessees. It is evident from the data that 51 per cent of the respondents stated that never was any additional income assessed by the tax department in their cases and 23 per cent of the respondents stated that they were not at all aware of any additions during the assessments. Only 13 per cent of the respondents stated that they were subjected to a penalty by the department. Though it was clarified during the interview, still it is likely that a few of them might have mistaken the interest charged as imposition of penalty. It is seen that the premises of 33 per cent of the respondents were surveyed and 7 per cent of the respondents were subjected to income tax searches. (called also as raids) The present sample contained a substantial number of cases where scrutiny, survey and searches were conducted. However, penalties were imposed in less

MAKING PEOPLE PAY

TB - 6.2

Ever poor taxpayer

It is said that during the colonial period, the income tax was administered by district collectors in India. Collectors used to personally assess the income of the persons by summoning them for personal hearings in his office. It is recorded that sometimes rich persons would come in tattered clothes, so that they would be considered poor by the collector and less tax be levied.

The collector of Agra noted on one occasion in the 1880s that one particular coat full of holes, stitches and ink-marks was used on the same day by more than a dozen assessees to impress upon the collector, their poverty and inability to pay higher taxes. Towards the close of the day, the wearer drew in so many words, the collector's attention to the condition of his coat; whereupon the magistrate remarked that he was familiar with the coat since he had been seeing it on many persons since morning. Thereafter the coat was abandoned.[5]

number of cases. This shows that the quality and success of the assessment proceedings were not at expected levels.

On an average less than 1 per cent of the cases are in fact scrutinized by the Indian income tax department every year. Similarly, only about 0.003 per cent and 0.00012 per cent of the cases are surveyed and searched respectively by the department. Unlike many other countries, in India, the scrutiny of Income tax returns (similar to what is called 'Audit' in several western countries) is considered by the assessees as a very mild form of enforcement. The reason is obvious. Even the Income tax department would admit that the scrutiny by its officers lacks depth and result-oriented investigation.[6] In most cases, the assessees would not have even stepped into the income tax office when his return for a particular year was being scrutinized. All explanations and clarifications are directly sought from his representative, who is often an external chartered accountant or an income tax practitioner. Thus, the scrutiny (whether it is detailed scrutiny or limited scrutiny) gets completed with certain routine disallowances and additions and only in rare cases would there be the detection of concealments, mostly trivial in nature. In effect,

		%
My returns were scrutinized by the department	Once	16
	Twice	12
	Three or more times	6
	Never	40
	I do not know	26
My returns have been assessed at a higher income than the returned income	Once	19
	Twice	7
	Three or more times	1
	Never	51
	I do not know	22
I have been imposed a penalty by the Income tax Department	Once	11
	Twice	2
	Never	68
	I do not know	19

Table T 6.13
Assessment experience of respondents

this enforcement measure passes off without any impact on the assessees. Rarely do they take any drastic corrective step and by and large no major change in the tax attitudes and tax behaviour is expected as a result of scrutiny.

Taxpayer service

As mentioned earlier, though many assessees deal with the tax department through the authorized representatives, some of the respondents in the sample had stated that they had personally visited the income tax office. Table T 6.14 shows the data regarding their experiences while at the income tax office. In this regard, many respondents felt that they were not always given a fair treatment.

Whenever I have personally visited the income tax office	Always got fair treatment most of the time	29
	I was treated fairly	23
	Neither good nor bad	13
	I had bitter experiences	15
	I have never gone so far	20
My refunds have been issued	Promptly always	21
	Promptly most of the time	29
	Only after I send reminders	16
	Only after the officials were bribed	15
	Yet to get refunds for returns filed more than three years ago	16
	Not applicable	3

Table T 6.14
Perception of taxpayer service

Table T 6.14 clearly indicates that only 21 per cent of the respondents received their tax refunds on time. It is important to note that 15 per cent of the respondents stated that they obtained the refunds only after the officials were bribed and 16 per cent of the respondents had not yet got the refund for the claims given three years earlier. This shows the poor service delivery of the tax department and that would definitely affect the attitudes and perceptions of the taxpayers about the IT Department.

Whether any income tax raid was conducted in your premises	No Yes	93 7
Whether any income tax survey was conducted in your premises	No Yes	67 33
Whether any income tax official visited your premises to make enquiries	No Yes	81 19
Whether you were called to the income tax office personally	No Yes	77 22

Table T 6.15
Past enforcement experience

Table T 6.15 gives the data regarding the number of respondents who had faced some type of income tax enforcement such as survey, search, personal enquiry, etc in the last several years. Only 33 per cent of the respondents stated that they were subjected to surveys or inspections by the tax department.

Insights from the study

Attitude and perception about the state and the governance

Citizens are not always silent spectators of the policies and activities of the government. There are umpteen number of sources through which they elicit information either collectively or individually. Collective gathering and sharing of information take place in the work place, peer group settings, meetings of the club, associations, etc. Apart from this, an individual is aware of what is happening in the official public domain through personal analysis of news, events and comments reported in the media. However, the most critical basis for opinion building would be one's own experience with any agency or apparatus of the government at any point in one's life. Opinions are formed on the basis of the assorted information gathered or chanced upon by the citizens from some or all of the above sources. The nature and extent of the depth and coverage of that information depends on various factors such as the educational status, political consciousness, the extent of public exposure, etc. Individuals with relatively high stakeholder awareness (those who feel substantially affected by the activities of the state positively or negatively) may make more conscious attempts to analyze information. There may be extreme cases where a few seek legal channels to obtain information, which are otherwise not parted to public in usual course.[7]

An average citizen is aware of the expected role of a government and he observes the activities of the government. The feeling of 'they' is predominant even when one knows that the government is both an abstract institution and a concrete organization with a large span of control and wide networks. Such abstractions and complexities attached to the government do not deter a person from evaluating the governance system as an outsider from his own little keyhole of perceptions. Throughout history, ideally governments all over the world are the institutions to ensure welfare and security of the people. In a democratic society, the government is considered as a trustee for the people and it is represented as an institution by the people and for the people, aiming at a feeling of 'we' than 'they' among the people. Thus, irrespective of the fact that one has paid one's tax or not, whether one has exercised one's franchise or not, or one has funded any one or anything in the government or not, one can still expect significant degree of accountability from the government.

Specific questions were asked during the interview to elicit the responses in this regard and the same have been already dealt with. An attempt was made to understand the respective correlation between the influence of the attitude of the respondents about the (a) tax system (includes responses on the concept of taxation, the power to tax, the preference for the type of taxation, etc), (b) tax policy (broader tax approaches and thrusts in terms of proportionate tax incidence and overall impact), (c) tax laws (specific tax laws and rates), and (d) tax administration (tax procedures and nature of enforcement and services). Queries were also raised on their attitude about a) role of the state, b) redistribution of the state, c) nature of governance, d) contribution of state to the respondent, and e) concept of welfare and equity. The overall correlated value for the taxpayer's perception of taxation (which signifies the attitudes and perceptions of the tax system, tax policy, tax laws and tax administration) with that of the tax payer's perception of state and governance (which signifies the responses about the role of the state, redistribution by the state, contribution of state to the respondent and concept of welfare and equity) is given in column 6 of Table T 6.16.

1	2	3	4	5	6
	Tax System	Tax Policy	Tax Laws	Tax Admn.	Taxpayers' perception of Taxation
Role of the state	0.379(**)	0.260(**)	0.115	0.345(**)	0.437(**)
Redistribution by the state	0.531(**)	0.272(**)	0.100	0.239(**)	0.432(**)
Governance	0.113	0.072	0.024	0.602(**)	0.385(**)
Contribution of state to the respondent	0.203(*)	0.145	-0.030	0.108	0.156
Concept of welfare and equity	0.538(**)	0.475(**)	0.129	0.110	0.438(**)
Taxpayers' perception of state and governance	**0.428(**)**	**0.302(**)**	**0.098**	**0.405(**)**	**0.491(**)**

Table T 6.16
Correlations between taxpayers' perception of state and governance & Taxpayers' perception of taxation

The above table clearly describes the first hypothesis of the study. The results indicate that there is a strong relationship between tax attitudes and perception of the respondents with their attitudes and perception of the state and governance.

As regarding the perception of the state's contribution to the respondent (in the context of exchange and reciprocity), it is found that a substantial number of respondents were not much worried about the extent of personal gain from the state. However, they were keen on evaluating the general gain for the society through redistribution, welfare and good governance. This can be a characteristic feature of a society with values of altruism. Another reason may be the people's realization of the fact that expecting a fair or proportionate treatment based on the amount paid as taxes is an impossibility in a highly stratified and unequal society. In this country where only a few find themselves in the tax bracket, the resultant compliance behaviour is neither based on any perfect altruism nor based on any *quid pro quo*. However, the fact that they part with a portion of their income as taxes makes them aware of their valuable support to the state for governance and they tend to evaluate the role performance of the state in terms of the redistribution and welfare.

Attitudes and perception about the tax evasion of others

Table T 6.4 showed the data related to the respondents' perception of the tax behaviour of others. It was found that 83 per cent of the respondents felt that most of the people were dishonest in paying the taxes. Similarly, 67 per cent of the respondents felt that most of the people they knew evaded their taxes. Thus, it is very clear that taxpayers themselves perceive that tax evasion is very widespread in society.

	TAX SYSTEM	TAX POLICY	TAX LAWS	TAX ADMINIS -TRATION	TAXPAYER'S PERCEPTION OF TAXATION
TAX EVASION OF OTHERS	0.222(**)	0.254(**)	0.150	0.105	0.271(**)

Table T 6.17
Correlations between perception of tax attitudes and behaviour of others & tax attitudes and perception of taxpayers

It was found that there is an association between the perception and attitude of respondents on taxation with their attitude and perception of tax evasion of others. (Table T 6.17)

Attitude towards state and governance & respondents' perceived tax behaviour

We have already seen in Table T 6.9 to T 6.12, the data showing the tax behaviour of the respondents as perceived by them in the past few years before the study. 21 per cent of the respondents admitted that they were not very regular in filing their tax returns. However, 70 per cent of the respondents stated that they were either 'very regular' (27 per cent) or 'regular' (43 per cent) in filing the returns for the earlier years (Table T 6.9). Though a mere filing of returns is not by itself an indication of actual tax compliance, the same is an indication of procedural compliance of the respondents. As was seen in Table T 6.10, a majority of the respondents admitted that a portion of their income was concealed from taxation. In Table T 6.11 and Table T 6.12 we have seen the data from the respondents indicating the perceived reasons for tax evasion and the nature of such evasion. The following Table (T 6.18) shows the correlations between attitudes and perceptions of State and Governance and perceived tax evasion. (income suppression)

Taxpayers' perception	Perceived tax evasion (income suppression)
Role of state	0.220(**)
Redistribution by state	0.320(**)
Governance	0.293(**)
Contribution of state to the respondent	0.193(**)
Concept of welfare and equity	0.162(**)
Overall perception of state & Governance	0.295(**)

Table T 6.18
Attitudes and perceptions of state and governance and perceived tax evasion

Current tax behaviour of the respondents and their past tax experiences

Current tax behaviour of the respondents in terms of return filing (data discussed in Table T 6.9) has been correlated with the data regarding their past tax experiences. (given in Table T 6.13 to Table T 6.15) The correlation value is 0.258 which indicates statistical significance. However, a similar positive correlation is not found when past tax experience was correlated with income disclosure. (-0.142) This shows that though the past tax experience had an influence on the procedural compliance, it had no influence on the actual compliance. (income disclosure)

	EXPERIENCE WITH IT DEPT
RETURN FILING	.258(**)
INCOME SUPPRESSION	-.142
REASONS FOR INCOME SUPPRESSION	-.228(**)
METHOD OF EVASION	-.065

Table T 6.19
Correlations of current perceived tax behaviour and past tax experience

Analysis with reference to background variables

Age

It is said that older people have greater motivation to pay taxes and greater pride in paying taxes. (Tittle, 1980) From the perspectives of criminology, it is indicated that as age increases compliance to the laws too increases. (Gottfredson and Hirschi, 1990; Hirchi and Gottfredson, 2000) However, there are no consistent findings among scholars as there are equal number of studies which conclude that there are no such relationships, between the two.

Respondents in the current study belonged to various age groups. Tax attitudes and perceptions of the respondents have been analysed with reference to the variable 'age' and it has been found that there is no significant correlation. (See Appendix-1 AT 6.1) No difference is found between the age groups with respect to their attitudes about taxation, tax evasion, state and governance. Similarly, no significant difference is found in respect of their current tax behaviour.

Level of education and tax attitudes

Respondents in the sample are from diverse educational backgrounds. Analyses were made to examine whether there were notable differences in their attitudes and perceptions about taxation among respondents with different educational backgrounds. While respondents without a degree-level educational background showed low mean score in respect of the positive perception of taxation, others showed a high mean score. In all the tables, where data on attitudes to tax policy and tax system are analysed, respondents with degree-level education showed high mean score and the respondents with pre degree/ undergraduate qualifications showed lowest mean score. The differences are found to be statistically significant.

Whereas the data showing the differences in the mean score on attitudes and perception of the respondents of different educational background about the tax system and tax policy are statistically significant, a similar association with the attitude and perception about the tax administration is not seen. As seen consistently in all the tables (See Appendix-1 AT 6.1), a positive tax attitude is visible more among the respondents with higher educational levels than among those with lower educational background.

The data regarding the attitudes and perceptions of the role of the state, redistribution by the state, governance, contribution of the state to the respondent, and the state in the context of the objectives of welfare and equity have been analyzed with respect to the educational background of the respondents. The relationship has been found to be statistically insignificant.

Tax awareness of the respondents

As mentioned earlier, a standardized tax awareness test was conducted during the course of the interview for all the respondents. The aim of the test was to examine the general awareness of the respondents on the preliminaries in fiscal policy, tax laws and procedures, etc. It was found that about 38 per cent of the respondents had relatively high tax awareness and 27 per cent of the respondents had moderate tax awareness. However, 35 per cent of the respondents had low tax awareness.[8]

It was found that taxpayers with high tax awareness score tended to think very positively about the state's contribution to them through services. To the statement that the State had failed in giving necessary services, respondents with low tax awareness score agreed whereas persons with high tax awareness score disagreed. Analyses have been made to examine whether there were any differences in the tax attitudes based on the level of tax awareness. It was found that there were no significant differences in their attitudes about tax system, tax policy, tax laws and tax administration. The overall attitude about taxation is the same irrespective of the level of tax awareness.

A similar trend is found in respect of the attitudes to the state's efforts for redistribution. Those with a high tax awareness score were positive about the state's redistribution activities whereas persons with low tax awareness tended to be less positive in this regard. Similar results emerged in respect of overall perception about state and governance.

Nature of occupation and tax attitudes

The current sample contained equal numbers of taxpayers from salaried, professional and business classes. An attempt was made to analyze the differences in their attitudes to taxation. While 70 per cent of the respondents from the business class did not consider tax evasion as a serious economic offence, only 42 per cent of the salaried class believed so. 46 per cent of the professionals also felt that it was not a serious economic offence.

Similarly, the attitudes of the sample of taxpayers about the state and governance have also been examined with respect to their occupational background. Analyses have not indicated any correlation between occupational background and the attitudes. (See Appendix AT 6.1)

Generational background and tax attitudes

India's taxpaying population is a microscopic minority. Most of the persons believe that income tax is something which has to be paid only by the most affluent sections of the society. As there are radical steps taken in the last few years to widen the tax base and to enforce total tax compliance, the number of new assessees has increased manifold. Thus, there are substantial numbers of first generation income tax payers in the country. It is significant to examine the attitudes and perceptions of these taxpayers and their nature of tax behaviour. This would also facilitate a comparative study of the attitudes, perceptions and behaviour of second generation and third generation taxpayers.

It was found that there is indeed a statistically significant difference between the first, the second and the third generation taxpayers in respect of their perceived tax evasion. Income suppression mean value is the highest for third generation taxpayers followed by the second generation taxpayers. The least mean value for income suppression is for the first generation taxpayers. However, analyses of the data regarding the attitudes about various aspects of taxation (tax system, tax policy, tax laws, and tax administration) showed that there were no major differences between the first, the second, and the third generation taxpayers. Data regarding the attitudes and perception about tax evasion in society also indicated that there were no major differences among the first, the second and the third generation taxpayers in this regard. (See Appendix Table AT 6-1)

Analyses of the data regarding the overall perceived tax behaviour of the taxpayers gave interesting results. This data included income suppression as well as other tax behaviour as revealed by them such as procedural compliance, past enforcement experience, scrutiny, and penalty. Here the third generation taxpayers perceived themselves as having high positive tax behaviour whereas both the first and the second generation taxpayers were not positive to that extent. The above analysis regarding the higher degrees of perceived tax evasion coupled with the perception of procedural compliance among the third generation taxpayers indicate the poor quality of tax enforcement. The taxpayers have realized over a period of time that what really matters for the administration is procedural compliance and tax evasion is not of serious consequence because of the lack of proper enforcement mechanism.

Data regarding the attitudes of the taxpayers about the role of the state, including, those in redistribution, and the state's contribution through services and governance, have been given in Appendix AT 6.1. As seen in these tables, taxpayers in the third generation category have more positive attitudes about the state and the governance as compared with the first and the second generation taxpayers. Their continuous faith in the state may be one of the factors in continuing as taxpayers for the third generation taxpayers.

Level of income

It is said that people who are in the high income tax brackets tend to evade more as the benefit out of non-compliance would be more compared to persons in the lower income group. The lower income persons may be at a higher disadvantage if they are caught and penalized proportionate to their income. (Jackson and Milliron, 1986) However, this may not be applicable in countries where there is weak tax enforcement system and low degrees of penalties and the tax system is not clearly progressive. In the current sample, there was no statistically significant association in respect of perceived tax behaviour and the income background of the respondents.

Insights in brief

The study has clearly shown that the tax attitudes and perceptions of taxpayers are influenced by their attitudes and perceptions about the state and governance. It was also found that tax attitudes and perceptions of taxpayers are influenced by their perceptions of attitudes and behaviour of significant others. One's tax behaviour is also influenced by the perceived behavioural pattern in the society. Past tax experience has influenced the procedural compliance and not the actual or substantive compliance. While age and level of income do not have much influence on tax attitudes and behaviour, the level of education, the tax awareness, the occupational background and the generational background are partly influential.

CHAPTER-7

A MATTER OF STICK?

Nabbing the Evader
The Trajectory of Indian Income Tax Enforcement

"Good name in man and woman, dear my lord
Is the immediate jewel of their souls
Who steals my purse steals thrash; 'tis something, nothing;
'Twas mine, 'tis his, and has been slave to thousands:
But he that filches from me my good name
Robs me of that which not enriches him
And makes me poor indeed"

(*Iago* said to *Othello*)

Even as trusting the people, particularly the taxpayers, is a welcome approach for governments, they cannot altogether do away with the tax watchdogs, ie. The tax enforcers. Tax administrations across the world keep a watch over the financial activities of taxpayers to ensure a true and complete disclosure of taxable income. Different tax administrations adopt different approaches in this regard. Some place emphasis on voluntary compliance through self-assessment with very limited random scrutiny and audits. Others stress on administrative assessment of substantial numbers of tax returns. Administrations in some countries enforce tax compliance through very stringent penalties while auditing. Mostly, developed countries enforce the penalty provisions strictly when violations are noticed. However, taxpayers may not welcome strict enforcement and penal proceedings. But widespread failure in enforcement creates resentment among the public against tax authorities and the government. In order to ensure proper compliance and nab the evaders, tax administrations employ various investigation strategies. In fact, some of these strategies may amount to the invasion of the privacy of the persons investigated upon.

One strategy used by enforcement agencies and also by private detective agencies is to tap personal information through various sources. It is true that quite a lot of information from the private domain tends to seep into the public domain. In this era of information technology, personal information of individuals is compiled, stored and exchanged across several institutions, with or without the knowledge of the individual concerned. For example, while filing a tax return, applying for a credit card, or engaging in a financial deal, several kinds of personal business information need to be disclosed, revealing the nature of activities engaged in by the individual. By electronic submission of such data, their dissemination across various agencies, both private and governmental, is easy unless there are sufficient steps taken to protect the confidentiality of the data and to curb any misuse. Such data can be transferred without any time or space restrictions with the current technological advancements. Information submitted for a particular purpose can be used or manipulated in another context.

Tax agencies use their statutory powers to gather data on financial transactions from various sources and these are used in investigating the affairs of the taxpayers. However, that would not be sufficient to pin down a tax evader. Tax enforcement agencies look for evidence to prove the evasion so that their actions are upheld by the courts of law. Therefore, in order to discover incriminating evidence indicating tax evasion, tax agencies adopt the strategy of searching the residential and office premises of the people suspected to be indulging in tax evasion. Search and seizure powers are widely used by the Indian income tax department for the past several decades to nab the tax evaders.

Tax enforcement measures in India

Tax enforcement measures in India are oriented towards two directions. One is aimed at non-filers of income tax returns and those who conceal substantial portions of their income in tax returns. The other is aimed at those return filers who indulge in fraudulent claims, wrong deductions, and inflated expenditure. In order to target the first set of assessees, the income tax department conducts searches (raids) and seizures and surveys in both the residential and business premises of the suspected taxpayers and their associates. And to detect the concealment in the case of the second set of persons, the department resorts to detailed scrutiny of their returns (similar to what is called 'audit' in countries like United States, UK, etc) and also conducts surveys in business premises.

A small percentage of income tax returns are scrutinized annually by the assessing officers as per the guidelines issued by the Central Board of Direct Taxes (CBDT). Detailed investigation and verification are conducted with respect to the claims of the assessees, after summoning all books of accounts and related documents. Arindam Das-Gupta and Dilip Mookherjee (Das-Gupta, 1998) have evaluated such scrutiny assessments and have observed: a) that there has been a marked drop in the scale of scrutiny assessments, especially since the 1980s due to limited manpower and paucity of time for making investigations of quality, b) that in the sample collected, three out of four scrutiny assessments result in additional demands, and c) that most of the cases fail in appeal due to lack of proper evidence gathered by the assessing officers and also due to less attention given by them for arguing the case before the appellate authorities. However, additional demands raised in scrutiny are not substantial and penalties are levied only in very small number of cases. As such, the assessees in general are not much wary of the scrutiny assessments as many officers do not use it effectively to detect concealment. As has been found in the study described in chapter 6, scrutiny assessments have not resulted in substantive compliance. Scrutiny, as a method of enforcement and deterrence, serves only a very limited purpose in the case of large-scale tax evaders. Therefore, the department has recognized the importance of the search and seizure provisions, in order to nab big tax evaders.

The power to search and seize

It is said that the power to search and seize was originally used by the enforcement authorities for recovering stolen goods from thieves. In

India, the Sea Customs Act, 1878 contained powers to search. The Income Tax Act, 1922, the first properly coded direct tax law of the 20th century, did not have any mention of the power to search and seize. The power to detect evasion was exercised as per the Code of Civil Procedure, 1908. It included the powers of discovery and inspection, enforcing attendance of witness, etc. In 1938, a bill was introduced to grant powers of search in business premises and for the seizure of account books and documents. However, due to opposition from several quarters, no amendment could be made. The Income-tax Investigation Commission, under the chairmanship of Sir Srinivasa Varadachariar, a former judge of the Federal Court was constituted under the Taxation on Income (Investigation Commission) Act, 1947. The Commission had recommended bestowing the powers to search and seize on the income tax authorities. In 1948, these powers were given but subject to certain safeguards.

The Taxation Enquiry Committee set up in 1953, recommended that in order to curb tax evasion and to detect tax evaders, the powers of search and seizure should be vested with the Income tax Department itself. Consequently, Section 37(2) was introduced by the Finance Act, 1956, conferring such powers on the Department. The powers were to be exercised under the Code of Criminal Procedure. The powers were restricted to search for any books of accounts or documents and their seizure if necessary, but seizure of valuables like cash, ornaments, stock, etc was not allowed.

The Finance Act, 1964, after long deliberations and debates in Parliament vested the powers of search and seizure with the Income Tax Department. The members had debated threadbare, each provision in the proposal, the apprehensions raised were clarified, and the bill was passed incorporating the suggestions. It is evident that the above powers have been conferred on the Income Tax Department after application of minds of several seasoned parliamentarians and legal luminaries. The search and seizure provisions are extremely powerful instruments but to be exercised with the utmost caution.

A MATTER OF STICK?

The Income tax (Amendment) Act, 1965, brought in the powers to seize valuables which represented undisclosed asset or income, under Section 132 of the Income Tax Act. Though Parliament has strongly recognized the need for this extreme enforcement action to unearth incriminating evidences and to nab the tax evaders, it is widely felt that the same should be exercised with maximum caution and only in the most appropriate circumstances.

The following are some of the observations, which underline the sensitive nature of the search provision and the directions for its careful use when it is absolutely necessary.

> *'A search and seizure operation involves the invasion of the privacy of an individual or family. The right to privacy and the guarantee that an intrusion into the privacy of an individual would be prevented is a fundamental right in a constitutional democracy and as valuable as any of the other fundamental rights. In the USA, courts have held that the right to privacy cannot be violated except for the strict purpose of discovering evidence of a criminal act. Constitutional barriers have been erected both at the federal and at the state levels against unreasonable invasion of privacy. It is well recognized in the USA as well as in India that the right to be free from unreasonable searches is a constitutional right. - Indeed, it is the essence of constitutional liberty.'*[1]

> *'.....Privacy is a very valuable right of a civilized society and violation thereof was not permissible except by authority of law and, therefore , the department should not only be slow but slowest in acting upon the information, being given by an informer.....No action should be taken on information based on surmises or guess. .....Therefore, it (information) has not only to be authentic but capable of giving rise to the inference that the person was in possession of undisclosed income which has not been or would not be disclosed. The authorities must comply with basic requirement of the section before they are permitted to invade the secrecy of one's home which is a violation of the citizen's right of privacy.'*[2]

> *'It is undoubtedly true that search and seizure is a drastic process and is bound to be associated with some amount of unsavory and inconvenient results. A sudden search and seizure may unnerve the inmates of the place where the search is made. But this is to be expected.'*[3]

The Search and Seizure procedure as per the Indian Income Tax Act

The search and seizure action by the Income Tax Department is conducted as per the powers conferred on them by virtue of Section 132 of the Income Tax Act, 1961 which is amended from time to time. It may not be possible to give a detailed picture of the various rules and procedures related to income tax searches here. It is also not relevant in the context of this study to engage in an academic discussion and appraisal of the powers and procedures under the Income Tax Act.

What needs to be kept in mind here is that the Income Tax Act is very clear on the powers related to search and seizure: Under what circumstances can a search warrant be issued? Who can issue the search warrant? To whom can the warrant be authorized for execution? Where can the search be conducted? What can or cannot be seized? What action is to be taken regarding seized documents and assets? When and how should the assessment order be passed? What penal action is to be taken? Apart from the above, Income Tax Rules (which are in the nature of a subordinate legislation) have stipulated specific procedures to be followed at the time of search and seizure. In line with various judicial pronouncements given from time to time, the Ministry of Finance and the Central Board of Direct Taxes (CBDT) have issued specific guidelines regarding the procedures to be followed on various aspects. Absolute satisfaction of the warrant issuing authority is necessary to initiate search on any person or premises. Details of the reliability of the information gathered and independent reconnaissance work by the investigating officers and their superior officers are to be recorded in writing independently by officers at various levels. In order to conduct the search in an environment of absolute discipline and order, the Union Government has codified a set of rights and duties of the person to be searched. (See Appendix - 2)

Thus, clear guidelines have been given to the officials of the Investigation wing of the Income Tax Department, which is the enforcement agency exclusively in charge of conducting the search and seizure operations. An understanding of the organizational structure of the Department would be helpful as we analyze the data gathered from the sample.

Search is generally authorized by the Director-General of Income Tax or the Director of Income Tax. The Additional / Joint Director supervises the search conducted by the authorized officers. After the search is conducted by such officers, they hand over the seized assets as well as the reports and documents to the organizing Deputy/Assistant Director. The Deputy/Assistant Director conducts the preliminary investigation and hands over the seized assets and documents to the assessing officer having jurisdiction over the searched case. This is followed by a detailed report called 'Appraisal report,' to be completed within the time prescribed.

After the search, further investigation and the passing of assessment order in the search case is done by the assessing officer under the close supervision of the Additional / Joint Commissioner. Every search case is subjected to detailed and comprehensive investigation covering the financial transactions of several years prior to the search. A series of independent enquiries would be conducted in respect of all connected cases where the assessees have had transactions. The decision regarding the retention and application of seized assets and documents are taken by the Commissioner and the Chief Commissioner.

The assessee has the option to approach the appellate authorities, if he is aggrieved by the order of the assessing officer. The department can approach the next appellate authority if it has not accepted the appeal order in favour of the assessee. The assessee and the department can file appeals up to the Income Tax Appellate Tribunal (ITAT) for the question of 'fact' and up to the Supreme Court in matters pertaining to the interpretation of law. Alternately, assessees can approach the Income Tax Settlement Commission, if there is any complexity in arriving at the undisclosed income by the assessing officer and if they are prepared to admit the concealed income directly to the Settlement Commission over and above their disclosure in the return.

A large number of searches have been conducted by the Income Tax Department since the enactment of search and seizure provisions and a substantial quantity of assets have been seized from the evaders. Table T 7.1 indicates the number of searches[4] conducted and the quantity of unaccounted income seized[5] by the Indian Income Tax Department in the last few years.

YEAR	No of Searches	Value of seizure in crores
1994-95	4830	381.42
1995-96	4612	458.14
1996-97	4299	405.63
1997-98	3653	306.85
1998-99	5746	300.54
1999-00	5670	412.84
2000-01	5321	512.36
2001-02	4358	344.33
2002-03	4902	515.87
2003-04	2492	231.37
2004-05	2377	202.28
2005-06	3364	351.70
2006-07	3534	364.64
2007-08	3364	411.45
2008-09	3483	625.50

Table T 7.1
Number of searches and total value of seizure

It is reported in the annual report of the Ministry of Finance that during the period from 1 January 2008 to 31 March 2009, a total of 4286 search warrants were executed leading to the seizure of assets worth Rs 748.29 crore. During the same period, a total of 8,695 surveys were conducted which yielded a disclosure of additional income of Rs 5858.5 crore (provisional figures).[6] During the period from 1 April 2009 to 31 December 2009, a total of 2282 search warrants were executed leading to the seizure of assets worth Rs 602.34 crore.

As per Section 132 of the Indian Income Tax Act, the authorized officer, along with his team, can enter and search any premises connected to an individual in whose case a warrant of authorization is issued by the prescribed authorities in the Income Tax Department. The team can seize evidences related to undisclosed assets and income. The power to search and seize is undoubtedly an overriding power of the state for achieving social welfare objectives. Courts have ruled that the effective enforcement of the law in a democracy is based on an equitable balance between the rights of the individual and the concept of the welfare state. The directive principles of state policy mandate the state to ensure that the ownership and control of the material resources of society are so distributed as to best serve the common good. Also, the state should see that economic activities do not result in the concentration of wealth in an uneven manner. Taxation provisions are enacted to collect from each one according to what they earn and to distribute it for public welfare. In order to check deliberate non-compliance in this regard, within the framework of the fundamental rights granted to the individuals, the state authorizes the designated authority, under appropriate circumstances, to invade the privacy of the individuals in the interests of the nation so as to detect undisclosed income.

The individual and the family who are subjected to such a search have to undergo the entire procedures and have to withstand the related yet unintended pressures and tensions of the proceedings. The search includes all the premises where one keeps or is likely to keep, the documents related to movable and immovable assets and undisclosed income. The searches are then followed by detailed investigation for about two years. The income tax search, as mentioned earlier, is called income tax raid in common parlance.

Income tax search undoubtedly creates a strong impact on individuals and their families. The family of the individual searched may feel as if a group of mighty strangers had suddenly arrived to ransack their personal space without any compelling reason. In many cases, that may be the first occasion where they are getting direct face-to-face exposure with the tax system in general and the income tax enforcement wing in particular. The enforcement agency with its vigorous enquiries into the minutest details and the rigorous procedures leave the individual and his family perplexed. They may worry about their inability to provide suitable explanations to the queries posed by the search team. They may also face a kind of mental block due to the unexpected enforcement action and related procedures.

The entire search action in the premises, may take more than a full day and extend to the whole night in most of the cases. The post search investigation may run into several months. All this would be a harrowing experience for the persons and their families whose premises are searched. During this time, the individuals may feel that there are lots of changes happening in relationships, in the business or professional environment and also in their familial and social networks. They may also introspect over the past behaviour regarding taxation and the business and professional activity in the light of the tax enforcement experience. Such a complex experience would also affect his tax attitudes and perceptions.

The objectives and focus of the study

An attempt is made here (called study -2) to delve deep into the lives of searched individuals, in order to understand their attitudes, perceptions and tax behaviour prior to the search and after the search. The focus is kept also on their account of the experience of the search and the immediate consequences it created for them, for their families and in their social and economic lives. At a macro level, the study would also indirectly provide insights on the responses and attitudes of the people in a situation where their personal lives were subjected to investigation by others and the subsequent long-term impact of that action on them.

The broad objectives of this study are to explore the sociological causes and consequences of tax evasion and tax enforcement and to analyse the social, psychological, and economic consequences that follow an income tax search on an individual. The key objectives are a) to understand the experiences of the income tax search as perceived by the respondents, b) to understand the emotional and health consequences of income tax search on respondents and their families, c) to understand the social and economic consequences of income tax search on the respondents, d) to understand the change in tax behaviour as perceived by the respondents before and after the income tax search, e) to know how the respondents' perception of taxation is influenced by their perception of tax compliance by others closely known to them, f) to understand and compare the extent of tax awareness of the respondents who underwent income tax search and those who did not, and g) to examine the sociological and economic significance of the actions of the enforcement wing of the Indian Income Tax Enforcement. The nature of the sample and the methodology were already described in chapter 5.

Details of all searches conducted in the last 15 years prior to the year of study were gathered. Statistics related to the total concealed income assessed as a result of the searches were not readily available because in most cases the assessments were made in the names of various persons and entities connected to the searched individual/concern. In a substantial number of cases the search assessments are still in appeal. Further, there are no compilations by the department on the total additional income sustained after all appeals in particular search cases. However, a random verification of a few search cases where all assessments and appeal proceedings are over indicates that the finally assessed income after all disputes are settled is much lower than the amount disclosed by the assessees during the search. The details are not discussed as this is not the primary focus of this study.

There were 257 searches (based on the number of groups searched and not the number of warrants issued) from 1985 to 2000 in the Coimbatore region of Southern India which is the area of the study. It was proposed to have 100 random cases of searched respondents for the study. However, some of the persons in the sample could not be traced because of various reasons such as unavailability of the main person who was present at the time of income tax search, shifting of business place, death or serious ailments of the main person, closure of business and failure in locating the residence, etc. In a few cases, schedules had to be abandoned due to the lack of a proper response. Thus, almost all the available cases have been considered and finally the number of cases selected in conformity to the standards for analysis is 74. However, the above 74 cases are representative in that they do have universal characteristics. As detailed previously, for limited purposes of analysis on selected points, responses of a sample of 74 respondents of non-searched cases were also selected at random from various districts of the same region to facilitate comparison. Thus, the total sample is 148.

Interviews were conducted successfully in respect of 74 cases selected at random (referred as Sample-A), out of the total 257 cases searched between 1985 and 2000. Interviews were conducted in respect of the sample of 74 non-search cases (referred as Sample-B) for limited purposes of comparison of attitudes, perception and behaviour related to taxation.

The conversational interview

As has been discussed before, the appropriate tool for data appraisal is a semi-structured interview (with minimized explicit pre-conceptions even at the outset of the data collection[7]) in the form of an informal conversation. Extra care has been taken to create this informal environment with an atmosphere of neutrality, so as to elicit genuine, frank, forthcoming responses from the interviewees. The respondents, in fact, fixed the time and venue of the interaction; this gave them enough time to relax from their routine work.

The interview schedule itself was finalized only after several rounds of checking and re-drafting with the help of a team of sociologists, social psychologists, tax experts and statisticians. Pre-tests were conducted in a few cases and consequently, relevant changes were made in the schedule to make it more clear and unambiguous. Each interview took an average of ninety minutes, with a minimum duration of 60 minutes to a maximum of about four hours. All interviews with the searched respondents have been conducted directly by the author, that too in an environment of utmost privacy and confidentiality as desired by the respondents.

Another set of respondents, who had not faced income tax raid, belonging to the same region and with relatively comparable demographic, geographic and business backgrounds were also selected for interviews. They were given another schedule with common questions related to tax attitudes and tax awareness as in the schedule administered amongst the sample of searched persons. This sample was then studied for limited comparison. Also, attempts were made to gather insights on the problem from informal discussions the author had with various scholars of the discipline and related fields that too after interactions with tax administrators and tax practitioners in the light of the primary data gathered.

Random samples were sufficiently representative and contained respondents of different age groups[8] and of different educational,[9] familial,[10] occupational[11] and generational backgrounds.[12] The samples contained respondents from different geographical backgrounds[13] and with varying occupational roles.[14] The majority of the respondents in sample A (86 per cent), had completed more than 10 years in the business or profession carried on by them. While 18 per cent had completed more than 30 years, 22 per cent and 47 per cent of the respondents had completed more than 20 years and 10 years respectively. Only 14 per cent had not completed 10 years in the business. In sample B, 51 per cent of the respondents had completed more than 10 years in the business or profession carried on by them. 75 per cent of the respondents faced income tax searches three to eight years before the interview and the rest during eight to fifteen years before the interview. The study was conducted (calculated on the basis of the date of interview) after a gap of three to fifteen years after the search.

Duration of search

Searches, no doubt, amount to invasion of the privacy of individuals. And its impact is felt more at the time of the 'physical' search on premises, especially in residential premises. Table T 7.3 contains the data related to actual duration of search in residential premises (except in two cases where residences were not covered under search, the data is of the main premises). This indicates the number of hours the members of the search team were continuously present in the residence of the respondents.

		%
Actual Duration of the first search in the residence	Up to 8 hrs	3
	8-16 hrs	39
	16-24 hrs	49
	Above 24 hrs	9
Group Total		**100**

Mean 18.69 S.D 8.01
Table T 7.3
Hours taken to complete the search operation

		%
No.of subsequent searches	Nil	27
	One	43
	Two	16
	3 & above	14
Group Total		**100**

Mean 1.24 S.D 1.17 (Range 1 to 5)
Table T 7.4
Number of subsequent searches

In 84 per cent of cases, the search party took more than 12 hours to complete the search and to leave the premises of the respondents. And in about 10 per cent of cases, the search party left the premises only after 24 to 72 hours. Thus, invariably all the respondents have stated that they had to face the search team for very long hours including the entire night.

As seen in the table T 7.4 in 73 per cent of the cases, the search party had not completed the search on the first day. In 16 per cent of the cases, the search party came twice after the first day of search and in 13 per cent of the cases, the search party entered the premises more than two times after the first day. In five per cent of the cases, the search party entered the premises of the respondents on another four occasions after the first day of search. In one case, it was reported that the search party continued the search five times after the first day of search.

Here, it is imperative that one should analyse under what circumstances the search party re-entered the search premises of the assessees. There are two different sets of reasons or circumstances for this. In the first situation, there may be cases where one or more of the rooms, cupboards or any other place in the premises could not be searched for want of keys and the assessee requested for time to trace the keys and to produce it before the search party. Another situation is that the search party could not complete the search in particular premises, since there were voluminous items or records to be perused. In this situation also, the search party may temporarily conclude the search (after putting a restraint under Section 132 of the Income Tax Act) to resume it on another day.

However, the second set of reasons, as narrated by some of the respondents during the interviews and case studies were as follows: In most of the cases, if the assessee failed to disclose undisclosed income before the search party, the premises would be 'sealed' to put 'pressure' on them for admission of the unaccounted income. In a few cases, it was reported that searches were deliberately kept pending for completing the cross verifications for exploring the possibility of further seizure from the same premises.

Here, one of the judicial observations in this regard is worth mentioning.

> *"search and issuance of a restraint order under Section 132 of the Income Tax Act, invade the rights of the owner or other person in possession, though the invasion may be of a temporary duration. Therefore utmost care must be taken by the authorities before exercising the power under Section 132. Even after the search, the subsequent enquiries and investigation should be concluded expeditiously, so that the person affected by the actions/orders of the authorities may be relieved of the hardship caused to that person by the exceedingly hard measure. The need to expeditiously conclude the enquiry after an order of restraint made under Section 132 is implicit in the very provision to dilute its harsh implications."*[15]

Almost all the respondents felt that the subsequent entry into the premises created a lot of inconveniences for them and that they faced embarrassment before the relatives, guests and clients due to the seals kept in the premises without any valid reasons. It was also stated that, subsequent presence and questioning in the premises created mental and physical strains for the respondents and the members of their families. The data indicate that in the majority of cases (94 per cent), this was the first ever income tax search in their lifetime. In 90 per cent of the cases, the respondents had never witnessed any income tax search even in the case of their close friends or relatives. It was found that there was no exposure for the majority of the chosen sample to any search action including those by any other government agency such as Customs, Enforcement Directorate, Police, or Commercial taxes.

Seizure of valuables

The primary purpose of any search action is to seize unaccounted assets. As per Section 132(1) of the Income Tax Act, apart from the books of accounts and other incriminating documents, money, bullion, jewellery or other valuable articles or things, which in the opinion of the authorized officer represent either wholly or partly the income or the property of the assessee which has not been or would not be disclosed can also be seized.

The success of any search action is generally measured in terms of the value of seizures made by the investigating team, though seizure of evidence in the form of books and documents is also important. Every search team, therefore, is eager to seize valuables *viz.* gold, cash, stock-in-trade, deposits, etc. Another reason for the emphasis given to seizure is that the same can be easily applied for clearing the tax dues consequent to the detection and assessment of black money. It is also often said that the search team was eager to seize a sizable portion of unaccounted assets in order to claim reward from the government, as seizure of a prescribed value of assets is a precondition for the sanction of the reward.[16]

However, this is an area of intense opposition, discontentment and controversy between the department and the assessees. The first and foremost area of discontent emerges from the disagreement between the both parties regarding the estimation of unaccounted assets. The basic step to find out the value of unaccounted assets is to find out the gap between what is written / reported in the books of accounts and income tax returns and what is found actually at the time of search. Here the contention centres around various points like the method of valuation, wrong quantification, and disputes regarding assets acquired from ancestors, gifts, loans and short term borrowings and assets held in *benami*[17] names.

In 60 per cent of the cases, the search party had seized a minimum of cash above Rs 1 lakh and in a few cases the seizure was above Rs 50 lakh. The mean amount of the cash seized was Rs 5,58,090/- (excluding the cases where no cash was seized). Apart from cash, other valuables such as gold jewellery, deposits, stock, etc were also seized, concluding the same as unaccounted. It has been found that in 79 per cent of the cases, the search team could seize unaccounted assets. (Mean 2014.93 lakh and S.D 2091.18 lakh). Only in 21 per cent of the cases, was there no seizure of valuables.

Seizure of personal jewellery and sociological significance

Out of the seizures of various categories of valuables or assets, sociologically the most significant effect is the emotional discontent and dissent experienced and manifested by the assessee and the members of the family at the time of weighment and seizure of personal jewellery and personal cash. Data indicate that in about 27 per cent of the cases, the search resulted in seizure of gold jewellery. The mean value of the jewellery seized was Rs 8.65 lakh (excluding the nil cases and the maximum being Rs. 30 lakh).

For almost all the respondents, the procedure regarding weighing and / or seizure of personal jewellery was an unpleasant experience. Even in cases where huge concealment was detected in other areas of business activities, the respondents felt more emotional when it came to seizure of even a minor quantity of personal jewellery. (See T.B.7.1) An analysis of the above takes us to the larger sociological and social psychological dimensions of income tax enforcement through search and seizure provisions. One reason could be the importance of gold jewellery in the

MAKING PEOPLE PAY

TB - 7.1

All that glitters is gold

Income Tax sleuths were busy conducting a raid on a big businessman in his residential premises. Unfortunately for him, the taxmen could gather several incriminating documents indicating large-scale tax evasion. Most shocking was the discovery of bundles of currency in gunny bags from various nooks of the house. Officials counted them with the help of counting machines which totaled them at two hundred and twenty five lakhs. Obviously, the man had to just sit helplessly while the taxmen sealed the currency in suitcases. The man had omitted to pay the taxes due by him all these years while sweating hard to earn every rupee of those amounts seized. Bad luck!

The silence in the house was suddenly broken with a sudden hue and cry from the man and his wife the moment the officials started another exercise. That was when the sleuths started weighing the gold jewellery in the house. Though the jewellery was worth only about five lakh rupees, both the husband and wife became very much disturbed by the process of weighing the jewellery. It was really surprising that similar emotional pressure and depression never surfaced at the time of counting and seizing crores of rupees from the residence. They begged the officials to not seize the jewellery and tried to give every possible explanation regarding the source of funds for the jewellery.

The above incident is just one of the manifestations of the extent of emotional bond Indians have to the yellow metal. As in many societies and cultures, the life of an Indian centres around a number of familial, social and religious functions. This is irrespective of and usually thrust upon by his primordial affiliations. In almost all functions, the presence of (or presents of) gold jewellery is inevitable. Even when the child is in the womb of the mother, a ritual called 'valaikappu' is performed on the pregnant woman in most of the places. All the elderly women and her parents adorn her with gold ornaments. Later, after the delivery it is a common tradition to feed the child with gold and honey (within hours of the birth). Gold chain is put on the baby's waist on the twenty-eighth day after the birth. After a few months, the naming ceremony is conducted wherein the child is given new ornaments by the close relatives. It is customary to receive gold jewellery during ceremonies and functions like tonsuring and ear-boring ceremonies, annaprasanam (first meal ceremony), vidyarambham (initiating the child to learning alphabets by writing on her tongue, mostly with gold), upanayanam (sacred thread wearing ceremony among the Brahmin community), puberty ceremony and marriage (where jewellery with thali or mangalsutra is tied and adorned on the bride by the bridegroom). All these are occasions for people to run to the nearest jewellery shop. Thus jewellery has become an important cultural artifact for Indians.

Apart from the above cultural significance attributed to gold, it is also a metal which brings along with it emotional and social security, empowerment and social status. For Indian women gold is both a source of security as well as power. Unlike many other family assets, women hold the role as the custodian of the gold jewellery in many homes. That has made the attempts of many men to dispose of the jewellery not as smooth as in the case of other family assets. It gives the women adequate emotional and economic security as they have the option to pledge or sell a part of the jewellery for personal emergencies.

The possession of gold as a valuable asset providing easy liquidity at the time of financial crisis is widely recognized by many Indian families. It is an asset which is transacted more widely and frequently than any other asset such as land, cash deposits, shares, debentures etc.

However, it is also a source for frequent fights between couples and between both families. Gold jewellery takes the form of a villain in many relationships. People make and break marriages in the name of the quantity and quality of gold jewellery. There are several instances were desperate fathers have adorned their daughters with gold coated imitation jewellery to keep up their status amidst financial troubles. Only misery awaited to those daughters who landed in the hands of equally avaricious in-laws. Relationships in society are embedded with several sovereigns of gold jewellery which in turn defined the nature of reciprocity between people. It is necessary that officials be sensitive to these sociological facts while engaging in the procedure of seizing the jewellery from residences.

cultural, social and even religious spheres of an Indian in this society. (Singh K S, 1997) Apart from the above ceremonial importance of gold jewellery, it is also a symbol of ancestral wealth as many Indians continue to own the jewellery passed on by their ancestors. However, many people have never felt the need to maintain any record of the quantity of such ancestral jewellery. Therefore, they fail to convince the authorities, regarding the explanation for possession of jewellery in the absence of proper evidence.

Another important sociological dimension that emerges is in the context of the unique gender relations and roles in the social structure. Even after recognizing the growing involvement of women and their empowerment in various areas of social activities in India, still in most Indian families, business and profession are largely male-dominated and the economic decision-making and management are left to the exclusive purview of male members. Thus, in most of the cases women in the family are unaware of the nature and procedures of their family businesses run by their male counterparts. Therefore, it is the womenfolk in the families who are more affected by shock, anxiety and surprises which they manifest in the form of anger, agitation and disappointment when faced with a situation where an enforcement agency intrudes for investigation into the malpractices of the business managed by male members. The sociological implication of listing, quantification and seizure of personal jewellery by the search party should be seen in this backdrop. Though, as mentioned earlier, they are not actually involved in the intricacies of businesses mainly managed by the male members, they are the custodians of the gold jewellery in almost all the cases. Invariably, in the case of most Indian families (and in the families of all respondents in the current sample), it is the women who decide on the purchase of jewellery according to their taste and they are emotionally attached to this, much more than to any other assets in their families.

Seizure of other valuables

Searches also result in seizure of other valuables such as fixed deposit receipts, documents related to money advanced, investments in various financial instruments, etc. Unaccounted fixed deposits were seized in 20 per cent of the cases. The mean value of deposits seized is Rs 22.92 lakh (excluding nil cases). In many cases, income tax searches had resulted in detection of investments of unaccounted money as stock in trade. In the sample of searched respondents it was found that 25 per cent had unaccounted stock which was seized during the search. In about 8.22 per cent of the cases, the value of such seized stock was more than 25 lakh.[18]

Interrogation, disclosure and retraction

The recording of the statement from the assessees and obtaining voluntary disclosure from them are usually considered as important procedures on the date of search. The search party, after gathering the evidence indicating the unaccounted income on the date of search, seeks the assessees' explanation towards the fag end of the search proceedings.

It is observed that 'there is an unfortunate tendency among the departmental officials, who are deputed to conduct searches to postpone the recording of statements to late hours in the night or past mid-night, in the early hours, when the person interrogated would be absolutely tired and will be a mental wreck' (Subramanian N, 1998). This may be true in a substantial number of cases. However, there may be several reasons for the delay. Evidence and information gathered during search at several premises conducted in the case of the main assessee are collected by the main team and he is interrogated at length on that. Normally by the time the physical search is completed and the information is collected from various premises, several hours would have passed. Invariably, in almost all cases the respondents have reported that statements were recorded only after midnight.

The interrogation of the assessees in the light of the evidence gathered during the search is considered to be crucial. This is done on the same day mainly to avoid manipulation and fabrication of evidence. Another reason may be to prevent the assessee from being tutored by consultants or other associates regarding the points gathered by the search team. A lot of unpleasantness develops at the time of the above interrogation which is done either in the respondent's house or in his office. It is stated by the respondents that such interrogations start only at the fag end of the search, and by that time they are totally exhausted as a result of the day-long proceedings. In 84 per cent of the cases, the search party took more than 12 hours to complete the search.

Disclosure of undisclosed income by the assessees is generally considered the most important measure of success of a case searched. Emphasis is laid on this by many in the department and outside. Thus, most often, the emphasis shifts from the value of seizure or the quantum and nature of evidence gathered during the search to the amount of disclosure of undisclosed income obtained by the search team. This may be one reason for the search teams to insist on substantial disclosure of undisclosed income from the assessees. In the current sample, the mean of the disclosure made by the respondents is Rs 74.74 lakh with a standard deviation of Rs 149 lakhs.

Subsequent retraction

In 62 per cent of the cases, respondents had disclosed a specific quantum of undisclosed income before the search team on the date of search. However, in about 40 per cent of the cases, the respondents had subsequently retracted from the admissions (disclosure) given on the date of search. And only in the case of 17 per cent of the respondents has there been any disclosure of undisclosed income after the search, i.e. mostly during post search investigations.

TB - 7.2

The Great Kitchen Raids

In Egypt, during the time of Pharoas, tax collectors who were known as scribes imposed a tax on cooking oil. In order to ensure that the citizens were not avoiding the cooking oil, these tax scribes used to inspect the households to ensure that appropriate amounts of cooking oil were consumed and that citizens were not using leavings generated by other cooking processes as a substitute for the taxed oil.[19]

It is the duty of the search team members to communicate the procedures of the search in a language which the respondent can understand. Therefore, during the recording of the statement, the officer has to properly communicate the questions with necessary clarifications so that the deponent can answer the questions clearly and completely. Questions cannot be asked to mislead the other person. At the same time, an environment should be created so that the respondent is able to state what he wants during the statement and not what the officer desires.

It was found that irrespective of the educational background of the respondents, 40 per cent had retracted subsequently from the statement given on the date of search. Thus, a substantial number of respondents had gone back from the statements. This clearly points to the suspicion that the statements given by the assessees and their disclosure of unaccounted income were not voluntary. Therefore, it is worthwhile to analyze the respondents' perception of the conduct of search.

ANALYSIS OF THE PERCEPTION OF THE CONDUCT OF SEARCH

Coercion and threat while recording statements

The person searched is examined on oath during the search proceedings. To the question as to whether they were forced to give any statement during the search, 39 per cent of the respondents stated that they were forced to give the statement in a particular manner as per the wish of the search party. 61 per cent stated that they were not forced during the recording of the statements. It is also understood that in about 40 per cent of the cases, the respondents perceived that the disclosures made by them cannot be said to be voluntary. Significantly, almost the same percentage of respondents had retracted from their earlier statements of disclosure made on the date of the search.

Similar responses were received from the respondents to the question whether the search party had threatened any family member during the search. Forty per cent of the respondents stated that they were threatened by the search party. In this regard, the respondents were asked to explain how they felt threatened at the time of recording of the statement. Out of the 29 respondents who stated that they were threatened, 19 respondents explained their feelings in detail. Some of the responses were (given in the order of response from maximum respondents to the minimum), a) 'if you do not answer in the way we suggest, there will be detailed investigation and that will be damaging for your business / profession', b) 'your premises will be sealed indefinitely if you don't disclose unaccounted income', c) 'we will not leave your premises unless you disclose', d) 'we will bring Police to your premises and apply force' and e) 'if you do not disclose and co-operate with favourable statements, you will be prosecuted.'

The overall atmosphere of the search environment and the behaviour of the search party during the search have a definite influence on the respondents and their family members. Statistical analysis shows that less educated people have felt marginally more threatened than their educated counterparts. However, irrespective of the educational status, a substantial number of respondents from each group have stated that they were threatened by the search party. If the respondent or any family member of the respondent felt threatened by the search team members that would definitely create emotional disturbances during the proceedings. A feel of threat has an irrational component in it and the respondents may feel insecure and a lack of trust on the search team would necessarily follow. Thus, there is consistency in the data related to the percentages of respondents who felt that the statement was forced, and those who felt that they were threatened during interrogation and those who have retracted from the statement and disclosure.

To a question about the overall behaviour of the search team, 73 per cent of the respondents stated that they were cordial. Only 19 per cent of the respondents felt that the behaviour of the search party was not cordial. Out of the above, 7 per cent of the respondents felt that the team's behaviour was aggressive. These data have to be seen in contrast with the data given earlier relating to the response of the respondents (40 per cent) that they were threatened during the search. It is clear from the data that while the respondents felt that the behaviour of the search team was cordial in general, their behaviour at the time of recording of the statements was very unpleasant and disgusting.

Unbecoming behaviour of the search party

Respondents were also asked to point out the unbecoming behaviour if any, perceived by them from the search party during the search. While 77.03 per cent of the respondents had nothing to pinpoint in this regard, about 22.97 per cent cited one or the other of the following incidents or behaviour perceived by them as unbecoming. Some of the incidents were, a) the team members abused the members of the family (reported in six cases), b) disrespect shown to the parents and elders of the house (three cases), c) the entire belongings of the premises were thrown about in a disorderly manner (three cases), d) entered the pooja room[20] wearing shoes (two cases), e) insulted the wife of the respondent by forcefully removing her managalsutra (thali - sacred piece of jewellery placed round the bride's neck by the groom at the time of marriage) for weighment along with other jewellery (one case), f) some officials came 'drunk' to the premises towards the end of the search and threatened the family (one case), and g) started smoking in the bedrooms (one case).

The results indicated in the above table can be compared with the data related to the threats given by the search party and their coercive behaviour. Interestingly, for the above two questions, about 40 per cent of the respondents perceived that undue threat and force were used by the search party at the time of interrogation and for getting a disclosure. However, 73 per cent of the respondents were happy with the general behaviour of the team. This indicates that the search parties were more active and aggressive at the time of interrogation and recording of statement. So, it cannot be said that the entire proceedings were conducted in an unpleasant manner. None of the respondents have pointed out any harassment on the part of the search team demanding any illegal favours during the search. Except for some particular instances reported by a few respondents on the unbecoming behaviour of individual team members, by and large, respondents were happy with the officials' behaviour.

As mentioned, the area of dissatisfaction relates to the way statements were recorded and the way the interrogation was conducted. The emphasis given to 'disclosure of income by the assessees' may be one of the main reasons for the aggressiveness or over enthusiasm of the search party at the time of interrogation and at the time of recording the statement.

It is possible that an impression may be formed in the minds of many, may be because of what is depicted and projected in the media that the searched persons may try to work out a deal with the searching team for a lenient approach. Here, it is pertinent to ask whether any illegal favours were demanded or received by any member of the search team during the search. However, the present study indicates that no such behaviour was experienced by any of the respondents. To the question 'whether the search party demanded any favour during the search,' all respondents stated that no such demand was made by anybody during the search.

Thus the analyses indicate that, though the overall behaviour of the search party till the time of final interrogation and recording of statement was good, the same was not at all smooth during the interrogation and at the time of recording the statement. It can be argued that search teams are supposed to be very offensive at the time of interrogation in order to extract truth and that such a procedure is an 'art of interrogation.' It can also be said that the physical search of the premises of the assessee is done in a highly polite and cordial atmosphere as it is an intrusion into the privacy of the individuals. However, the same kind of soft attitude may not be appropriate at the time of interrogation with reference to the incriminating evidence that may have been found against the same individuals.

Unequal numbers: The presence of a larger search team

Several respondents reported that the huge presence of the search team in the residential premises had created an environment of fear, panic and terror in the minds of the members of the family, including children. The number was so large in some cases that the family members lost count of the people who came and went. There were cases where even outsiders sneaked in to 'watch' the events happening, out of sheer curiosity, and the officials did not prevent them. It was also reported that personnel, including the drivers (of the taxis hired by the officials), who were not part of the search team had often entered the residence and had gained unauthorized entry even into bedrooms. A few respondents have stated that even the members of the police personnel, who were accompanying the search team for security purposes, entered the house, thereby creating further psychological disturbances for the families of the respondents.

The paired sample test shows the extent of disproportion in this regard. However, the actual number of personnel present in the search premises was much more than this, considering the fact that several officials (also police personnel) who are not part of the search team, also enter the premises often during the search.

It is evident here that in a substantial number of cases, the search teams out-numbered the residents in the house, creating a situation of helplessness and insecurity if not panic. However, it was found that proper care had been taken by the search organizers to include at least one lady member in every team while covering residential premises.

Here one might pause to ponder, how far a question regarding the

	Minimum	Maximum	Mean	S.D	t	df	Sig.
No. of persons belonging to family	0	11	3.9730	2.0472	-8.968	73	**
No. of members in the Search Party who entered the residence	3	20	7.9189	3.0778			

Table T 7.5
Paired sample t-test indicating the number of persons in the search party

extent or nature of co-operation offered by the respondents at the time of search is sociologically relevant. It is a situation where an interaction is taking place in a skewed environment, between the powerful investigators at one end and the searched party who are at the receiving end. Respondents have reported aggressive and threatening behaviour by the search team during interrogation. However, successful steps were taken by both the parties to create a conducive environment during the search action. The perception of the respondents is that they have fully co-operated with the search party (93 per cent) during the search. The conclusion derived here is that though there is a strong feeling and perception in respect of the threatening and coercive behaviour of the search party (as mentioned by about 40 per cent of the respondents), the dissent or protest was not expressed in any form by the respondents in the highly charged environment. Thus, the co-operation offered by the search party is partly characterized by circumstantial compulsions.

Presence of witnesses

The presence of two independent witnesses is one of the important statutory requirements in the search and seizure proceedings. The entire proceedings of the search are recorded in the most important document called 'panchanama' and the witnesses affix their signatures in all the documents related to the search including the documents seized. The presence of the witnesses throughout the search action is mandatory so as to ensure that the search party follows the procedures properly. The witnesses are supposed to witness the search proceedings from the beginning to the end, so that no excesses are committed by any member of the search party. Rule 112(6) of the Income Tax Rules makes it incumbent on the authorized officer (one who leads the team) to call upon two or more respectable inhabitants of the locality of the search premises, to attend and witness the search. The witnesses are also necessary in order to ensure that a conducive atmosphere is provided by the searched persons to the search party.

Considering the significance of the above, a question was put to the respondents whether two independent witnesses were present at the time of search. 93 per cent of the respondents had stated that the searches in their premises were carried out in the presence of two witnesses. However, at the time of detailed interview and during the case study, a few respondents stated that witnesses were not at all present during the search. They had left after signing the warrants of authorizations in the beginning of the search and returned at the time of conclusion of the search for signing the documents. One of the reasons for this is the long duration of search, and witnesses, with the permission of the officer, leave in between to attend to their personal work. Though it is not procedurally correct to do any search action in the absence of witnesses who signed the warrant at the time of execution, assessees themselves may prefer that the witnesses be away at the time of the search. In most of the cases, the witnesses are neighbours and the respondents are not comfortable with their continuous presence at the time of search, listing and counting of valuables, interrogation of family members, etc. Thus, the sociological impact of the presence of neighbours at the time of search is very much relevant.

In many cases, especially in cities, it is very difficult to get proper witnesses for searches. The assessees, by and large, are reluctant to call their neighbours as witnesses to the search proceedings for numerous reasons. The first and foremost reason is the privacy factor. Second, it may lead to a flow of information of whatever happened in the house during the search to the immediate social circles. The assessees generally do not wish others to witness the social and psychological strains faced by the family members during the search, seizure and interrogation. The risk of flow of information, sometimes exaggerated, would further aggravate the emotional disturbances faced by the assessees on account of the search. Therefore, in several instances, the respondents themselves had requested the search party either not to call the neighbours as witnesses, or if they were called, to allow them to be away during the time of physical search and at the time of interrogation and recording of statements. In most of the cases, the respondents had made a plea for selecting their own illiterate servants, drivers or employees as witnesses for which the search parties were reluctant because these persons were not considered to be independent witnesses. Initiation of the search was delayed in many cases due to the delay in getting independent witnesses.

Thus, the analysis shows that the inevitable procedures relating to the presence of witnesses create sociological and psychological strains on the respondents. However, the search parties, by being considerate to the assessees, compromise on the proper procedures. By being liberal in terms of the selection of witnesses and their presence during the search, it cannot be said that the interests of the respondents are rightly protected and that the search procedures are followed systematically and not arbitrarily. Therefore, there is a lack of transparency and there is a possibility of unreasonableness in this procedure. And there is ample scope for intimidation in the absence of independent witnesses during the search and interrogation. This may be the price paid by the assessees in their efforts to protect their social status and prestige in their immediate social circles. There cannot be any doubt that the behaviour of the search party in the presence of independent witnesses will be different from their behaviour to the respondent and their family members in the absence of the witnesses or in the presence of uneducated servants or employees or drivers as witnesses. However, the presence of independent witnesses as a third party may ease out lots of tensions created between the searched family and the search party. However, as our study shows, urban respondents, by and large, do not prefer their neighbours as witnesses. The reasons may be the lack of intimacy, sincerity and mutual dependence in the relationships in urban settings as compared to those in towns and villages.

Conduct of the search: What the officials say

It would be interesting to find out the responses of the officials of the enforcement wing on the feedback given by the respondents. Most of the officials who were party to income tax searches had admitted that the sternness and firmness that are required for such an enforcement action were shown during searches. It is evident from the data that the respondents had perceived harshness from the search team only during the interrogation. The officials pointed out the fact that 73 per cent of searched respondents felt that the search proceedings were cordial. According to them, it would be too much for any investigating agency to expect a 'good conduct certificate' from the persons investigated upon. Therefore, any responses from the searched persons on questions about the behavioural pattern of the searched party need to be analyzed in the context of the role performance of the investigators.

A successful investigator is the one who gathers truth from a person who has concealed certain facts from appropriate authorities. It is not always possible to gather evidence from anyone through mere conversation. He needs to engage in intelligent and systematic interrogation. This involves cross examination, re-examination, verification, repeated questioning, counseling etc in the light of various pieces of evidence gathered. He needs to employ various investigative tactics to gather the truth and to obtain an explanation or admission of the same from the persons being investigated. Therefore, interrogation cannot be a very pleasant experience. In spite of this, the fact that substantial number of respondents felt that the search proceedings were cordial, is perceived by most of the officials as a pat on the back of the enforcement wing.

Views of the enforcement officials were also gathered on the fact that about 40 per cent of the respondents had subsequently retracted from the statements given to the search team. Most of the officials perceived the same as not unusual. In any crime, whether it is civil or criminal, the accused tries to explore whatever legal channels and resorts to diverse steps to wriggle out of the charges. During the course of this the person who was charged with any offence musters assistance from various experts and consultants. It would also be possible that some of the searched persons could not provide certain vital facts and explanations before the search team due to various reasons and circumstances. Thus, according to the officials, the retraction from the statements before the

TB - 7.3

Confidentiality of the search action

Income tax searches are conducted in the most unexpected time and the surprise element is a part of all searches. It is noteworthy that information is very rarely leaked from the department regarding the proposed search. The reason may be the highly motivated officials of the investigation wing who are mostly chosen specifically by the higher authorities after careful evaluation of their credentials and capabilities. Unlike the searches by other enforcement agencies where searches are conducted after a scam or an irregularity is reported by the media, income tax searches are generally conducted after months and years of careful planning, reconnaissance and confidential verifications of allegations or information about evasion.

Though search actions are planned in the most confidential manner, still there is a general impression that information is leaked to the assessees before a search. In order to verify this, a question was asked to the respondents whether they expected an income tax search in their premises during that time. 88 per cent of the respondents stated that they never expected a search in their premises. One may be curious regarding the rest 12 per cent of the respondents. To the question why they expected a search in their premises, none of the respondents stated that they got any information in this regard. The responses include 'huge expansion took place in the business', 'aggressive advertisement campaigns catching public attention', 'construction of palatial buildings with inadequate asset disclosures in the IT returns', etc. This has to be contextualized in the backdrop of the fact that the data gathered clearly indicated the surprise element of the search and that it underscored the extreme care and confidentiality of the pre-search processing of search cases by the enforcement wing of the Department.

search team cannot be viewed as a failure of the enforcement authority. Similarly, it would not be appropriate to arrive at a conclusion that the statements were forced. However specific misconduct if any reported by the searched persons by any official of the search team is neither intended nor tolerated by the investigation wing of the Department. All such incidents are viewed very seriously by the Department and disciplinary action is taken against the erring officials. But it is not clear how many such incidents are actually brought to the knowledge of the Department.

Financial strains consequent to the search

Income tax procedures are perceived as very complicated for the individuals and they necessarily seek the help of specialists who charge substantial amounts as fee and other expenses. No assessee escapes from the acute financial strains that follow a search. No doubt, the most important strain, would be the huge tax liability determined consequent to the search. However, the financial strain on account of payments other than the tax liability is another difficulty that even the respondents who got a clean chit (where no incriminating evidence was found or seized) during the search would also face. These include various payments made to lawyers, chartered accountants, travel and other expenses related to various hearings, illegal payments made to various persons for 'smooth' proceedings at various levels within the department or outside, etc.

A question was put to the respondents to state what the total expenditure incurred by them was, consequent to the search action, apart from the payment towards tax liability. A direct question was deliberately avoided regarding the huge fee paid to the auditor or lawyer or the unauthorized payments made to any officials at any time during the investigation, assessment or appeal proceedings. The respondents were asked just to recall the total expenses incurred by them apart from the tax, interest and penalty payments.

About 51per cent of the respondents had paid at least Rs. 1 lakh and

MAKING PEOPLE PAY

TB - 7.4

Some great hide-outs

It is pretty easy to make money. However it is extremely difficult to hide the same. Tax evaders find several ways and means to conceal their undisclosed assets. In India, substantial amounts of undisclosed income are invested in immovable properties as both sellers and purchasers find it the best avenue to conceal part of the consideration through undervaluation. One gains on the tax on the source of investment and stamp duty and also on the capital gains tax. It is very difficult for the taxmen to find out the hidden consideration.

There are many who invest in *benami* names (in the names of other persons) in various movable and immovable assets. A few high-end evaders park the funds in overseas tax havens or try ingenious methods to convert the same into clean money. Some blow their slush money on expensive vacations and other intangible luxuries. But the most common and less sophisticated method is to hide the hard cash.

While some construct secret chambers within the residential or business premises, some others maintain safe deposit lockers to keep the cash. It is reported in the case of one person that he used to keep a large quantity of cash under the kennel where he maintained ferocious Alsatian dogs. Thus, people hide their valuables not only from the eyes of thieves but also taxmen. Some find it secure to keep the funds with private money lenders who pay handsome interest as they charge exorbitant interest from their clients.

above in this regard. About 47per cent of the respondents incurred expenses of over Rs. 1 lakh up to Rs. 10 lakh. It is to be noted that some of these payments had been made a few years ago and the value of the rupee during those years was much more than what it is today. In two cases they paid more than Rs. 25 lakh as expenses in this regard. Thus, it is seen that the respondents incurred substantial sums as miscellaneous expenditure as a result of the search apart from the additional tax liabilities. Though the exact figures of final tax liabilities (after the completion of all appeal proceedings) are not available for all cases, an analysis conducted in respect of a few available cases indicates that the miscellaneous expenses incurred by the searched persons (Mean Rs. 3.25 lakh, S.D Rs. 5.24 lakh) are substantial as compared with their total tax liability. Thus, financial strains are more on account of expenses which are actually unwanted but are perceived by the respondents as inevitable expenses. Substantial amounts had to be spent by the respondents for expenses other than the additional tax burden consequent to the search. In some cases, the amount spent was very high when compared with the value of unaccounted asset seized. The above facts clearly indicate the extent of undesirable economic consequences perceived by the respondents as a result of search.

Emotional disturbances consequent to the search

The income tax search is an extreme enforcement measure by a government agency. It has only a very limited purpose of detecting the undisclosed income and all procedures and steps are aimed at gathering evidence from the particular premises. However, the data gathered reveal that the income tax search had overwhelming and devastating consequences on the emotional status of the individual and their families.

Emotional disturbance for the individual

Table T 7.7 provides us the data on the extent of emotional disturbance

TB - 7.5

Post-search proceedings and appeals

Search is not an end but only a beginning of long legal battles. The data gathered both from the assessees as well as from certain records indicate that in a substantial number of cases, the search resulted in long legal battles between the respondents and the Income Tax Department at various levels *viz.* Commissioner of Income Tax (Appeals), Income Tax Appellate Tribunal (ITAT), Settlement Commission, High Court, Supreme Court, etc. It was found that in 68 per cent of the cases, the assessees preferred appeals against the findings of the search team and consequent assessment orders. (Chart C 7.1)

Accurate data are not officially available on the exact undisclosed income finally assessed in each search case due to the multiplicity of assessments in each search case and the appeals at different stages. A question was put to the respondents to understand whether the assessed income (the status as on the date of interview) was higher or lower than the income disclosed by the assessee in each case. While 31 per cent of the

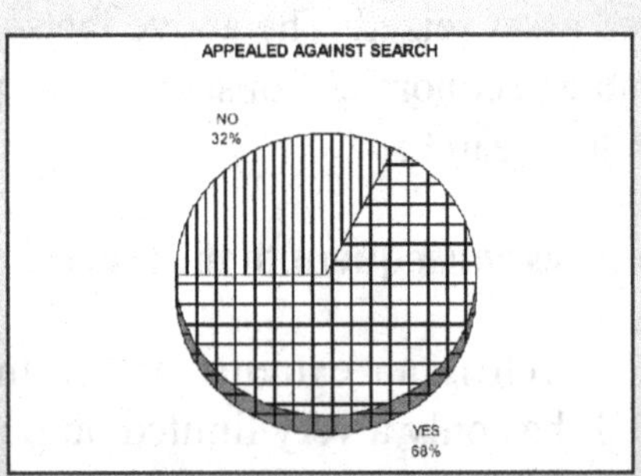

Chart C 7.1
Number of cases where appeals has been filed against the search assessment

respondents chose to be indifferent to the above question (partly because of either ignorance or difficulty in estimation), 54 per cent stated that the income was assessed at a higher quantum (before the same was contested in appeals) than the amount of undisclosed income admitted at the time of search. Out of this, 80 per cent of the respondents stated that the assessed income was exorbitantly high. Only 3 per cent of the respondents stated that the assessed income was lower than the unaccounted income admitted at the time of search.

Appeals against search and search assessment

The data gathered during this study indicate that most of the cases were locked for more than 5 years in appeal on an average and a few cases were dragged on for more than 7 years and some even up to 14 years. Table T 7.6 shows the level up to which appeal had been filed in respect of these cases.

Appeal filed up to	%
Nil	32
Commissioner	31
Income Tax Tribunal	19
High Court	3
Supreme Court and Settlement Commission	15
Group Total	100

Table T 7.6
Appeals filed by the respondents

Punitive action after the search

It is reiterated here that the provisions of search are exercised only in most fit cases where there is valid reason to believe that substantial amounts have been concealed by any person. The search and seizure provisions are considered as an effective deterrence measure to large-scale tax evaders. The legislative intent is clear when it had incorporated various penalty and prosecution provisions in the Income Tax Act. Thus, it is expected that the persons who are caught with huge undisclosed income are punished appropriately. However, it was seen that only in 14 per cent of the cases were any penalty proceedings worth mention conducted. Of this, only in a very small number of cases was the penalty amount (at least a portion of the levy) paid.

The prosecution proceedings are conducted only in one case out of the present sample of respondents. This shows that ultimately the searched persons got away by paying only the tax dues on the concealed income.

experienced by the respondents during and immediately after the search. 88 per cent of the respondents stated that they were emotionally disturbed as a result of the search. Out of the above, a sizable number of respondents (61 per cent of the total respondents) stated that they were very much disturbed because of the search process. Only 8 per cent of the respondents stated that there were no emotional disturbances at all. These data clearly show that the search created certain serious sociological problems, though unintended.

It is appropriate to get necessary data on the duration of the above emotional disturbance in order to assess exactly the intensity of the

Emotional disturbance	%
Not disturbed	8
Little disturbed	4
Disturbed	27
Very much disturbed	61
Group Total	**100**

Table T 7.7
Emotional disturbance (self) as a result of search

Period of disturbance	%
No disturbance	8
Till completion of search	11
Few months	45
Till proceedings completed	22
Not recovered fully	14
Group Total	**100**

Table T 7.8
Period of emotional disturbance

problem. It can be argued that any unexpected or random bizarre happenings in life, however small and strange they are, can create certain immediate but short term (lasting a few minutes or even hours) disturbances. Therefore, a question was put to the respondents to ascertain as to how long they experienced this emotional disturbance continuously from the date of the search.

As seen in Table T 7.8, the emotional disturbances experienced by the respondents were not limited to the day of the search but for a significant period after the search. 45 per cent of the respondents felt that the experience was traumatic and lasted for a few months after the search. About 22 per cent of the respondents stated that they could experience normalcy only after the completion of all the proceedings connected to the search (primarily investigation and assessment, excluding appeal) which took more than two years. 14 per cent of the respondents stated that they still had not recovered from the emotional impact that followed the search. In the case of all these respondents, assessment and investigation proceedings had been completed. It is significant to note that though the intense proceedings were over, the respondents still felt that they had not emotionally recovered even after several years. Out of the total respondents, 11 per cent stated that the emotional disturbances had lasted only till the completion of the physical search.

Emotional disturbances to the individual's family

The bond between the individual and the family in Indian society is strong and deep. It can be said that the emotional or social problems experienced by one member of the family have a close impact on the entire family. Even in cases where the members carry on business or profession independent of other members of the family, any success or setback is shared by the members of the family emotionally if not financially.

In most Indian families, occupational and familial roles are very much closely connected. More so in the case of families that engage in business activities. Thus, relationships are built in business through family networks and *vice versa*. The perceptions and attitudes of the individuals are influenced to a greater extent by the familial, social, and economic environment. Likewise, whatever happens in respect of the business or profession affects the entire families and their kin networks.

Therefore, it is relevant to collect data to find out whether the search process had any emotional impact on the family of the respondents as well.

The following table shows the data related to the extent of emotional disturbance experienced by the family, as perceived by the respondents, as a consequence of the search.

Family emotional disturbance	%
Not at all	9
Little extent	9
Some extent	23
Greater extent	59
Group total	**100**

Table T 7.9
Emotional disturbances to the family members

91 per cent of the families of the respondents experienced emotional disturbance in varying intensity as a result of the search. About 59 per cent of the respondents stated that their families experienced emotional disturbances to a greater extent (extreme point on the five point scale). 23 per cent stated that their families experienced emotional disturbance to some extent. 9 per cent of the respondents stated that there was emotional disturbance for their families to a little extent.

The data on emotional disturbances to self and family are compared below with respect to certain key variables. Though statistically not significant, the data indicate slightly more emotional disturbance for respondents who were below the age of 35. ANOVA results showed high mean values for less educated respondents. Similar significance is observed for the combined date of self and family emotional disturbances. Analysis also showed that the emotional disturbance of businessmen was more than that of the professionals. Similarly, ANOVA results indicated that the directors had the least emotional disturbance when compared with partners and proprietors. It is a general assumption that those individuals who are having more social exposure may feel less disturbed emotionally in stressful circumstances. However, this is not true in the present context. Here it was found that irrespective of the level of social exposure, the respondents experienced emotional disturbance consequent to the search.

Emotional Disturbance and some key variables	
Younger respondents	More emotional disturbance for self and family
Less educated respondents	More emotional disturbance for self
Businessmen	More emotional disturbance than professionals
Directors of Companies	Less emotional disturbance for self
Partners and Proprietors	More emotional disturbance for self
More years completed in business and profession	More emotional disturbance for self and family

Health disturbances consequent to the search

As body and mind are inseparable, the changes in the emotional status of an individual have definite and direct link with his health status, and *vice versa.* Analysis of data related to emotional disturbances shows that both respondents and families have had experienced emotional disturbances in varying intensity as a result of the search. Table T 7.10 and Table T 7.11 contain the aggregates of data collected regarding the health consequences of search. About 69 per cent of the respondents stated that they faced health problems in varying intensities as a consequence of the search. 28 per cent of the respondents stated that their health was affected to a great extent after the search.

Similarly, data was gathered relating to the extent of health consequences on the members of the family as a result of the search in the case of the respondent. Table T 7.11 indicates that 70 per cent of the families of the respondents experienced health problems as a result of the search in one way or the other. This may be for one or more than one member of the family and the damage ranges from mild health problems to loss of life. It is very significant to note that an income tax search conducted in the case of one (mostly) of the family members, that too for the exclusive purpose of detecting evidence related to undisclosed income or asset, is perceived as one which has created a strong emotional and health impact on the entire family. In 11 per cent of the cases, the respondents stated that they have experienced more or less permanent damage (including loss of life of a member) as a result of the search. 19 per cent stated that the income tax raid had resulted in health disturbances to their families to a great extent.

Health disturbances to the individual

Health disturbances	%
Not at all	31
Little extent	19
Some extent	22
Great extent	28
Group Total	**100**

Table T 7.10
Health disturbances on the respondents

Health disturbances to the family

Family health	%
Not at all	30
Little extent	18
Some extent	22
Great extent	19
Permanent damage	11
Group Total	**100**

Table T 7.11
Health disturbances to the family

In two cases, it was reported that persons in the family committed suicide which the respondents perceived as a consequence to the emotional and health disturbances because of the search proceedings. In one of the above two cases, it was stated that the son who was present at the time of search was blamed by the father who was absent during the search for giving a wrong statement under the compulsion of the search team. Later, fearing the serious consequences of the statement and the intense emotional disturbances caused by the search and further proceedings, the son committed suicide. In many cases, the respondents stated that they believed that they were affected by ailments like high blood pressure, diabetes, skin allergies, cancer, etc because of the tension and physical strains of the search.

Health disturbances of the self and family consequent to the search were compared with respect to the selected variables. Businessmen have stated that they have had more health disturbances than professionals. Similarly partners and proprietors have had more health disturbances than the directors.

Familial and social support

Indian families are by and large considered to be closely knit and the members of the family are closely bonded to each other even as they grow old. The remnants of the joint family system that prevailed in India may be one of the reasons for this emotional and physical proximity and bonding.

Singer (1996) who has studied the Indian joint family system in modern industry, has interviewed a sample of Madras-based business men. He found that what he called adaptive processes of compartmentalization, vicarious ritualization, separation of ownership and control and household management in industry are very much in existence in the sample. He found also that, while there have been striking changes within three generations in residential, occupational, educational and social mobility, as well as in patterns of ritual observances, these changes have not transformed the traditional into isolated nuclear families. On the contrary, he found that the families maintain numerous ties and obligations. Thus, individuals look for emotional support in their families and the families in turn share and interact with their kin network.

Our sample contained 39 per cent joint families and 51 per cent nuclear families and the rest others. (In sample B, the distribution is 38 per cent, 40 per cent and 22 per cent respectively). Not withstanding the above dispersed percentages of family structure, a substantial number of the respondents had looked for family support at the time of the present problem and a majority of them received unlimited comfort and support from the family members. It was found that 96 per cent of the respondents got support from their families during and after the search. Out of this, 66 per cent got total support and 29 per cent got support to a greater extent. Only 3 per cent of the respondents stated that they had not got any support from their families after the search.

Similarly, questions were also posed to know the respondents' perception of the support and sympathy they received from their close relatives. 23 per cent of the respondents stated that they never discussed the search matters with the relatives. Interestingly, 15 per cent of the respondents stated that their relatives were very happy to hear about the raid on them. The validity of the above data can be seen in the analysis of data related to the reasons perceived by the respondents for the income tax raid on them. It was found that 15 per cent (the same percentage of respondents stated that some of their relatives were quite happy on the raid on the respondents) of respondents stated that the department might have conducted the raid based on the information passed on by their own relatives. However 26 per cent of the respondents stated that their relatives were very sympathetic towards them. At the same time, data gathered relating to the support and attitude of the friends as perceived by the respondents, give a slightly different feedback. In the case of friends, 46 per cent of the respondents stated that they got total support from their friends. Likewise, 4 per cent of the respondents stated that their friends were really happy over the raid; whereas about 15 per cent of the respondents stated that their relatives were quiet happy over the raids. Thus, it can be said that the assessees, by and large, felt that they received more sympathetic response and support from friends rather than from relatives (excluding their own family members).

Predictably, responses consistent with the above findings have come out for the question regarding the nature of the relationship with the relatives after the search. About 24 per cent of the respondents stated that the relationships with relatives got strained consequent to the search. 9 per cent of the respondents stated that the relationships were severely strained. (See Table T 7.14)

Why was I searched?
Perceived reasons for search

Man is a rational being. Though the degree of rationality differs between individuals, all are eager to find the reason for whatever happened or is happening to them within their level of understanding of the situation. One may ultimately console oneself by treating them as *'fait accompli.'* Nevertheless, every individual endeavors to search for the factors responsible for an event that occurred in one's life or in the world around.

Therefore, it is natural for anyone to ponder over any major happening in life and to come to conclusions or answers which may or may not be nearer to the truth. However, the person believes them as true and directs possible future behaviour and actions based on such belief. Thus, any data collected in this regard is very important.

Respondents were asked the question, 'In your opinion what could be the reason for the department to conduct Income Tax search in your premises?'

They were given a set of possible answers prepared based on the opinion of experts, our preliminary study and the data gathered during the pilot study. (see Table T 7.12) They were given twelve options and were requested to rank them according to their perception of possibility. They were also allowed to give any other reasons which were not listed in the schedule.

All the respondents had ranked at least one reason out of the 13 options given. That means, all the respondents had given their first choice. 70 per cent of the respondents had chosen the second choice, and 31 per cent had listed the third choice as well. Only 11 per cent and 4 per cent of the respondents had selected the fourth and fifth ranks respectively. And no respondent had given more than five ranks. This shows that the choices regarding reasons are limited and therefore it can be concluded that they had already eliminated several possibilities. Since a substantial number of the respondents believed only in one or two possibilities, it can be inferred that they were more or less focused in their own 'search' for the reasons and not just giving wild guesses.

Let us analyze the reasons given by the respondents. It is seen that 28 per cent of the respondents had given first rank for the reason that the search had happened out of enmity or jealousy of competitors or others. 12 per cent of the respondents had given Rank No. 1 for the reason that the Department had acted based on the information given by their own (respondents') staff or business associates. And, 11 per cent of the respondents ranked as No.1, the reason that 'they understand that the Department had gathered the information themselves and studied the respondent's business activities clearly before doing the search'. Thus, 41 per cent of the respondents felt that the raid was a result of information passed by people known to them. However, no respondent gave the No.1 rank to reasons like 'out of political pressure' or 'personal vengeance of an official in the Department'.

Now, let us analyze the ranks given by the respondents to various reasons. The popularity of the statements and the rank weights are given for the first three ranks. (See Table T 7.12)

	Reasons for search	RANK			Popularity	Rank weight
		1	2	3		
1	Incorrect disclosure	5	5	3	28	2.15
2	Default in return filing	3	6	1	22	2.2
3	Some assets concealed	4	3	6	24	1.84
4	Dept acted on false presumptions	2	6	0	18	2.25
5	Out of enmity /jealousy of competitors	21	9	4	85	2.5
6	Information by own staff or associates	9	10	2	49	2.33
7	Information by own relatives	7	2	2	27	2.45
8	Out of political pressure	0	2	0	4	2
9	Personal vengeance of the officials	0	0	0	0	0
10	Consequential raid connected to another search	7	3	0	27	2.7
11	Not known	7	0	0	21	3
12	Department has acted based on its own study	8	6	5	41	2.15
13	Any other reason	1	0	0	3	3

Table T 7.12
Popularity and rank weights of perceived reasons

It is clear that the most popular reasons are 1) Out of enmity or jealousy of the competitors or others (Sl No.5), 2) Information by own staff or associates (Sl No.6) and 3) Department had acted on the basis of its own study (Sl No.12). However, both the popularity and rank weight are nil for the reason given in Sl No 9 as all respondents had not given any rank to it.

If reasons no. 6 and 7 are taken together (irrespective of the ranks given), it can be said that 78 per cent of the respondents felt that the information was passed on by their own relatives or staff, or close business associates. As per the comments by a few respondents, the department was stated to have acted on the explicit or implicit request of these individuals. Some respondents expressed the extreme view that the department has 'played' into the hands of these 'unscrupulous' elements without independent study or verification. Though they do not admit that they were totally honest in matters related to tax compliance, still they felt that they were not as 'mendacious' or 'fraudulent' warranting an income tax raid on them.

The above mentioned view point may be a response from a minor cross-section of the respondents. But it points to certain other revelations as emerging from the data. Income tax searches are supposed to be preceded by months (and sometimes years) of pre-search investigation, reconnaissance, and study of various documents and cross-verification of information. The search is carried out only when there is absolute information verified by at least two levels of officers as true and total satisfaction by the warrant issuing authority, that the case is fit for search. Assessees are hardly aware of these procedures and plans. The above table shows that only 26 per cent of the respondents had given in their first three choices, the possible reason that 'the department had gathered information itself and studied my business activities clearly before doing the search.' And only 11 per cent had given it as their first possibility. This is an indication of the general thinking that the Income tax search action is not based on careful independent investigation and examination of records by the officials, but mostly an act based on hearsay or petitions sent by people to settle scores with the assessees.

Why was I non-compliant? : Perceived reasons for income suppression/ tax non-compliance

Even as the respondents had attributed reasons for search action on them on various factors other than their own degree of non-compliance with tax provisions and concealment of income, most of them were not confident to say that everything was in order before the search. In order to get clear data on the perception of the respondents in this regard, the following specific question was asked deliberately as a 'leading' question: 'What were the reasons for not showing the true and correct income for taxation before the Income tax search?'

The non-compliance leading to stringent enforcement can be in

Reasons for concealment	RANK 1	2	3	4	5	Popularity	Rank weight
1 I had thought that though there are rules related to taxation nobody follows them strictly	10	2	4	1	1	73	4.05
2 Majority of taxpayers do not disclose the income correctly	7	13	3	0	0	96	4.17
3 Tax rates are very high and therefore unable to show the actual income	9	9	3	1	1	93	4.05
4 Unaware of the tax provisions	14	4	4	2	0	102	4.25
5 Never thought that the concealed income will be detected	4	2	0	3	1	35	3.5
6 Considered that paying tax is to be avoided to the greater extent possible because it is a burden	0	2	0	0	0	8	4
7 Did not maintain proper books of accounts	8	5	1	1	0	65	4.33
8 Thought I will pay when I am caught	0	1	0	1	0	6	3
9 Because my CA/IT Practitioner advised me so	5	4	2	0	0	47	4.27
10 Any other	0	1	1	0	0	7	3.5

Table T 7.13
Popularity and rank weights of perceived reasons

diverse ways: non-filing of returns, suppression of actual income, wrong or inflated claim of deductions and allowances, deliberate incorrect computations, etc. There may be several reasons for the above non-compliance. It can be the general apathy towards tax payment, the influence of the tax behaviour of others closely known, lack of awareness, heeding the advice of tax representatives or auditors, etc.

After analyzing various possible reasons gathered during the literature review and the pilot study and the pre-test, the following seven 'reasons' were given as options to the respondents at the time of the interview. They were also allowed to state any reason other than the options given.

In the response to the question regarding 'perceived reasons for search' discussed earlier, all respondents had given at least one reason. However, in response to the present question regarding the reasons for concealment, about 27 per cent of the respondents did not give any reason. They stated that they had not perceived any concealment of income, though they were searched by the department.

An analysis of the responses shows (see Table T 7.13) that, statements 4, 2, 3 and 1 have got maximum responses from the respondents. Based on the percentage of respondents who opted for a particular reason and the ranks given, comparative scores have been arrived at to gauge the responses.

Unawareness as a reason

As seen in the Table T 7.13, a sizable number of respondents stated that they concealed their income due to lack of awareness about tax provisions. By this, they might be implying that they were not guilty since their actions were not deliberate. The assumption is that they would not have concealed had they been clear about the tax provisions.

It is not clear in this context whether they were unaware of even the existence of something like income tax on income earned by them. But the data gathered regarding the pre-search tax compliance perception and pre-search tax awareness perception had indicated that there was a lack of awareness about various provisions, but most of them were aware of the existence of income tax as a direct tax on income. The Table shows the extent of tax awareness before the search as perceived by the respondents. 31 per cent of the respondents stated that they were not at all aware about the tax laws before the search. They had only a vague idea about the taxation before the search. Only 11 per cent of the respondents stated that they had very good tax awareness before the search. Almost consistent figures emanate from the data gathered as to the awareness of respondents regarding tax rates before the search. Most of them were not aware of the correct tax rates before the search.

About 18 per cent of the respondents did not know what accounts to be maintained and 39 per cent of the respondents knew only to some extent about this. 40 per cent of the respondents stated that they were totally ignorant of the penalty provisions for concealment of income before the search. About 15 per cent of the respondents never had any idea about any penalty being imposed by the Income tax Department for concealment of income. Only 9 per cent of the respondents were well aware of the penalty provisions under the Income Tax Act before the search.

The above responses to the question regarding the perceived reason for concealment is consistent with the data gathered earlier regarding pre-search tax compliance perception and pre-search tax awareness perception.

Influence of perception of tax behaviour of others

The second reason (Rank No 2) stated by the respondents as reason for concealment of income is that a majority of the tax payers do not disclose the income correctly. This is almost similar to the reason given (Rank No 4) that 'I had thought that, though there are rules related to taxation, nobody follows them strictly'. This indicates that the respondents' perception of tax behaviour of others has an influence on their own tax behaviour. Here also there is no element of guilt perceived as the action is suitably justified by the respondents. They do not treat this as a deviant behaviour as most of the people they know conceal their income. Thus, their action takes the form of a conformed behaviour without any fall-out on the normative structure of the society. They feel that they are not at odds with the behaviour of other people and consequently, there is no question of any culpability in the action. 76 per cent of the searched respondents agreed to the statement that 'there is nobody who pays his tax honestly'. Another statement on similar lines was put forth with slightly different wordings and meaning: 'Most of the assessees are dishonest in disclosing their income'. 87 per cent of the respondents agreed to this statement, with just 4.05 per cent disagreeing and 8 per cent not responding to it. To the statement that 'Most of the people I know are large-scale tax evaders,' 62 per cent of the respondents nodded their agreement, out of which 36 per cent agreed strongly.

The above sociologically relevant data regarding the social influence in tax behaviour is a very valuable piece of information for detailed analysis and follow up by the policy makers and administrators of taxation. The same is more relevant in a country like India where there is very close kin and social network with a host of intermingled primary relationships. The fact is that the tax behaviour of individuals is very much influenced by their perception of tax behaviour of others.

How do people perceive the tax behavior of others? There may be several ways and avenues for this - direct experience from the interaction with close friends and relatives, what is depicted in the media regarding widespread evasion, widespread publicity regarding the existence of a huge quantum of black money in the country, awareness of the historical and cultural data on tax evasion, etc. Thus, most of these sources of information cannot be treated as completely reliable and accurate. The internalization of such information along with the perception of the lack of effective enforcement may lead to tax evasion by individuals and the further rationalization of the same.

High tax rates as reason for concealment

Regarding concealment, a few respondents gave the reason that high tax rates prevented them from disclosing the income fully for income tax evaluation.

It is true that there is a general perception that tax rates in India are comparatively high. However, this view is not based on any scientific analysis or verification. It is a type of situation like, 'since everybody says, I also.' Even in the case of present set of respondents, 77 per cent of the respondents felt that the rates of income tax were very high and therefore it was very difficult to comply with. And 89 per cent of the respondents felt that there should be a further cut in income tax rates, though there has been a reduction in tax rates over a period of time.

This particular reason of high tax rates was given by the respondents for concealment before the search. Let us analyse whether their answer is based on their own finding, from experience, or whether it is based on their perception of the general perception of the people around them. Earlier, when a question was asked to the respondents whether they were aware of the tax rates before the search, only 15 per cent stated that they were well aware of the tax rates before the search. Therefore, it can be concluded that though statistically no association could be made, their perception of high tax rates as the reason for concealment was not based on any concrete understanding of the rate structure, but mostly based on their general belief from what they heard from others.

Analyses with respect to variables such as educational background (self), total educational background (self and family), generational background and geographical background, indicate that above responses are by and large uniform irrespective of the variables. Here, no significance can be reported.

Relationships after the search

Individuals maintain a relationship network in society. Though the extent, intensity and nature of relationships vary with personality traits, all persons regard social relationships as an asset, more so by people in business or professional settings. The personal relationships of friendship are seen as providing a context within which most of the basic human needs can be met. Kahn & Antonucci (1980) identify three different classes of provisions of friendship: a) information and practical assistance, b) emotional support and enjoyable association, and c) validation of self-worth. Bell, in his interview studies on friendship has identified 'emotional support and understanding' as one of the major gains for the individuals from social interaction. (Bell RR, 1981)

Search action does have an overwhelming impact on the individuals and their families. As has already been observed, there were lasting sociological, psychological and health consequences on a substantial number of respondents and their families as attributed by them as consequential to the search process. The following data was collected to ascertain whether there was any significant impact on the relationship networks of the respondents. Questions were put on their nature of relationships with their other partners or directors, their relatives, clients or customers, *et al* after the search. Indeed, there was a significant change in the nature of relationship with the relatives after the search. Though we cannot arrive at a clear explanation for the strains reported after the search, an analysis of the feedback received from some of the respondents during interview and the case studies point to the latent sociological consequences of the income tax searches.

Relationships-relatives	**%**
Very strainful	9
Slightly	24
No change	54
Cordial	11
Very cordial	2
Group Total	**100**

Table T 7.14
Relationships with relatives after the search

It is evident from Table 7.14 that for 54 per cent of the respondents there was no change in the nature of relationships with the relatives after the search. 24 per cent of the respondents stated that they were having slightly strained relationship with their relatives after the search. This change in the nature of relationship can be attributed to the misunderstandings that crop up after the search and also as a result of the response of the relatives to the respondent after the search. Interestingly, it was found during interviews that 15 per cent of the respondents felt that their close relatives were happy when they heard of the income tax search on them.

Relationships-partners	%
Not applicable*	39
No support	2
Slightly strained	9
No change	47
Cordial	3
Group Total	**100**

* These are proprietary concerns

Table T 7.15
Relationships with partners after the search

Clients/customers etc	%
No support	3
Slight strain	42
No change	50
Cordial	5
Group Total	**100**

Table T 7.16
Relationships with clients and customers after search

There is little compartmentalization of economic and social roles and functions in Indian society. Business and social relationships are often interlinked and not mutually exclusive. This inter-connectedness is observed in diverse ways. First, there are situations where the close kith and kin join together in a particular venture, or more than one business activity (family owned business houses). Second, partnership businesses with close friends are common. As distinct from corporates, partners and the partnership concern (firm) are inseparable and there is a close and intimate bond between the partners which totally bind them to the business. The third situation is where the individual enters into major transactions with a friend, a relative or any other close associate for raw material purchases, product sales, manufacturing activity, marketing, finance, etc. The fourth situation is where an individual chooses a friend or a relative or a person of one's own sub-caste, who has qualified in accounts, as his tax consultant.[21] The fifth situation is where one employs one's close friends or relatives as managers or key employees. There may be several other possibilities also. In all these cases, there would be considerations other than merit in choosing respective persons for the roles or transactions.

Thus, the relationship is not built in a purely professional manner but characterized by social obligations and wider kin networks. Consequently, the above relationships happened to be binding, creating (for the most part) inescapable claims and obligations. The result is that the individual either has to be silent or has to soft-pedal in matters related to inefficiency or dishonesty in service, compromise in quality, or violation of financial discipline. In both ways, the individual has to suffer. If one is silent, that might affect the business and may lead to various problems.

The above point can be illustrated by drawing examples gathered from our sample. If one's tax consultant (who belongs to any one of the above-mentioned categories) is inefficient or is a person who lacks financial discipline, then invariably the individual lands in trouble, including tax problems. In many cases (66 per cent), the respondents stated that they received poor or inadequate advice on tax matters before the search. In response to the question regarding the reasons for not showing the true and correct income for taxation before the income tax raid, 15 per cent of the respondents cited the reason as, 'because my chartered accountant or income tax practitioner advised me so.' This clearly indicates that the respondents have perceived the problem as partly created by their own chartered accountant or tax consultant. Though there is no specific question asked as to whether their tax consultant was a close friend or relative or was selected on pure merits, it was gathered during the interviews that in a substantial number of cases, the key accountants or consultants were either distant relatives or friends or persons referred by them. Thus, the respondents naturally felt reluctant to reprimand such persons for the wrongs, for if that were done, the relationship might have got strained. Thus, search becomes a turning

MAKING PEOPLE PAY

TB - 7.6

Making People Pay: The Role of Tax Practitioners

People yearn to earn income from whatever sources possible. Tax would be last in their thoughts while engaging in the income earning activity. Just before filing the tax returns most of them run towards a group of professionals who would then spend sleepless nights to set right the records, accounts and liabilities. Their main challenge is to make people pay their taxes on the income earned by them. These professionals are the Chartered Accountants, Certified Public Accountants, Advocates and Tax Consultants. All of them can be collectively called as Tax Practitioners. Some of them engage in the task of preparation of accounts, some do the auditing and some provide just consultancy. There are many who do all these for their clients.

They do remarkable service in making people tax compliant. However their contributions are grossly underplayed. The general perception is that they are instrumental in making their clients avoid as much tax as possible. This may be true to a limited extent. However present analysis indicated something to the contrary.

The study revealed that more than 90% of taxpayers in the professional and business categories had to necessarily depend on tax practitioners for finalizing their accounts and to compute the tax liability. In fact, these practitioners had promptly reminded their clients about the advance tax due dates, tax withholding rules, return filing etc. It was interesting to hear from some taxpayers that their chartered accountants had forced them to comply with rules, many times to their dislike. It is seen that substantial number of taxpayers had found the need to take the assistance of a competent chartered accountant or consultant to make the accounts systematic after the search.

In countries where taxpayers perceive legal and procedural complexities, tax practitioners play decisive roles not only in tax decisions but also in professional and business strategies of their clients. Thus most of the taxpayers repose their faith in their auditors and tax consultants giving them unrestricted power of attorney. In India, Priyamvada Birla, widow of businessman M P Birla bequeathed about Rs 5000 crore of assets to her chartered accountant R S Lodha, who was neither a family member nor a relative.

However questions have been raised in several quarters about the ethical issues in auditing and consultancy in the context of corporate governance. The decisive roles played by auditors in major corporate scandals such as Enron, WorldCom, Sun Beam, Satyam etc have raised questions on the credibility of established audit firms. Cases were registered against the auditors of many tainted companies for collusion with the management. Recently it was reported that a practising Certified Public Accountant was charged and convicted for his own tax evasion in Singapore, which is first of its kind in that country. Regulations such as Sarbanes-Oxley Act, self regulatory boards like Public Companies Accounting Oversight Board (PCAOB) in US and implementation of International Accounting Standards etc have brought in systematic reforms in the last few years. Institute of Chartered Accountants of India (ICAI) has its own disciplinary body, which initiates proceedings and imposes penalties. ICAI has already initiated steps to ensure auditor independence, auditor rotation and effective peer review.

point in business, when skeletons come out of the cupboard, and the assessee who has faced the 'worst', gains the necessary courage to take strong steps against the key accountants or consultants.

Thus, as seen already, a substantial number of respondents have chosen better professional advice (77 per cent) after the search. The steps taken include change of tax consultants or the chartered accountant. There is definitely a change in the relationships in this regard.

Similarly, several other instances have been reported by the respondents indicating the impact on the relationships consequent to the search. Some such experiences shared by the respondents are given below:

1. There are a few cases where the search team happened to find substantially high quantity of cash and jewellery in the rooms of one brother as compared to what was found with the other brother. Both (and their wives) are partners in the joint business venture with equal share. However the disparity in the assets found had created a mis-understanding between the partners, one accusing the other that the business money was diverted. Strains slowly spread to the wives and other members of the family which resulted in serious rifts.
2. Similar experiences have been shared also by partners who are not related by blood. If the search leads to detection of evidence related to any misappropriation of funds or accounting or financial frauds, the partner who is in charge of that particular activity is questioned by the other partners and then relationships get strained.
3. It is the practice of several businessmen, to do at least a part of their business activities without accounting for them. During the course of this act they may transact in cash with persons or concerns known to them. However, if one party who has been raided tries to explain the presence of the cash, credits, or assets as given by the other party, the latter, in all likelihood, would deny the transaction. In spite of the fact that the person has indeed given the goods or lent

the money, the person might refrain from owning up the same fearing consequential action from the Income tax Department. The same is the case with real estate transactions also, where substantial unaccounted money passes hands. All these lead to strains in the relationships among the persons.

4. There are several cases where the respondents had to face severe problems in the relationships with their clients or customers after the search. Some of them are narrated below:
   i. The customers/clients stop or considerably reduce the transactions with the respondents.
   ii. The debtors conveniently default on payments. (This happens in many types of cases, more often in cases of financiers)
   iii. Creditors become aggressive in collecting the amounts payable to them without any leniency.
   iv. Banks and other financial institutions become suspicious about the credentials of the respondents and adverse decisions on overdrafts, letters of credit, and loans follow.
   v. During the time of post-search investigation and assessment, the officials may summon or investigate several persons connected with the assessee and his business. This exercise leads, in some cases, to the development of strains among them and the respondents because the former blame the latter for the inconvenience and possible harassment meted out to them by the investigating officials.

Social exposure and activity before the search and after

Man is essentially a social being. His myriad social activities in various fields have a definite influence on his attitude and behaviour. The nature and extent of the sociability of a person is very relevant in a sociological study. The individual, during his interaction with others in society, develops concrete social relationships in the social settings wherein one lives and works. In the process, one contributes as well as receives ideas, information and resources and thus becomes part and parcel of a world of sharing and reciprocity. However, the nature and extent of involvement of individuals in society varies among individuals and among cultures. Various other factors such as educational background, geographic location, inherent qualities, past experience, etc determine one's propensity to socialize. The 'roots and causes' of the nature of relationships in society are 'complex and intertwined'. (Duck and Perlman, 1985) The social interaction and participation in various social, religious and charitable activities and social entertainment provide a platform for individuals to relax and to gain more exposure to the information and the happenings all around.

> "Simmel sees in sociability a capacity for transferring the 'seriousness and tragic to a symbolic and shadowy play-form' which can reveal reality obliquely. Thus, although much social interaction involves elements of sociability, the purer play-forms of sociability, e.g. parties or picnics, or mere talk, can be seen as possessing their own specific importance in social life. Although apparently and necessarily 'undirected' and 'unserious', they form a definite role, first in providing relaxation, distraction, etc but also in throwing a fresh light on 'serious' endeavours" (Jary and Jary, 1991:574).

Social interactions within the community, organizations, and clubs and intimate sharing in immediate social circles give individuals ample opportunities not only to project themselves but also to get regular updates and feedback. It is pertinent to examine the extent of social participation and exposure[22] of the respondents before and after the

Organizational Activity *before* Search	%	Organizational Activity *after* Search	%
Not a member	27	Decreased to a great extent	11
Passive member	43	Decreased to some extent	15
Active member	26	No change	65
Very active member	4	Increased to some extent	9
Group Total	**100**	**Group Total**	**100**

Table T 7.17
Organizational activity before and after search

search. Table T 7.17 shows the extent of participation in trade or commerce or professional association by the respondents before and after the search, as perceived by them.

It is seen here that 26 per cent of the respondents stated that their organizational activities decreased after the search. Similarly, 24 per cent of the respondents stated that there was a decrease in social and charitable activities after the search, whereas 8 per cent of the respondents stated that there was an increase in social and charitable activities. (See Table T 7.18)

Social and charitable activities *before* search	**%**	**Social and charitable activities *after* search**	**%**
Most disinterested	2	Decreased to a great extent	11
Not participated	28	Decreased to some extent	14
Passive participation	35	No change	67
Active participation	30	Increased to some extent	7
Very active participation	5	Increased to a great extent	1
Group Total	**100**	**Group Total**	**100**

Table T 7.18
Social and charitable activities before search

The extent of social activities of the respondents before the search was worked out on the basis of their responses regarding the participation in organizational activities, clubs, social and charitable activities, etc. The same were compared with the selected variables in order to verify the influence. However, it was found that only the generational background and years in business were significant. Again, the ANOVA results show significance at 5 per cent level. It is seen that the respondents from the first generation have low mean values of pre-search social activities than those from the second and the third generations. However, the ANOVA results show significance at 1 per cent level while comparing the variable 'completed years in business.' It was found that there was an increase in the extent of social activities when the respondents had completed more years in the business. Data given in Table T 7.19 show the change in the religious activities after the search.

Religious activities	%
Decreased to a great extent	3
Decreased to some extent	4
No change	72
Increased to some extent	9
Increased to a great extent	12
Group Total	**100**

Table T 7.19
Religious activities after search

It is often said that individuals' attachment and dependence on supernatural powers or God increases at the time of any crisis or important happenings. A question was put to the respondents to understand whether there was any significant change in their religious activities after the search. As shown in Table T.7.19, as many as 72 per cent of the respondents stated that there was no change in the religious activities after the search. The extent of devotion and intensity of the faith continues to be the same for a majority of the respondents. 21 per cent of the respondents stated that there was an increase in religious activities after the search and seven per cent of the respondents stated that there was a decrease in religious activities after the search.

Response about the departmental proceedings after the search

Undoubtedly, no assessee receives a search team with a smiling face. However clean one might be in respect of the accounts and tax compliance, the very presence of the search team on one's premises creates great mental tension to the individual. In the same way, however nice and polite the behaviour of the search team, still they have to necessarily carry out certain well laid out procedures in an impersonal way. The action may be perceived by the respondents as perfunctory and surreptitious from the side of the search team.

Questions were put to the respondents in order to understand what they felt about the income tax proceedings after the search. 65 per cent of the respondents stated that the post-search proceedings were systematic.

34 per cent felt that it was not systematic. However, 77 per cent stated that the proceedings were very lengthy and 23 per cent stated that it was not that lengthy. 51 per cent felt that the income tax proceedings were very complicated. But 49 per cent felt that the proceedings after the search were not that complicated. To the question whether the proceedings were less cumbersome than expected, 77 per cent of the respondents answered in the negative and 22 per cent stated that they were less cumbersome than expected.

In the background of the data collected relating to the respondents' perception of aggressive behaviour by the search party, a question was put to the assessees whether they had any vengeance towards the income tax department at present, that is, after the years of search. 86 per cent of the respondents stated that they did not have any feeling of vengeance towards the department or towards any officials but 14 per cent still bore a sense of vengeance against the department who searched them.

IT Department proximity before the search and after

Though a substantial number of assessees perceived that the search and post-search experiences were emotionally disturbing and unpleasant, it is important to note that they have shed their inhibitions in interacting with the Department after the search. They have become more confident in communicating with the departmental officials and there are no strains in the relationships. In contrast to their earlier position, they feel more familiarity with the departmental environment. Proximity to Income tax Department is calculated on the basis of the awareness as well as the interaction of the respondents with their jurisdictional income tax office prior to the search. This was compared with the geographical background and it was found that respondents with city backgrounds were more proximate to the IT Department than the respondents from towns. Those from the villages were the least proximate to their income tax office prior to search. Thus, there is significance at 1 per cent level. It was also found that highly educated respondents had more proximity to IT Department prior to the search. 81 per cent of the respondents stated that they were more confident in interacting with the income tax Department after the search. This shows that the search was an important milestone in their lives and in their business and the respondents felt that there were certain positive roles played by the above action.

Two questions were put to the respondents in order to examine their emotional status related to their approach towards the department and the proceedings, that is, after the completion of the major proceedings. Firstly, they were asked to respond on a five-point scale to the question whether the anxiety and worry about the income tax matters increased or decreased after the completion of the search process. To this question, 66 per cent of the respondents stated that their anxiety and worry about the tax matters had decreased.

Anxiety	%
Decreased to a great extent	24
Decreased to some extent	42
No change	20
Increased to some extent	12
Increased to a great extent	2
Group Total	**100**

Table T 7.20
Anxiety about tax matters after completion of all search proceedings

Anxiety about tax matters after completion of all search proceedings

Out of the total, 42 per cent of the respondents stated that the anxiety about tax matters had decreased to some extent and 24 per cent stated that their anxiety and worry had decreased to a great extent after the completion of all search proceedings connected to the search. While 20 per cent of the respondents stated that there was no change in this respect, 12 per cent stated that their anxiety and worry related to tax matters had increased. Though attempts were made to gather data giving possible explanation for this, no clear conclusions could emerge from it.

Another question, a similar one and carefully worded, stressing on the income tax proceedings, was asked subsequently, but only after sandwiching both questions with several other questions. The respondents were asked whether they felt that they carried less tension and fear as far as income tax proceedings were concerned after the raid. Though this may be criticized as being a leading question, it was posed deliberately in order to set off the possible bias related to a couple of questions posed earlier, stressing the emotional consequences of search proceedings.

Tension and worry	%
Totally scared	3
Carry a little tension now	16
No difference	20
Reduced to some extent	34
Reduced to a great extent	27
Group Total	**100**

Table T 7.21
Tension and worry after the completion of all proceedings

Table T 7.21 indicates that 61 per cent of the respondents stated that they carried less tension and fear as far as IT proceedings were concerned. Out of the total, 34 per cent of the respondents stated that the same was reduced to some extent and 27 per cent stated that tension and fear related to IT proceedings had declined to a great extent. While 20 per cent of the respondents stated that they felt no change in this aspect, 16 per cent stated that they carried a little tension and fear still, but without giving any clear reasons.

As has already been seen, a majority of the respondents perceived that they had experienced intense social, psychological and physiological strains due to the search process. However, it is interesting to note that a substantial number of respondents did not bear any vengeful feelings against the department now, years after the search. What would be the reason for that? Does that mean they have also gained something from the whole process? This is examined in detail below.

Perceived impact of search on financial well-being, business management, and fiscal compliance

Financial well-being, good business management and fiscal discipline are interlinked if one has the intention to comply with the business laws. It is significant to examine the impact of the income tax search in the above context on the searched individuals. Since the ultimate aim of this extreme income tax enforcement is to detect undisclosed income and to curb unaccounted money, the action is predominantly economic in nature. All the consequences as discussed earlier *viz.* social, emotional, and health consequences are only indirect results of the income tax enforcement. They are mostly unintended also. However, there is a close and direct link between the income tax raids and the economic status of the assessees. The search action may result in the detection of huge concealment of income and consequently substantial tax liability for the individuals. It may also disturb the normal business activities for a significant period of time and thus adversely affect the fund position of the individuals. Even in cases where the assessee maintains the position that he is correct in tax matters, still he may have to spend considerable amount of time and money for litigation. This would invariably affect the business activities of the assessee.

Perceived status*	Before Search		After Search	
Accounts maintenance	Correct to some extent/maintained to some extent	66	Better maintained	32
	Very correctly maintained	23	Very correctly maintained	47
Sought professional advice	Not received	26	Better advice	51
	Some extent	34	Excellent advice	26
Promptness in filing the tax returns	Very prompt	32	Very prompt	68
			No change	7

***Percentages of the sample. Other responses are not very significant**

Table T 7.22
Compliance before and after search

The above table indicates that the respondents have perceived radical improvements in fiscal compliance. Comparative analysis was made with respect to geographical background (village, town or city) and pre-search tax compliance perception. The ANOVA results indicate significance at 1 per cent level. It is seen that respondents from cities had more mean values for pre-search compliance perception than those from villages and towns. It was also found that the pre-search tax awareness perception of respondents from cities was higher as compared with those from villages and towns. A comparison of the associated capacity relating to the business or profession indicates that directors of companies were more pre-search tax compliant as compared to the proprietors and partners. Analysis also indicated a slight association between the completed years in business and pre-search tax compliance. However, the same was not statistically significant.

From the responses, two things are clear. Firstly, there is a significant improvement in the way accounts are maintained after search. Similarly, they have become much more procedurally compliant. The respondents admitted that they had less tension and fear in respect of tax matters and were more confident in dealing with tax authorities. Does that mean there is less tax evasion and concealment of assets and income?

It is quite natural for anyone to be inquisitive, to know about the perception of the respondents regarding their present disclosure of their income. One question was put, but after exercising utmost caution, to get as honest a reply as possible. The question was also framed in such a way that the assessee may without much reluctance respond to the question in a frank way. The question was, 'Do you think that you are able to disclose your true and correct income ***now?***' (Emphasis added on now) By stressing the words 'do you think,' the aim was to get a response which was straight from the respondent's mind, without thinking twice about what others perceived or what his auditor would have told him. By adding the words 'are able to,' the respondent was given an impression that the process of making a disclosure was not a smooth, automatic, natural process or normal action, but one which required personal initiative amidst several possibilities and choices. The words 'true' and 'correct,' stressed that the 'disclosure' implied that the respondents have disclosed their true income (i.e. not part of his total income), and that 'correct income' meant one has correctly computed one's total income without any excess or incorrect claim of the statutory deductions and allowances. In spite of these deliberate strong wordings, the question was put in an appropriate manner and tone, with necessary clarifications to ensure an honest reply.

Present disclosure	%
Totally impossible to disclose fully	2
Not possible to disclose fully	2
No difference	3
Discloses to a great extent	37
Able to disclose fully	56
Group Total	**100**

Table T 7.23
Perception of present disclosure

Table T 7.23 contains the data relating to the responses to the above question. Even after the completion of the major part of the search proceedings and even after stating that they had less tension and worry relating to tax matters and income tax proceedings, it is significant to note that only 56 per cent stated that they were able to fully disclose their income. 37 per cent of the respondents stated that they were able to disclose the true and correct income to a greater extent at present. While two per cent felt that it was not possible to disclose the true and correct income, another two per cent stated that it was totally impossible.

Two important points emerge from the above data. A comparison of the disclosures shows that there is significant improvement in the tax compliance as respondents tend to disclose more as compared to the period before search. More importantly, the assessees are more clear and confident about what they disclose now. Secondly, this apparently sensitive question was answered more or less honestly. It is a basic human tendency to hide the crime or the serious deliberate omissions done. Respondents may boldly and frankly give their attitudes and opinions on any sensitive issue. However, frank admission of an apparent omission or malpractice can happen only in a free and frank environment. In this case about 40 per cent of the respondents stated that they still failed to disclose fully their true and correct income to the Income Tax Department. The study was thus successful in gathering honest responses from the respondents as is abundantly evident from all the responses.

As we saw earlier, a substantial number of respondents had stated that there was remarkable improvement in their tax compliance and tax behaviour after the search. Apart from the specific questions already discussed, certain other questions were asked with yes/no options as summary responses.

The respondents were asked to comment on their business activities after the search. To the question 'how is your business now', 32 per cent of the respondents stated that there was no difference as compared with the period before the search. 24 per cent stated that the business had gone bad

Consequences of IT raid on economic activity		No	YES
Helped me to organize my business activities in a better way	%	27	73
I became more systematic in recording and maintaining the accounts	%	16	84
I got better control of the business activities	%	31	69
I am aware of the tax provisions and the procedures	%	18	82
I could achieve better financial results after the raid	%	47	53
IT raid has disturbed my entire business/profession and there is no recovery expected in the near future	%	70	30
I lost faith in the tax authorities	%	78	22
IT raid has made me almost bankrupt	%	85	15
My clients/customers left me after the raid	%	68	32
I lost control of my business activities	%	78	22

Table T 7.24
Other consequences of search

after the search and 12 per cent said the business was worse now. However, 23 per cent of the respondents stated that their business had improved and 8 per cent stated that their business had become much better now.

Though the question was put in order to measure the impact of search and post-search proceedings on the businesses of the respondents, it may not be proper to arrive at any conclusion by narrowly interpreting the responses. There may be various other reasons for the upward jump or sharp decline in the businesses of the respondents. Bearing this in mind, the respondents were asked to give the reasons, if any, for the response to the above question.

23 per cent of the respondents had given reasons other than search for the present status of their business. Out of the 36 per cent of respondents who said that their business or profession had come down, more than 85 per cent stated that it was because of the emotional disturbances consequent to the search. However, out of the 31 per cent of respondents who stated that they did better after search, about 75 per cent gave factors other than search as the reason.

Thus, though the search had made the respondents more systematic in the business/profession and accounts, a substantial number of respondents did not feel that they could achieve radical economic progress after the raid. The factors for the economic progress reported after the search in some cases were extraneous to the search impact. But most of those respondents who had not done well after the search preferred to put the blame on the disturbances caused by the income tax search on them and their business activities. To the question, 'have you expanded the business or profession after the raid?' 49 per cent of the respondents stated that there was no change. 22 per cent stated that there was only moderate expansion and 9 per cent stated that there was considerable expansion. Significantly, 15 per cent of the respondents stated that there was reduction in the business and 5 per cent stated that they stopped the business after the search. Respondents were also asked whether they had ventured into any other area of business or profession after the raid. 86 per cent of the respondents said 'No' and only 14 per cent stated that they had ventured into fresh business or profession other than the business or profession carried on by them before the search.

Perceived pre-search tax awareness and actual post-search tax awareness

The table above shows the extent of tax awareness before the search as perceived by the respondents. 31 per cent of the respondents stated that they were not at all aware about the tax laws before the search. They just had only a vague idea about the taxation before the search. Only 11 per cent stated that they had very good tax awareness before the search. Almost consistent responses emanate from the data gathered regarding the awareness of respondents regarding tax rates before the search.

Respondents were also asked a specific question as to whether they knew the basic exemption limits. Only 41 per cent of the respondents knew the basic exemption limits before the search. About 18 per cent of the respondents did not know what account books were to be maintained and 39 per cent of the respondents knew only to some extent about this. 39 per cent stated that they were ignorant of the penalty provisions for concealment of income before the search. About 15 per cent of the respondents never had any idea about any penalty being imposed by the Income tax Department for concealment of income. Only nine per cent of the respondents were well aware of the penalty provisions under the income tax act before the search.

Tax law awareness	%
Not aware	31
Wrongly understood	1
Some extent	41
Great extent	16
Well aware	11
Group Total	**100**

Table T 7.25

Pre-search tax awareness perception

In the five point scale (1 to 5), the mean is 2.89

Pre-search tax awareness perception was analyzed comparatively with respect to key variables and it was found that some of them had significant associations. Though pre-search tax awareness increased with an increase in educational qualification (of self), the same trend was not seen at the highest level. As the Total Educational Background score increased (self and family), there was marginal, proportionate increase in the pre-search awareness. There was considerable variation observed between businessmen and professionals in respect of pre-search awareness perception. Professionals had more mean tax awareness score than businessmen. Analysis also showed that there was significance at 1per cent level, between the pre-search awareness perception and the geographical background. The pre-search tax compliance perception was higher in the case of respondents from cities as compared with respondents from villages and towns. No significance was found in respect of the generational background.

Post-search tax awareness

The pre-search tax awareness perception of the searched individuals before the Income tax raid has been analyzed already. Post-search tax awareness of the respondents are analyzed now. This was gathered by administering a set of standardized tax awareness questions covering all points to the respondents. Twenty-five standardised questions covering all areas were put to the respondents to test their actual tax awareness. Tax awareness of the respondents on various topics/area were separately analyzed. The analysis of the data on actual tax awareness indicated that the level of awareness of respondents on tax laws is low when compared with their awareness on income tax and accounting procedures. This is almost in tune with their responses when general questions were asked before administering the tax awareness questionnaire. Though, clear data could not be gathered about the actual tax awareness of the respondents before the search, it is indicated that the respondents had perceived that they were more aware of tax laws and procedures after the search.

Subjective tax awareness and objective tax awareness of sample-B (respondents who have not undergone income tax search)

The data shows that the perceived tax awareness of the respondents regarding tax laws was in line with their actual total tax awareness. The Chi square results indicated significance at one per cent level.

	Group	Mean	S.D
Total Tax Awareness Score	Sample B	26.6753	10.0413
	Sample A	29.5000	11.2691

t = -1.628   df = 149

Table T 7.26
Comparative tax awareness scores of sample B and sample A

Though statistically insignificant, it is observed that the mean score of sample B (searched group) is more than the mean of sample A (non-searched group). Thus, the tax awareness of the persons who were searched is higher than the tax awareness of others. Analysis also made in order to verify the association between the variables of the study with the actual tax awareness. There are two significant findings in this regard. It is seen that total tax awareness score increases along with an increase in TEB values, with a slight fall at the highest level. Secondly, there is an increase in tax awareness from first generation respondents to third generation respondents.

CHAPTER-8

TAX COMPLIANCE AND TAX ENFORCEMENT

Problems and Prospects

This chapter is consciously retrospective. In the light of the findings in chapters six and seven, an analysis of the problem of tax compliance in general and tax attitudes and behavioural perceptions of the taxpayers in a developing country in particular is attempted here. Though some of the issues might be exclusive to countries where the Tax-GDP ratio and the Taxpayer-Citizen ratio are comparatively low, the attitudinal and behavioural patterns of both taxpayers and tax enforcers as delineated in the empirical studies provide ample insights for researchers as well as policy makers, around the globe

Though the empirical studies have several limitations both in terms of the geographical constraints as well as the fact that the data gathered might not be very exhaustive, yet the results have given new insights into understanding the tax compliance. By geographical constraint, one would mean the difficulties in generalizing the data gathered from a specific geographic setting. The data gathered may not be very exhaustive and there would always be a feeling of inadequacy of data in studying areas such as tax attitudes and tax behaviour where the author squarely depends on the ability to gather as much truth as possible from the respondents. Though both these problems are inevitable in the current project settings, they do not hinder valid interpretation and generalization. The Indian Income Tax Act is uniform all over the country and both the tax administration and enforcement follow uniform patterns everywhere. The geographical area of the sample is also a neutral place where no major incidents of tax protests, political movements, large financial scams or unique tax evasion patterns have been reported in the past several decades. The extent of tax enforcement and tax compliance in the past several decades is the same as the national averages. Therefore the results may be a strong indication of the overall tax attitude and behaviour in the country.

The second concern was how far one was able to get genuine data about the tax behaviour. As the data themselves indicate, the respondents were very frank and forthcoming in narrating their tax behaviour. The fact that a substantial number of respondents had openly admitted about their dishonesty in income disclosures is a strong indication of the genuineness of the data. Similarly, the consistency in the views while answering statements put to them in different ways too indicates the seriousness shown to their responses. Thus, it may be safely said that the interviewer was successful in gathering as genuine and as clear data as possible. Now, let us examine the results that emerge from the empirical studies conducted.

Procedural compliance and substantive compliance

Data reveal that the taxpayers gave more importance to procedural compliance as they felt that the tax administration was more visible in enforcing the procedural compliance. Thus, taxpayers were keener to file their returns promptly. Past tax experiences of the respondents also prompted them to be procedurally compliant. However, actual or substantive compliance (where all incomes are disclosed correctly and completely) is lacking. The same trend is seen when an analysis was made on the third generation taxpayers. They tend to have low degrees of substantive compliance (they admitted to have shown more income suppression than the first and second generation taxpayers) and at the same time perceive their act to be highly procedurally compliant. This clearly indicates the taxpayers' perception and realization that tax administration and enforcement are either not keen or weak in enforcing substantive compliance. They felt that procedural compliance was what mattered.

It is interesting to note from study 1 (given in chapter six) that while 66 per cent of the respondents had admitted to concealing their income from taxation, only about 25 per cent of the persons had ever found their admitted income disturbed by the tax authority during assessment proceedings and only less than 14 per cent of the persons had paid some penalty for the concealment. In study 2 (given in chapter seven), about 67 per cent of the respondents had maintained incorrect accounts for the purpose of taxation prior to the search. 43 per cent of the respondents had admitted to concealing their income even years after they were subjected to search. Penalty proceedings were conducted only in 13 per cent of the cases searched and penalty could ultimately be levied in still less number of cases only. However, the majority of the searched respondents became procedurally more compliant after the search through prompt filing of returns, auditing the books of accounts, responding to notices for hearings, etc. Thus, it is evident from the data gathered from both sets of respondents that taxpayers showed more procedural compliance than substantive compliance in the face of income tax enforcement.

The problem of enforcement

As tax regulator and tax administrator, the State has a twin role - a watchdog of the economy as well as a service provider. In the context of income taxation, the government needs to curb all attempts at concealing the income from taxation and it has to provide satisfactory service to the taxpayers in processing their returns and settling their claims and grievances. Taxpayers orient their actions based on the nature of tax administration and enforcement. As Kelman (1961) suggests, the regulated people, in any given situation, have many options. They may co-operate, withdraw, practice defiance or find ways of circumventing - all depending on the nature of the regulator. If the taxpayers feel that the focus of the tax administration is only procedural compliance and not substantive compliance, their natural response would be in that direction.

It was found in the study that a substantial number of respondents felt that the income tax department was not well equipped to detect tax evasion. Coming from the 'horse's mouth', it needs to be taken seriously. The extent of unaccounted money and the number of tax evasion methods have increased manifold over the last few decades. The strict enforcement regarding due dates for filing returns, furnishing of audit reports, quoting of PAN, deduction of tax at source, advance tax payments, etc has helped in ensuring procedural compliance among the taxpayers. However, weak scrutiny of assessments, investigations of poor quality, and lack of evidentiary value for the documents gathered against errant taxpayers have resulted in the perception that the entire enforcement system is weak. While about 75 per cent of the respondents in study-1 felt that penal provisions for tax evasion should be strictly followed, it is a fact that penalties are levied only in very few cases and the number of cases where tax evaders are prosecuted is much less. Thus, the public opinion is not in favour of a soft tax administration while dealing with evaders.

Audits (scrutiny) have a crucial role to play in detecting tax evasion and in ensuring substantive compliance. Studies done in the context of several advanced countries show that most taxpayers who had been audited once are more likely than those who have not been audited to comply with their tax obligations, even though the risk of their being audited again is no higher than before. (Jenkins *et al*, 1993) However, such a trend is not visible in India due to obvious reasons mentioned earlier. The perception that the tax enforcement is weak has made taxpayers think in terms of utilizing the possible avenues for tax evasion.

An examination of the income tax enforcement measures is appropriate in the light of the facts reported in study 2. Income tax searches are, undoubtedly, one of the important deterrent measures in India. However, a fresh look at the whole process of income tax searches is necessary in the light of the findings of the study. The enforcement strategies and the outlook and approaches of the enforcing officials need a re-orientation. As found in study-2, searches had resulted in serious emotional and health consequences for a substantial number of searched persons and their families. The focus of the search process should be exclusively on the desired objectives ensuring minimal latent consequences of such action on the other party. The study also indicates the relevance of formulation and effective application of alternate deterrent strategies and measures other than the income tax searches. Some such measures like collection of information on investments and income from various sources and immediate matching of the same with the returns, quality investigation through detailed scrutiny of records furnished, etc are to be streamlined effectively. These would be much more result-oriented in curbing evasion by a large cross section of people with least latent consequences, consequent to the income tax searches as reported in this study.

Taxpayer-tax authority game

There is a strong perception among the taxpayers that the tax enforcement is weak in the country. Taxpayers are also aware of the extent of investigation conducted during the scrutiny assessments and also have some basic idea of the functioning of the enforcement wing. Similarly, tax authorities are, to a much greater extent, aware of the nature of tax evasion prevailing in their vicinity. It is also true that several taxpayers know that the tax authority is aware of the tax behaviour of the taxpayers. However, to a limited extent, there are areas where both these 'groups' are unaware of each other's strategies. Taxpayers tend to comply with the procedures, as they perceive stricter enforcement for procedural compliance by way of notices, charging of interests, etc.

Also, the respondents do have a strong faith in the ideology of taxation and they consider taxation as an instrument for achieving development and welfare in the country. However, taxpayers do not consider the tax department as an institution that effectively facilitates this objective. There is a long gap or distance between the tax department and the taxpayers. As Natalie Taylor argues, (Taylor, 2003) at a super-ordinate level, where there is a 'we' feeling by the tax payer about the tax department, there will definitely be more tax compliance. However, at a sub-group level of identity where there is only a narrow perspective about the tax department there will be less compliance. If the tax authority is perceived by the taxpayers as an institution doing a fair job and not as an extra-territorial authority out to harm the income earners, then there would be better co-operation and tax compliance. Such an atmosphere can happen only if the tax administration takes systematic steps to demonstrate its fairness, efficiency and firmness before the public.

Inter-group comparison and fairness perception

Perception of fairness is an important factor in tax behaviour. Data gathered from both the sets of respondents in studies 1 and 2 have revealed that a substantial number of the people were of the view that the tax administration was not always fair. About 35 per cent of the respondents felt that the Income Tax Department had not taken action against all types of evaders. 65 per cent of the respondents felt that political and bureaucratic interference made tax administration unfair. The searched group of respondents, though it had agreed in the same proportion to the former view, had disagreed substantially with the latter view. Unlike what is projected in the media, a majority of the searched respondents vouch that with political or bureaucratic interference, anyone who gets caught in an income tax search cannot easily get away. That is definitely a complement for the investigative agency as the views expressed are from the own experience of the searched respondents. However, both the sets of respondents perceived that the tax system is not neutral to all categories of taxpayers. This response points to the perception that some are taxed, some are not and some are taxed too much and others too less due to various political and related reasons. Thus, the problem is not only rooted in enforcement, but also at the policy level.

Inter-group comparison is very much a fact when tax decisions are taken by the people. One of the most common comparisons is the one between the 'rich' and the 'poor'. There may be a feeling by the 'rich' that they are supporting the vast majority financially even as many in that majority can afford to pay. The feeling that they are overburdened for the sake of a vast non-paying majority would create a negative tax attitude. On the contrary, the 'poor' may also perceive unfairness when they feel that they pay the indirect taxes and other local taxes on equal rates along with the 'rich' group who tend to conceal their income from taxation.

Similarly, various occupational groups such as the business class, the salaried class and the professionals would also feel that they are not being fairly treated. In the present sample, though the attitudinal differences among the above three groups were not found to be statistically significant, the interviews have revealed the apprehensions of each group in terms of the others' tax compliance and tax liability. While the salaried class felt that they paid the tax correctly as the same is deducted at the source itself, they perceived that the business and the professional classes concealed their income in spite of the fact that they enjoyed several deductions which are unavailable for the salaried class. Interestingly, and quite surprisingly, the salaried class also perceived that they indulged in income suppression. Though the quantum may be small, there is definitely a concealment of non-salary income (such as interest, rental, etc) from the employer while the employer makes computation for source deduction.

There is also a perception of unfairness among different business categories. While the trading sectors felt that the manufacturing sectors were given several tax incentives, the small-scale sectors felt that they were not given adequate concessions. Similar grievances were also raised between concerns engaged in domestic sales and those in the export sector. There is a plea that income has to be taxed source-neutral so that there is fairness across the trade and industry. Thus, the inter-group comparison by each group has led to a perceived inequity (horizontal, between occupational groups and vertical, between income groups). This has also resulted in a type of relative deprivation and consequently it has a bearing on the tax behaviour.

The framing and overflowing

The perceived inequity by the taxpayers discussed earlier can be analyzed through the concepts of framing and overflowing. While the concept of framing has been developed by E Goffman, (1971) the term was linked to the concept of overflowing by Michael Callon (1991.) The frame establishes a boundary (may be a set of rules and laws) within which interactions take place more or less independently of the surrounding context. Callon identified two approaches characterizing diametrically opposed attitudes. In the first approach, framing is the norm and the overflows are the exceptions, which must be contained and channelled with the help of appropriate investments. In the second approach, the overflowing is the rule. Here, framing is a 'fragile, artificial result based on substantial investments'. (Callon, 1998)

It is an undisputable fact that Indian tax laws are characterized by several exemptions and deductions as tax incentives for taxpayers. Some of them are available to all types of taxpayers, while others are limited to particular categories. Therefore, the various subsystems in the tax system have to customize themselves in order to cater to particular requirements. Thus, discretions and liberal constructions and interpretations of rules become part of the system. In 'framing', all laws, rules, procedures, enforcement subsystems, assessments and service subsystems, etc would be uniform and static across the taxpayer categories, that too for a long period. However, in a tax system characterized by 'overflowing', there would be discretions, subjectivity, loopholes, liberal constructions and interpretations of statutes, etc. Political patronage and pressure groups play a significant role in such an overflowing.

However, the above overflow can be positive or negative. It is positive when it is applied for ensuring social justice and equity. This happens in situations where particular statutes are disadvantageous to a section of the taxpayers by virtue of their economic or social positions. It is negative when such overflowing creates negative externalities and also amounts to favouritism and inequity. It is necessary that the tax system be flexible to the needs of various categories of taxpayers, but that flexibility has to be based on consistent, fair and rational analyses of the demands and the needs and not based on narrow political or bureaucratic considerations and the influence of any pressure groups.

Multiple determinants of tax attitudes and resultant cognitive dissonance

The tax attitude study clearly indicates that tax attitudes of the people are shaped by multiple factors. The cognitive component is based on beliefs and ideas about the tax system as a whole (rationale of taxation, awareness of tax system, tax structure, etc). It depends on their perception of the role of the state and an awareness of the concept of social welfare. It is also based on an awareness of personal needs and responsibilities. The affective component of the tax attitudes is based on the perception of what is actually happening around them and this is ultimately based on personal judgements of situations. It is also based on citizens' own tax experiences. Thus, there is a tendency either to empathize, or to be passive or aggressive in their attitudes. The third element of the tax attitude is behavioural. The attitudes formed may lead to a predisposition to act in a particular manner. However, since several factors are involved in shaping the attitudes, the characteristics of most of these factors are in flux and not static; that means the behaviour cannot be predicted with precision and also it may be subject to change. In many cases therefore, the taxpayers who express a particular type of attitude may not behave in the same way in a real-life decision-making situation. As Massey (2002) describes, 'consistency of thought and action implies a rationality and thoughtfulness that does not always occur in the behaviour of individuals in everyday life.' Tax attitudes are in a flux and are therefore not enduring. Particular individuals and groups may form attitudes, which they may themselves change in different periods of time and circumstances depending upon their experience and exposure to causal factors.

Individuals strive towards consistency within themselves. Their opinions and attitudes tend to exist in clusters that are internally consistent. There is the same kind of consistency between what a person knows or believes and what the person does. But there are exceptions. Often, an individual would face difficulties in 'maintaining the face.'[1] What captures one's attention here are the exceptions to otherwise consistent behaviour. There may be inconsistencies between a person's opinions and beliefs and the actual behaviour. As seen in the data gathered, the respondents were well aware of the constructive role of the state in achieving development and welfare for the country. They also did not have any doubt regarding the necessity of taxation as a tool for raising revenue for developmental and welfare initiatives of the state. Thus, at the cognitive level, there is a positive perception and a consequent predisposition to act in consonance. Therefore, in these cases, cognitive consistency could be expected. However, as seen from the data on perception of self-tax behaviour, a substantial number of respondents admitted that they evaded the taxes. As inertia sets in over a period of time due to continuous non-compliance, it becomes increasingly difficult for the non-complier to change his habits. (Spicer, 1986) What interferes with the positive predisposition originating at the cognitive level is the affective component. This is a synthesis of what is perceived to be the behavioural pattern in society, one's own past experiences and one's judgement of the functioning of the State and the tax system. Thus, the taxpayers' experience what may be termed as cognitive dissonance,[2] leading to unintended tax behaviour.

Endogenous and Exogenous Stimuli

Tax attitudes consist of cognitive, affective and behavioural components and this multiplicity of factors often creates dissonance. There are both personal and situational factors that contribute to tax behaviour. The analysis shows that there are both endogenous and exogenous factors, which induce particular types of tax behaviour. Some such key factors are enumerated in Text Box TB - 8.1

As the tax administration and enforcement are perceived to be weak, tax-system-generated exogenous factors do not contribute much to tax compliance. The endo-exogenous factors are important and decide strongly in favour of either tax compliance or tax non-compliance. As seen from the data gathered in the studies given in earlier chapters, taxpayers have strong perceptions about the tax behaviour of others.

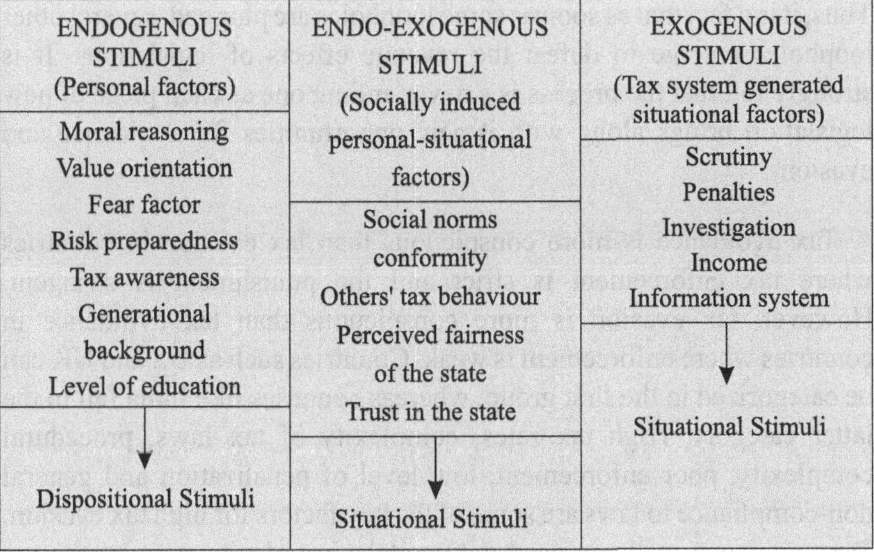

Text Box T.B.-8.1

They are also very much aware of the role performance of the State. This awareness is integrated to their own personal (endogenous) factors such as value, orientation, ideology, perception of the role of the state and general awareness. Factors such as generational background, educational background and occupational background also exert an influence, though marginally.

The evasion-avoidance ambiguity

In both the studies, a substantial number of taxpayers had identified shortcomings of the income tax laws and rules among the reasons for the low tax compliance. High prevalence of tax evasion often has its roots in liberal interpretation of laws and rules for avoiding taxes. The meanings of tax evasion and tax avoidance are almost indistinguishable to many taxpayers. However, tax authorities feel that both tax evasion and tax avoidance are unfair as the latter is perceived as a direct result of exploiting loopholes in the existing laws and rules. There is always a long time lag between several instances of tax avoidance behaviour and consequent plugging of the loopholes with necessary legal amendments.

Thus, it is a fact that as soon as some loopholes are plugged, several other loopholes emerge to defeat the revenue effects of legislations. It is strongly felt that the process is a never ending one as each piece of new legislation brings along with it new opportunities for avoidance and evasion.

Tax avoidance is more conspicuous than tax evasion in countries where tax enforcement is strict and the punishment is stringent. However, tax evasion is more conspicuous than tax avoidance in countries where enforcement is weak. Countries such as US and UK can be categorized in the first group, whereas countries like India fall in the latter category. High tax rates, complexity of tax laws, procedural complexity, poor enforcement, low level of penalization and general non-compliance to laws are some of the key factors for high tax evasion. Tax avoidance methods used deliberately in order to defraud the tax department are also as serious as tax evasion. What is being emphasized here is that the economic consequences of both are the same. (Cross and Shaw, 1982)

Reciprocity and the perception of corruption

In study-1, it was found that about 40 per cent of the respondents felt that the government had failed in its role as a service provider for the people. This view came out of a sample which felt that taxation is necessary for the overall development of the country (92 per cent) and that income taxation is an appropriate measure to raise revenue for the nation (72 per cent). Though the people are aware of the rationale and necessity of taxation, still there is large-scale non-compliance. One of the reasons as seen from the current study is the perception of poor reciprocity in terms of State's services. Here, there are three possibilities: a) 'I do not perceive the reciprocity from the State in terms of personal goods to the extent of my contribution.', b) 'I do not perceive the reciprocity from the State in terms of public goods to the extent of my contribution.', and c) 'I do not perceive that the contribution of others is proportionate to mine.' The data showed that the respondents were not very keen about what they got personally from the state. However they were worried about the state's contribution to society as a whole. Therefore, the attitude is not that since one is not utilizing the collective goods in proportion to his contribution, one need not pay up. On the contrary, non-compliance is attributed more to what society fails to get from the state. Thus, the taxpayer is concerned about the inadequate visibility of investments in public goods. In both studies, substantial numbers of respondents felt that corruption in the government was the main reason for low tax compliance. This definitely indicates their personal perception, which would have contributed to their own tax behaviour.

Nature of state and taxpayer behavioural response

As discussed in Chapter four, many political scientists are of the view that tax policy evolves as a result of the ideology of particular political parties in power as well as the views of the dominant pressure groups. Scholars have also argued that the taxation and tax compliance have deep political significances as there are different degrees of compliance under different political systems.[3] If one classifies states very broadly, in terms of their nature of responses to public opinion, the following would be some prominent labels appropriate for them: welfare state (state which works for overall welfare, including a coalition state where no single group has substantial public support); representative statc (state ruled by a group with a clear mandate and which got elected on the basis of particular ideologies); authoritarian state (state with absolute power which cannot be questioned); societal state (ruled by various competing social groups founded primarily by primordial collectivities); partisan state (state ruled by and for a particular dominant group); and abusive state (which wields power illegitimately and acts solely for those in power). Different countries would have different types of authority in different periods in history. While some countries continue with the same types of elite circulating in different forms (as described by Pareto[4]), other countries face contrasting types of governments.

The stimulus for tax behaviour	Ideology/basic premise	State and tax governance	Characteristic features of the tax system
COMMITMENT	Sense of duty to state and society	Welfare state	Fairness Patriotism justice
RESPECT	State has the legitimacy to collect taxes	Representative state	Well laid out rules. Lack of loop-holes
FEAR	State wields unquestionable power to enforce taxes	Authoritarian state	Strong penal measures and enforcement Fairness not important
SOCIAL SANCTION	Social institutions and groups influence taxpayer attitudes and behaviour	Societal state (in conformity with the public opinion rather than its own stable policy)	Affected by the social sentiments and groups' behaviour
APATHY	State is unfair and not trust worthy	Partisan state	Tax system is perceived as inequitable and biased
PROTEST	Illegitimate tax laws and abusive power and misuse	Excessive?/ abusive? state	Unjust and unfair tax collection

Text Box T.B.-8.2

India is an example of a country which has witnessed different types of authority over a period of time. The fiscal policies evolved in India over a period of time with marked changes in the nature and objectives as a latent result of the dominant factors and characteristics of each period. While the system of taxation in ancient and medieval India had predominant cultural and religious moorings, with an inherent disparity based on caste, community and religion, the system in the colonial period had taken a purely 'economic' character with an unquestionable bias favouring the interests of the British government. Later, we see that the ideology and rationale of taxation in the post-independent India was radically different from the preceding tax history. Taxation had become a social legislation and it was projected as an instrument for social welfare, equity and justice. Redistribution was one of the primary objectives of the State in an economically stratified society. Thus, the very same nation (or group of nationalities) can be seen to have oscillated between societal state, partisan state, authoritarian state and welfare state under different rulers and governments. Compliance of the citizens under different regimes was also in tune with the nature of authorities and the fiscal policies thereof. In contrast to the 'conventional economic explanation' summarized by the term *Homo economicus,* scholars are of the view that (Bowles and Gintis, 2000) people support the welfare state because it conforms to deeply-held norms of reciprocity and conditional obligations to others. The size and nature of the factors influencing compliance may be different in different countries.[5] Our analysis of the literature of tax behaviour under various types of governments has indicated that there is a strong nexus between the nature of the State and the corresponding tax behaviour of the people.

India is attempting to achieve the ideal of a 'welfare state'. The tax system of a welfare state would ideally be characterized by fairness, patriotism and justice. As the data gathered in the present study reveal, there is a perception among a substantial number of taxpayers that the tax system is not totally fair. Though there is a sense of duty to the State and society, the taxpayers' perception of the role performance of the State and the general tax behaviour in society have resulted in a feeling of apathy along with the desired feeling of commitment. The dissonance is manifested in unexpected tax behaviour, which is rationalized by the view that tax enforcement is weak. Also issues of fairness and reciprocity are projected. Thus, trust in the State and the tax system gets eroded and that leads to tax non-compliance. However, the sense of commitment at the cognitive level tries to reduce the dissonance and accounts for the tax compliance. A mixed behavioural pattern emerges out of these contrasting predispositions (mixed perception of state as 'welfare state' and 'partisan state').

In a perfectly competitive economy, the individuals are guided exclusively by self-interest in respect of their tax compliance. However, in markets which are substantially competitive, the taxpayers are guided both by self-interest as well as by reciprocity. Thus, conditionality in compliance is a very predominant trait in highly competitive markets. In India, the tax compliance would be based on both reciprocity and a pro-social behaviour. As seen from the data gathered in this study, taxpayers are concerned about what is coming back to society from the taxes collected, and not much worried about what are the personal gains in the exchange. The other extreme situation is where people pay taxes just because of their pro-social attitudes. But both the egoistic extreme (in perfect markets) and altruistic extreme (in zero-competitive environment) are only just ideal types to a great extent.

Information on tax compliance in the public domain

Information regarding the compliance level of others is important for self-compliance. In both the empirical studies, the taxpayers had stated that most of the people they knew were dishonest in disclosing their income. The above information need not be necessarily based on any first hand information. In many cases such inference is coming out of what is generally talked about in public or based on what is projected in the media. One cannot deny the fact there are substantial tax evasions taking place in the country. However, it is also pertinent to think in the other dimension. There is also an increasing tendency among people to pay tax voluntarily and there is a growing realization that tax compliance can be less burdensome if there is proper tax planning. Respondents are also not unaware of the increasing compliance in the recent years. In study -1, seventysix per cent of the respondents agreed that there was better voluntary compliance to income tax in the recent years.

In a laboratory experiment by Trivedi, Shehata and Lynn (2003), it was found that standard enforcement policies based on punishment alone should be supplemented by an information system that would acquaint taxpayers with the compliance level of other taxpayers. What is required in India is an organized and systematic information flow from the tax department to the public about exemplary cases of tax compliance in various sectors and also information regarding stringent punishments imposed on evaders.

Musgrave (1997) rightly commented that 'what reason is there to expect that good taxation - taxation that is equitable as well as efficient - should offer a haven of simplicity in an increasingly complex world?' Taxation is becoming more and more complex as the economy gets complex with the rapid rise in business opportunities. The challenge before the tax administrators is to make it as simple and transparent as possible for the taxpayers because complexity should not be a reason for tax non-compliance.

CHAPTER-9

TAXATION IN A GLOBALIZED WORLD

Transitional and Transnational Challenges

Taxation continues to be an inevitable instrument to raise resources for a nation. As we saw in the earlier chapters, parting a portion of the earnings as income tax is not always a pleasant experience. Factors affecting affirmative tax behaviour are many. The universal apathy towards taxation is rooted in the original objectives of income taxation as a means to perpetuate war on communities and nations and to consolidate the power of the ruling elite. The discriminatory and inequitable character of taxation in various historic stages resulted in protests and dissent in many parts of the world. Of late, as democratic ideology found popular acceptance and legitimacy, there is an increased recognition of the rationale of taxation and consequent acceptance as an important economic institution benefiting the individuals and the states. Thus the policies, strategies, structure and methodology of taxation and tax enforcement were derived from an economic utilitarian perspective. Political and sociological determinants in tax behaviour have been grossly underplayed. As discussed in the preceding chapters, tax compliance, to a larger extent depends on various non-economic factors and utilitarian and rational taxpayers are only ideal types. Tax compliance is not just an action based on tax rates but also influenced by various other historical and sociological factors. Therefore, various social-structural determinants in tax behaviour need to be appropriately considered while making policies and procedures related to taxation. This is the main thread of all the descriptions and discussions in this book. However, our discussion cannot be complete without looking at the trajectory tax systems all over the world are taking in the wake of globalization. There are far-reaching consequences in the entire gamut of taxation as territorialities related to business transactions are becoming increasingly fluid.

MAKING PEOPLE PAY

Globalization has brought in radical transformation in every aspect of life. There is hardly any sphere of life that is untouched by the forces that are unleashed in the wake of this global revolution. Businesses spread their wings far and wide. Firewalls that insulated the economies broke down. Relationships and social behaviour found new meanings in the virtual world. The leaps in technology and communication have changed the way people do business. An improvement in overall quality of life is visible, though one is not sure whether the growth is equitable or not within and between the nations.

Is globalization good for tax systems?

There are contrasting views on this.[1] While some argue that globalization would fatally undermine the national tax state, others argue that it hardly constraints tax policy choices. Genschel (2005), after a comparative analysis of the first three decades of the 20th century to the last three decades, find that the effect of globalization is not so much to force change upon the tax state as to reduce its freedom for change. Though procedural and legislative changes are inevitable for many countries, what is more serious, particularly for the developing countries, is the fear about erosion in tax base. Tanzi (2000) used the words 'fiscal termites' while analyzing the impact of globalization. Studying a large number of industrialized countries, he has found that the work of these termites will eventually bring serious damage to the fiscal houses.[2] The study by Garret and Mitchell (2001) of 18 countries in the OECD showed that measured by volume of the exchanges or the opening of the financial market, economic globalization does not decrease tax on capital, but it reduces the total public expenditure.

Most of the countries depend on income taxation as a source of substantial revenue. The power to tax is the sovereign power of the states and they survive on the due share from every citizen who earns his income from whatever sources and many times irrespective of the place of incidence of income. States also consider it their right to demand a share from every person and entity that earn income within their territorial jurisdiction irrespective of their citizenship or domiciles. However in this era of trans-national mobility and transactions in virtual space, the fear of states losing out on the much-needed tax revenue is not totally unfounded.

Tax competition

Countries have been quick in formulating rules and procedures related to international taxation. There is no uniformity in the tax treatment across countries on taxation of income earned outside their own countries. Countries such as the US, the UK, and Japan use a worldwide system of taxation with a foreign tax credit. Countries such as France and Netherlands use a territorial system that exempts foreign income from taxation. In India, residence-based taxation is applied for residents and source-based taxation for non-residents. Some countries have specific tax rules based on the tax treaties signed with other countries. Differences in tax incidence between countries encourage many multinational firms to alter their transfer prices.[3] Though transfer pricing norms have been enacted in several countries, there is enough scope to manipulate the norms as the arms-length prices are always in a flux due to the difficulties in their determination for many intermediate goods and services and also for intangibles.[4] In a competitive economy, business entities may find it difficult to go for flexible pricing to retain the clients or to canvas new clients because of the transfer pricing norms. Though there are discussions on the scope of transitioning to a global formulary apportionment system as compared with the arm's length approach, there is no consensus on the same within many countries. However, neither the formulary apportionment nor the arm's length system can effectively tackle the issues of tax loss or double taxation.[5]

Strategies such as raising capital through loans from a high tax country for their entire business operations to realize a reduced net profit as compared with earning a higher net profit in a low tax country are also widely adopted. Companies tend to incorporate themselves away from their home countries just on tax considerations. Such strategies would reduce the taxable revenues of particular countries, without necessarily making other countries better off. Thus there could be an overall dip in global revenues from income tax due to lack of uniformity in taxation across the countries. Most affected would be the countries that cannot reduce their tax rates beyond an optimum level due to low tax -GDP ratio, low tax compliance and substantial welfare commitments.

Withering welfare state?

Surviving the waves of globalization is not an easy task for many developing countries. Most of these countries are in the category of low tax-GDP ratio, low tax compliance and substantial welfare commitments. They are compelled to focus on two areas, though both eventually may lead to erosion in tax base. First is the attempt to reduce the tax burden on home country businesses that face tough competition for their products and services from players originating elsewhere. This will affect the overall tax revenue. At the same time, it is necessary to create a level playing field to attract more businesses from outside the country in order to overcome the stiff inter-country competition to attract investments. On this count also, countries lose substantial tax revenue. Thus there would be an overall dent in the tax revenue of several developing countries. That would affect social sector allocation. Optimistic views such as, less developed countries still have distinct welfare regimes, demonstrating a capacity to formulate different social policies,[6] are too far - fetched.

Many states are under constitutional obligation to create an environment that promotes prosperity and well-being of the people. India, like many such states, has a constitutional commitment to be a welfare state. Directive Principles contained in the Constitution of India contemplate measures to secure equitable distribution of resources. Article 47 obligates the State to regard, as among its primary duties, the raising of the standard of living of its people and the improvement of public health. As a country with more than 28 per cent of the population below the poverty line,[7] it depends substantially on its direct tax collections for fulfilling the constitutional obligations.[8] Similar is the case with many other developing countries. Therefore, determined efforts are needed to ensure sufficiently adequate tax revenue.

The rules relating to the transfer of capital and taxability of international transactions need to be formulated and applied after considering the overall deficiency in the home economy. The question would be whether particular countries can afford to provide such freedom at the cost of scaling down the funds for welfare.

The need to see beyond tax rates

Though thcrc is an environment of tax competition as businesses look for countries that offer most favourable tax treatment, it is imperative to ponder whether that is the only factor that can promote businesses in another country. It is prudent for the business entities to think beyond tax rates and analyze the opportunities and strengths in the destination country as compared to those available in the home country. Factors such as the nature of the government, political stability, regulatory systems, law and order, infrastructure, wage rates, and quality and efficiency of the labour force are crucial while arriving at a decision. It is necessary to have a clear understanding of the factors mentioned above before deciding on any trans-national venture or planning for any business transplantation.

An analysis of the empirical studies about the status of particular businesses and evaluation of the socio-political and economic environment of the interested countries is required. Apart from periodic reports of various international bodies such as the IMF, the World Bank, and the OECD, studies conducted by individual scholars and research institutions, may be perused before taking decisions. There is a need for in-depth empirical studies examining the net tax loss or tax gain in the overall global economy due to the internationalization of business transactions and tax flight. Governments and business associations need to do systematic risk analysis and accordingly guide the entrepreneurs and businessmen on the potential and challenges of international ventures.

Relevance of a Global Tax Research and Analysis Organization (GTRAO)

Taxes are ubiquitous. There are more commonalities than differences among tax systems of various countries in terms of tax objectives and tax policies, though there are major differences with respect to tax structure and the extent of tax compliance. In a globalized business and professional environment, tax policies can no longer remain insulated within a particular state territory. Policies, rules and procedures of countries get influenced by one another and tend to congruent with common and interconnected issues. However, there are possibilities of disputes and misunderstandings between business entities and also between tax systems. Many small and developing countries may require factual and legal guidance on global tax matters. There need to be uniformity in international taxations so that no country loses out on the tax revenue. There is relevance for a Global Tax Research and Analysis Organization (GTRAO) to study the issues relating to global taxation and to update the countries by disseminating the results of its analyses.

This is not a suggestion for a global regulatory authority. Tax sovereignty of the states cannot be undermined through any global authority. There was a proposal in the late 1990s for a 'Global Tax Organization' (GTO)[9] on the lines of World Trade Organization (WTO). What is needed is not a regulator, but a nodal agency at the global level which is purely a body that engages in research and analysis on taxation for all countries. It can work as surveillance and reporting body to detect tax leakages globally as well as related to particular states. The body can also work to ensure tax co-ordination among the countries facilitating exchange of information and verification.

Varying degrees of tax compliance

While thinking of a congruence in tax treatment in the context of international taxation, one major worry is the varying degrees of tax compliance across countries. Though tax evasion is a universal phenomenon, the extent of evasion in some countries is much greater as compared with low degree of evasion in some other countries. This is discussed in detail in chapter 3. As we saw in chapter six and chapter seven, more than 65 per cent of the respondents of the studies had admitted that they evade part of their taxes. It is surprising to find that more than 40 per cent of taxpayers continue to conceal their income even after an income tax search on them. In very few cases detailed audits have been done that resulted in detection of suppression of income and imposition of penalty. However, there is a sharp increase in procedural compliance (such as obtaining Permanent Account Number issued by the Income Tax Department, filing of tax returns within the due dates, deducting tax at source, and payment of advance tax). What is lacking is the substantive compliance where one discloses the full income for the purpose of income taxation. Strengthening of the enforcement system is necessary to ensure substantive compliance among the taxpayers. In a globalized economic environment, countries need to have strong enforcement systems to plug tax leakages that have a bearing on the tax revenues of other countries as well. Though a hundred per cent tax compliance may be a utopian expectation, systematic efforts to increase the tax compliance level by developing countries will be rewarding for them as that will boost their welfare agenda. These countries can attract businesses and investments by providing a rationalized tax structure, simplified tax laws, transparent procedures and service oriented administration.

Making People Pay

The first chapter of this book started with the following question. Is paying taxes a matter of money or mind? As we come to the end of this book, it is amply clear that tax compliance is more a matter of mind than a matter of money. As we analyzed the historical origins and growth of taxation of income in different parts of the world and in India, it was found that the 'mentalities' of the people which got shaped by historical experiences had a bearing on the attitude towards taxation. Popular psyche has been ingrained over generations with apathy towards taxation as it was either discriminatory or used for selfish interests of the authority or for financing unjust wars. Taxation continues to be the major and constant revenue source all over the world. For the last several decades taxation has been approached, analyzed and redesigned from a utilitarian perspective and mostly considered as an exclusive terrain of economists. Though there was growing academic interest to examine tax evasion from the angles of criminological and social psychological approaches, these did not translate into appropriate policy interventions. In recent years there is a clear shift to the utilitarian school in the wake of economic globalization. Inappropriateness of such an approach for tax-states of the developing world has been underscored in this book. Political context of taxation, which is described in detail in chapter four, has both positive and negative ramifications for compliance and evasion. It can play a very constructive role in pluralistic societies to ensure equitable and objective tax system.

No analysis is complete without empirical back up as detailed in chapter six and chapter seven. Data collected from taxpayers themselves have revealed that the tax attitudes and perceptions of taxpayers are influenced by their attitudes and perceptions about the State and governance. It was also found that tax attitudes and perceptions of taxpayers and consequent tax behaviour are influenced by their perceptions of tax attitudes and tax behaviour of others. It is found that money is not the crucial factor in tax decisions. What mattered was one's perception of the State and the society. Similar results have emerged from the study on the sample of taxpayers who faced income tax search for alleged tax evasion. The study has pointed out the sociological causes and consequences of tax evasion and tax enforcement. Detailed analyses of the studies and policy suggestions are already given in chapter eight.

The entire gamut of tax non-compliance has been analyzed at both macro and micro levels under four broad headings: A Matter of Time, A Matter of Money, A Matter of Power and A Matter of Mind. The attempt was to examine the significant role played by each in influencing tax attitudes and tax behaviour. The theoretical critique, the historical review, and the empirical analyses have pointed out the predominant role played by the economic-sociological factors in shaping tax attitudes and behaviour. While tax decisions are made by people, what matters more are not costs and benefits, but their attitudes and perceptions of the State and the society. In this universal exercise of making people pay without any proportionate reciprocal benefits, the states can only cash in on people's altruistic spirit, empathy and tolerance. Such virtues will be plenty only when the exercise is fair, efficient, transparent and reasonable.

NOTES

CHAPTER - 1

1 A brief review of studies where tax compliance costs for the taxpayers of different countries have been estimated by various scholars has been given in Jenkins, Glenn P and Edwin N Forlemu (1993).

2 The term 'tax gap' is used to indicate the extent of unpaid tax out of total tax due from the taxable income generated in any country.

3 See a detailed discussion on this in John and Li (1999).

4 Swedberg (1998) has given a detailed description on the evolution of idea of economic sociology from the days of Max Weber. Also see Smelser and Swedberg (1994)

5 New Economic Sociology as a branch of study emerged in the 1980s at Harward. Though it started as a counter to economists who believed in perfect rationality, the conceptual foundations are appropriate while analyzing interdisciplinary issue like tax evasion.

CHAPTER - 2

1 Writings by Brownie, 2004; Bartley and Richardson,1998; Brown and Mary,1996 contain description of the characteristic features of the systems of taxation in each period

2 Such interesting tax snippets as mentioned in this book can be seen in www.taxworld.org/history/tax History. htm

3 Officially titled the "People's Initiative to Limit Property Taxation," and popularly known as the "Jarvis-Gann Amendment," Proposition 13 was placed on the ballot through the California ballot initiative process. The U.S. Supreme Court declared in *Nordlinger v. Hahn* that Proposition 13 was constitutional. Justice Harry Blackmun, writing the majority opinion, noted that the state had a "legitimate interest in local neighborhood preservation, continuity, and stability", and that it was acceptable to treat owners who have invested for some time in property differently than new owners

4 See Sears, D.O., and J Citrin (1985), and Beito, D.T. (1989). Also see Peter (1991)

5 See Haws Robert J (1983) in Phillip Sawicki (1983).

6 According to Hinduism, Manu is the oldest law giver. The code of Manu is known as *manusmriti*. *Smriti* means "that which has to be remembered".

7 As mentioned in the book 'Hundred Years of Income-tax Department 1886-1985', Directorate of Inspection, Central Board of Direct Taxes, New Delhi,1985, p.3-4

8 Detailed description can be seen in Laws of Manu, Chapters VII to IX http://www.hinduwebsite.com/sacredscripts/hinduism/dharma

MAKING PEOPLE PAY

CHAPTER - 3

1 E F Schumacher proposed the idea that 'small is beautiful' as early as in 1973. However his suggestion for maitaining 'smallness within bigness' has become an impossibility in the wake of globalization.

2 Public goods are narrowly defined as goods that are 'non-excludable' as well as 'non-rival'. According to this definition, it is not possible to exclude individuals from the goods' consumption. Examples of such public goods are clean air, information in public domain, public transport, law enforcement, etc. But in the current context, a better term for provisions by the government for the needy people would be 'publicly provided goods'.

3 A review can be found in Slemrod (1990)

4 See for example, 'The Elasticity of Taxable Income: Evidence and Implications' *(NBER Working Paper No. 7512)*, NBER Research Associate Jonathan Gruber and co-author Emmanuel Saez, http://www.nber.org/digest/jul00/w7512.html

5 See details in the Report of the Joint Economic Committee (1986), Also see Mitchell, Daniel J. (2002)

6 Details are available in http://www.huppi.com/kangaroo/L-taxcollections.htm

7 http://home.att.net/~rdavis2/taxcuts.html

8 http://www.oecd.org/document/11/0,2340. See also Table AT 3.1

9 However it is important that there is no uniformity on what constitutes taxes while arriving at the percentage of the GDP. Most estimates are based on the total direct and indirect taxes and state and federal taxes.

10 Please see, Tanzi, Vito (1987), 'Quantitative Characteristics of the Tax Systems of Developing Countries', in David Newbery and Nicolas Stern, eds., The Theory of Taxation for Developing Countries, World Bank, Oxford University Press

11 See the report of the World Bank (1998)

12 This view can be seen in, James and Nobes (1994)

13 See the details in the report, 'Confronting the Problems of Tax Avoidance and Evasion: Selected Countries in Asia and the Pacific' (1987), Project of the Study Group on Asian Tax Administration and Research, National Tax Research Center, Philippines, Department of Finance

14 A committee headed by Dr E.A.S Sarma was set up in 2000 in order to recommend draft legislation on fiscal responsibility. The committee submitted its report in the same year. Indian parliament enacted the law in 2003. Under Section 7 of the Fiscal Responsibility and Budget Management Act, no deviation is permissible in meeting the obligations cast on the central government under the Act, without the approval of the parliament.

NOTES

[15] Quoted in the statement laid before parliament during union budget 2008 by the Minister of Finance, P Chidambaram (February 2008)

[16] As per the Indian Public Finance Statistics 2008-09, Government of India. It can be viewed at http://finmin.nic.in/reports/index.html

[17a] It is reported in the Annual report of Ministry of Finance and can be viewed at http://finmin.nic.in/reports/index.html

[17b] Please see the Discussion paper on the Direct Taxes code, issued by the Department of Revenue, Ministry of Finance, Government of India (2010). Details can also be found is www.incometaxindia.gov.in

[18] The views of Stigler in this regard is well-known. See, Stigler, George J. "The Theory of Economic Regulation," Bell J. Econ., (Spring 1971), 2, 3:21.

[19] The author is reluctant to use the terms 'black economy', 'black income', 'black money' etc as that would amount to associating the word 'black' to things which are undesirable and has negative connotations. However, wherever the terms are quoted from other sources, they are reproduced in the same manner to avoid misrepresentaion of facts.

[20] See Burton, John, 'Underground Economy in Britain', in Owen Lippert and Michael Walker (eds), The Underground Economy: Global Evidence Of Its Size And Impact, Canada ,The Fraser Institute Vancouver, British Columbia

[21] Quoted in Winkler, Raymundo, The Size and Some Effects of the Underground Economy in Mexico, in Owen Lippert and Michael Walker (eds), The Underground Economy: Global Evidence Of Its Size And Impact, Canada ,The Fraser Institute Vancouver, British Columbia

[22] "Roots of Gorbachev's Problems: Private Income and Outlay in the Late 1970s," Joint Economic Committee, US Congress, Gorbachev's Economic Plans, vol. 1, Washington, DC, 1987, pp. 213-229 quoted in Owen Lippert and Michael Walker (eds), The Underground Economy: Global Evidence Of Its Size And Impact, Canada ,The Fraser Institute Vancouver, British Columbia

[23] Please see, Cuccia, Andrew D (1994), 'Economics of tax compliance: What do we know and where do we go?, Journal of Accounting Literature, 1994, Vol 13.

[24] Studies are conducted in the related area by Blumenthal, M , Charles Christian and Joel Slemrod (2001). They have found that there is no evidence that normative appeals will bring in additional tax revenues and thus impact tax compliance

[25] See a review of studies in Richardson, M and Sawyer, A J 'A Taxonomy of the tax compliance literature: Further findings, problems and prospects' (2001) Vol 16, Australian Tax Forum, pp 137-320}

[26] See Milliron, Valerie C and Daniel R Toy,1988; Mason, Robert and Lyle D Calvin(1984); Poterba, James(1987). Contrasting findings are given by Slemrod, Joel (1985) and Dubin, Jeffrey A and Louise L Wilde (1988).

[27] http://www.irs.gov/businesses/article/0, id=205889,00.html

[28] The Wall Street Journal 10/12/09

29 See details in Kellner, Martin (2006) Tax Amnesty 2004-2005-An Appropriate Revenue Tool?, German Law Journal, Vol.5, No.4, 2006

30 The details of the study can be found in 'A review of the tax amnesty scheme', http://www.pakistaneconomist.com/issue 2000/issue29

CHAPTER - 4

1 A detailed analysis can be seen in Bird and Eric (2003)

2 See for example, Tomasic and Pentony (1990)

3 The concepts of horizontal equity and vertical equity have been challenged by many scholars as incomplete and misleading. Individuals can have different tastes and differential capacity to earn income. At the same time the status is not constant and there will be wide fluctuations within even a short period. It is also not very clear how the differences can be defined in different contexts.

4 Summarized from Clemen, S (1961). A Mysterious Visit, The Complete Humorous Sketches and Tales of Mark Twain, 145 (www.readbookonline.net)

5 This was underscored in detail in, Adams, J.S. (1965).

6 Please see Spicer and Lundstedt, (1976) ; and Etzioni, A (1986).

7 Gujarat state is ruled by the opposition party Bharathiya Janata Party and as against the central government led by Congress Party. The conflict clearly indicates the political context of tax policy. See Times of India, New Delhi, June 11, 2008

8 A detailed analysis has been given in Page, B I (1983)

9 'Electoral trust' as an entity has been recognized for the purposes of Indian Income Tax Act quite recently. See also, 'How do parties collect money?' http://www.rediff.com/election/2004/mar/ 25espec.htm .

10 'Corruption and the funding of UK Political Parties', Report of the Transparency International(UK), October 2006

11 See the details in http://indiaelectionwatch.net/whatisnew.htm , June 13, 2008

12 The Department of Economic Affairs in the Ministry of Finance issues detailed budget circulars to the concerned departments much before the budget exercise detailing the steps to be taken in the budget planning , proposal and formulation.

13 Revenue budget consists of the revenue receipts of government (tax revenues and other revenues) and the expenditure met from those revenues. Capital budget consists of capital receipts and capital payments. They are loans raised by government from public, called market loans, borrowings by government from Reserve Bank of India, loans received from foreign governments and bodies etc.

14 This is also found in, Pen, J (1987), Expanding budgets in a stagnating economy: The experience of the 1970s. In C.S. Maier (ed.), Changing Boundaries of the Political. Cambridge: Cambridge University Press.

15 Budget speeches of various Finance Ministers are available in http://indiabudget.nic.in/bspeech/bs196869.pdf

NOTES

CHAPTER - 5

1 Some such studies are Caroll (1987;1992), Kent (1990), and Etzioni (1988).

2 Also see Klepper,S and Nagin D (1989a, 1989b); Warneryd, K E and Walerud, B (1982); Clotfelter, C.T (1983); Porcano, TM (1988) and Wallschtzky, LG (1984) etc.

3 See for example, Ciadini, R B 'Social Motivations to Comply: Norms, Values and Principles', in Roth, JA, Scholz, J T and Witte, AD (eds) , Taxpayer Compliance Social Science Perspectives (1989), Vol 2, Philadelphia, PA, University of Pennsylvania Press, pp 200-227

4 Carter and Marco (2002) have given a detailed analysis of the economic impacts of altruism, trust and reciprocity with an experimental approach to the concept of social capital. Also see Fehr and Gachter (2000); Frey and Meier (2002); Bowles and Gintis (2002)

5 Alan H Plumley in his commentary (Slemrod, 1992) on the above study has stated as follows. 'The change in the voluntary compliance exhibited in subsequent years by those who have been contacted for enforcement purposes (which we call the 'subsequent year effect' and which Kinsey calls the 'special effects' of the 'personal contact') and the change in voluntary compliance exhibited by those who have not been contacted directly, but who form perceptions of the likelihood and severity of enforcement through indirect means such as others who have been contacted directly. We call this 'ripple effect', and Kinsey calls it the 'general effect' of the 'vicarious contact'".

6 See for example, Falkinger, J and Watter, H 'Rewards versus Penalties: On a New Policy on Tax Evasion' , Public Finance Quarterly, 19 (1991) pp 67-79

7 It may not matter what is happening as a whole in society. What matters for the individual is what he perceives as the behaviour of his group or his reference group. Objective relativism is the view that the beliefs of a person or group of persons are "true" for them, but not necessarily for others.

8 Looking-glass self is a conception of the 'social self' as arising 'reflectively' as the outcome of the reaction to the opinion of others. This term was coined by Charles Cooley.

9 Two most known studies are by Friedland, Maital and Rutenberg (1978) and Spicer and Becker (1980) who used laboratory settings to study income reporting.

10 Schwartz and Orleans (1967) administered three types of surveys to three different types of high income taxpayers. First group was given inputs on morality and second group was given inputs on sanctions prior to filing the returns. There was no inputs for the third group. Fourth group was not surveyed at all. It was found that the first group showed an increase in reported income compared to earlier years. Such

improvement was not found in other groups. Also see Bazart and Pickhardt (2009), Alm, Jackson and Mckee (1992).

11 The concept of 'self' is of interest to sociologists and psychologists. The perspective of symbolic interactionism of Mead is rooted in the concept of self. For Mead, it is the self that makes the distinctively human society possible.

CHAPTER - 6

1 Theorists whose work stands predominantly within the tradition of symbolic interactionism include Mead, Cooley, Becker and to a greater extent Erving Goffman. Intensive interview is an important methodological tool in this approach.

2 There were about 99500 taxpayers in the study area as per the computerized data base. Out of the above, random sample of 500 taxpayers were taken with the help of a software to ensure that the list is cutting across various circles and wards and different categories of assessees, and to ensure the representation as per selected variables. Out of the above list, fifty each of salaried, professional and business categories that fulfill the criteria were selected at random for interviews.

3 Quoted in Peters (1991) p.208

4 Proportionate weightages have been given to the statements for which first three ranks given by the respondents (First rank is given three points, second rank is given two points and the third rank one point).

5 Quoted in 'Hundred years of Income-tax Department 1886-1985' Directorate of Inspection, CBDT, 1986, P.10-11

6 Please see the study by Das-Gupta and Mookherjee (1998) where the scrutiny assessments of the Income tax department have been critically analyzed with data from the assessing officers.

7 The Right to Information bill passed recently by the Indian Government is a radical step in this direction. The above Act is aimed to provide for setting out the practical regime of right to information for citizens to secure access to information under the control of public authorities, in order to promote transparency and accountability in the working of every public authority

8 Out of the total score of 50, 38 per cent persons scored more than 32 points, and 35 per cent of persons scored less than 20 points. 27 per cent persons got scores between 21 and 31.

NOTES

CHAPTER - 7

[1] This is discussed in detail in the Report of Raja J. Chelliah (1991)

[2] (Dr Nanda Lal Tahiliyani vs Commissioner of Income Tax and others -Allahabad High Court), Income Tax Reports (India) Vol 170 Page 592

[3] Poorna Mal etc Vs. Director of Inspection (Investigation) of Income tax (1974), All India Reporter, 348

[4] Number of searches means number of search warrants executed in the main cases. In most of the cases more than one warrant will be issued to search the connected companies or firms and the individuals

[5] Most of the searches result in seizure of unaccounted assets such as cash, jewellery, deposits, stock etc. Total value of such seized assets are given in the column.

[6] Annual report of the Ministry of Finance for the year 2008-09. It can be viewed at http://finmin.nic.in/reports/index.html

[7] This is akin to the, 'reality construction business' propounded by Schwartz. See Schwartz and Jerry (1979)

[8] Out of the 74 searched respondents, 8.11 per cent were below 35 years, 28.38 per cent belong to the age group 36 to 45, 41.89 per cent belong to the age group 46 to 55 years and 21.62 per cent of respondents were more than 55 years old. There is comparatively less number of respondents in the age group of up to 35 years. In sample B, 36.36 per cent of the respondents were from the age group up to 35 years, 19.48 per cent of respondents were between 36 and 45 years, 31.17 per cent were between 46 and 55 years and the rest were above 55 years of age. Obviously, there were more young respondents in the sample B, unlike sample A where very few from the age group of below 35 years were searched. This variation does not affect analysis as 'age' is used as a variable only for very limited purposes in this study.

[9] The educational backgrounds of the respondents and their parents and grandparents have been analyzed in this study to understand the influence on tax awareness and also the attitudes and perceptions related to taxation. Following are the categories: Up to class 10, Plus Two (Pre Degree), Degree, and Post Graduates and above. The mean has been calculated after giving scores from 0 to 20. The mean score for all respondents is 11.6450, with a standard deviation of 5.5470; whereas the scores of the father and the mother are 5.2569 and 2.7770 respectively. Thus, it is seen that educational background of the respondents are much higher than their parents and the educational background of fathers are better than the educational background of mothers. In analysing the data gathered regarding the respondents' perception of search, the Total Educational Background (TEB) of sample A has been compared.

The TEB has been arrived at by totaling the comparative scores given to the educational qualification of self, parents and the grandparents. As per the data, 35.1 per cent of the respondents were from high TEB, 40.5 per cent were from medium TEB and 24.3 per cent of the respondents were from low TEB.

10 The families of the respondents have been categorized into three: Joint Family (where either more than one generation or more than one married sibling live in the same house hold), Nuclear Family (wherein the family unit consists of spouses and their dependent children), and Others (those families which are neither joint nor nuclear). Indicative of the general trend in modern Indian Society, both samples contain more persons from the nuclear family (51.35 per cent and 41.56 per cent) and 39.19 per cent and 38.96 per cent respectively from the joint family. The rest 9. 46 per cent and 19.48 per cent respectively, stated that they live neither in a joint family nor in a nuclear family. However, in the present sample, there are substantial numbers of joint families where members jointly engage in business.

11 In sample A, 87.84 per cent of the respondents were from the business category and 12.16 per cent were professionals. It is seen from the statistics related to the total number of searches conducted in the region that the majority of the respondents searched were business people and the number of professionals searched was less than 10 per cent. In sample B, 87.01 per cent were business people and 12.99 per cent were professionals.

12 Efforts were made to examine the influence of the familial business or their professional backgrounds on respondents. The respondents were divided into three groups, based on the data on their familial business or professional background: the first generation, the second generation and the third generation. If at least one of the parents was in the similar occupation as the respondent, then the person was categorized as the second generation. If at least one person from either of the maternal or paternal grand parents was also in similar occupations, then the person was categorized as third generation. If there is no similarity in occupational background in any of the above cases, the respondent was categorized as first generation. In sample A, 55.41 per cent, 29.73 per cent and 6.76 per cent were first, second and third generation respondents respectively. In the sample B, 52.70 per cent, 28.38 per cent and 18.92 per cent were first, second and third generation respondents respectively.

13 Data was also gathered regarding the geographical background of the respondents. They were asked to state the location of their continuous stay or principal place of business for the last fifteen years. In all cases, the location of the main business and the residence were in the same location. In the sample A, 56.76 per cent of the respondents stayed within the municipal limits (designated as town), 36.49 per cent of the respondents resided within the corporation limits (city) and 6.76 per cent

resided in the Panchayat area (village). 44.16 per cent of sample B were from the city, 48.05 per cent from the towns and 7.79 per cent of the respondents were from the village limits.

14 The perception of the search process and the consequent experiences may vary between persons who do business alone and those who engage in the business activity along with other partners or directors. The sample of searched respondents contained 47.30 per cent who were partners along with others in business. 13.51 per cent of the respondents were directors of Companies and the rest (39.19 per cent) were proprietors of their businesses. In the other sample, 60.81 per cent were proprietors and 22.97 per cent were partners in their businesses. 8.11 per cent each were either directors or salaried personnel in businesses. It is significant to note that most of the searched respondents were partners in the businesses, whereas most of the respondents in the unsearched sample were proprietors. It can be seen that 61 per cent of searched respondents did business jointly with others as against 31 per cent in the non-searched sample.

15 The court's observation is given in, Income Tax Report, Vol. 210, Page 786

16 In the report submitted by Vijay Kelkar to Government of India, it was mentioned that the practice of giving rewards has contributed to obtaining forced confessions of undisclosed income and seizure of money, jewellery, stock or other assets recorded in accounts or acquired from disclosed sources of income. However such claims are not generally made by officers as rewards are sanctioned after thorough scrutiny as per reward guidelines by a committee headed by very senior officers.

17 *Benami* means investing in assets in the names of other persons

18 As per the recent amendments in the Indian Income Tax Act., seizure of stock is not allowed

19 www.taxworld.org

20 It is customary for many people to keep one room in the house as a pooja room where photos and statues of deities are kept. No one enters this room wearing footwear. In fact, in many Indian houses, people remove their shoes while entering the houses.

21 It is very common among family owned businesses and also in the cases of partnership firms to have a person from the caste or sub caste of the promoters be appointed as the accounts officer or the auditor. The reason is not only the element of trust but also compelled by an obligation to give an opportunity to a person from one's own caste or sub caste.

22 Social exposure was measured based on the data on the extent of social activities engaged by the respondents

CHAPTER - 8

1 This is a term used by Erwin Goffman. According to him face is the image of the self that is presented. Face is what other assumes and it is the image that others see or consider to have been expressed by the actor. An internally consistent face is one whereby the actor is in face or maintains face

2 Cognitive dissonance is a theoretical concept propounded by Leon Festinger (Festinger,1957). The theory addresses competing, contradictory, or opposing elements of cognition and behaviour.

3 See for example, Tomasic R and Pentony B (1990) Defining Acceptable Tax Conduct, Discussion Paper 9 No.2), Centre for National Corporate Law Research, University of Canberra

4 The theory of circulation of elites by Pareto is significant here. Though the rulers change, the characteristics remain. Sometimes successive governments tend to adopt the traits of predecessors bringing out continuity in political culture consciously or unconsciously.

5 See the study by James Alm and Jorge Martinez-Vazquez, 'Institutions, Paradigms, and Tax Evasion in Developing and Transition Countries', in Martinez-Vazquez and Alm, eds., Public Finance in Developing and Transitional Countries (Cheltenham, UK: Edward Elgar, 2003)

CHAPTER - 9

1 Philip Genschel has examined this issue in detail (Genschel.2005). He did not find any indication that globalization spells the beginning of end of the national tax state. It is argued by scholars that the globalization process is making it more difficult to tax the full range of economic activities, hence making it increasingly difficult to attain 'fiscal sustainability' (Asher and Rajan (1999))

2 Eight fiscal termites were identified by Tanzi. They are a) electronic commerce and related transactions, b) use of electronic money, c) intra company trade, d) off-shore financial centres and tax havens, e) derivatives and hedge funds, f) inability to tax financial capital, g) growing foreign activities and h) foreign shopping.

3 Common strategy is to underprice sales to their affiliates in low-tax countries and to overprice purchase from them and thus shift taxable profits to those countries to reduce the tax burden.

4 See discussion in the context of US taxation (2009) by Tax Policy Center, Urban-Brookings Tax Policy Center, www.taxpolicycenter.org/briefing book. It is reported that the US tax system encourages US multinationals to locate assets and economic activity, and earn and realize profit, in other countries where taxes are lower.

NOTES

5 Steve Christen has examined this issue and suggested that if the factors such as simplicity and theoretical fidelity are considered, the formulary apportionment system could be a viable alternative to current arm's length pricing system.

6 Rudra has examined the issue of globalization and the decline of the welfare state in less-developed countries. See Rudra (2002).

7 As per the Report of the Indian Planning Commission 27.5 per cent of people are below poverty line in 2004-05. However World Bank estimates it at 42 per cent.

8 See Appendix-1 for the details of direct tax collections in India

9 Vito Tanzi (formerly with the World Bank) had suggested a 'Global Tax Organization'(GTO) that monitors and regulates taxation on international transactions.

ABBREVIATIONS

ANOVA	Analysis of Variance
CBDT	Central Board of Direct Taxes
EIC	East India Company
FRBM	Fiscal Responsibility and Budget Management
GST	Goods and Services Tax
GTO	Global Tax Organization
GTRAO	Global Tax Research and Analysis Organization
IMF	International Monetary Fund
IT	Income Tax
ITAT	Income Tax Appellate Tribunal
OECD	Organisation for Economic Co-operation and Development
PPERA	Political Parties Elections and Referendum Act
SD	Standard Deviation
TCMP	Taxpayer Compliance Measurement Program
TEB	Total Educational Background
US IRS	United States Internal Revenue Service
VDIS	Voluntary Disclosure of Income Scheme
TIE	Taxable Income Elasticity

APPENDIX-1

Table AT-6.1

Correlation for key variables

Attitude/Perception	AGE	EDN	OCC	TA	GEN	INC
Attitudes about tax system	NS	S**	NS	NS	NS	NS
Attitudes about tax policy	NS	S*	S*	NS	NS	NS
Attitudes about tax laws	NS	NS	NS	NS	NS	NS
Attitudes about tax administration	NS	NS	NS	NS	NS	NS
Perception of tax evasion as a crime	NS	NS	S*	NS	NS	NS
Perception of tax evasion of others	NS	NS	NS	NS	NS	NS
Role of the State	NS	NS	NS	S**	S**	NS
Redistribution by the State	NS	NS	NS	S*	S**	NS
Governance	NS	NS	NS	NS	S*	NS
Contribution to the individual	NS	NS	NS	S**	S**	NS
Return compliance	NS	NS	NS	NS	NS	NS
Income suppression	NS	NS	NS	NS	S**	NS

(EDN - Educational level; OCC - Occupation (Salary, Profession, Business); TA (level of tax awareness); GEN (Generational background); INC (Income level); NS (No significant correlation); S*(Significant correlation- at 0.05 level); S**(Significant correlation-at 0.01 level). Wherever there is significance, the same have been discussed in the relevant chapter.

Direct Tax - GDP Ratio (India)						
Year	Net collections of direct taxes (Rs.crore)	GDP at current market prices (Rs.crore)	Direct tax-gdp ratio	GDP Growth rate	Tax Growth Rate	Buoyancy Factor
1990-91	10947	568674	1.93%			
1991-92	15207	653117	2.33%	14.85%	38.91%	2.62
1992-93	18142	748367	2.42%	14.58%	19.30%	1.32
1993-94	20299	859220	2.36%	14.81%	11.89%	0.80
1994-95	26971	1012770	2.66%	17.87%	32.87%	1.84
1995-96	33564	1188012	2.83%	17.30%	24.44%	1.41
1996-97	38895	1368208	2.84%	15.17%	15.88%	1.05
1997-98	48280	1522547	3.17%	11.28%	24.13%	2.14
1998-99	46600	1740985	2.68%	14.35%	-3.48%	-0.24
99-2000	57959	1952035	2.97%	12.12%	24.38%	2.01
2000-01	68305	2102376	3.25%	7.70%	17.85%	2.32
2001-02	69198	2281058	3.03%	8.50%	1.31%	0.15
2002-03	83088	2458084	3.38%	7.76%	20.07%	2.59
2003-04	105088	2754621	3.81%	12.06%	26.48%	2.19
2004-05	132771	3149412	4.22%	14.33%	26.34%	1.84
2005-06	165208	3580344	4.61%	13.68%	24.43%	1.79
2006-07	230181	4129173	5.57%	15.33%	39.33%	2.57
2007-08	312213	4723400	6.61%	14.39%	35.64%	2.48
**2008-09	333818	5321753	6.27%	12.67%	6.92%	0.55

** Figures of 2008-09 are provisional, GDP for 2008-09 are based on Advance Estimates
GDP for 2007-08 is based on Revised Estimates

Table AT-9.1

(Source : Govt. of India, Ministry of Finance, Annual Report 2009-10)

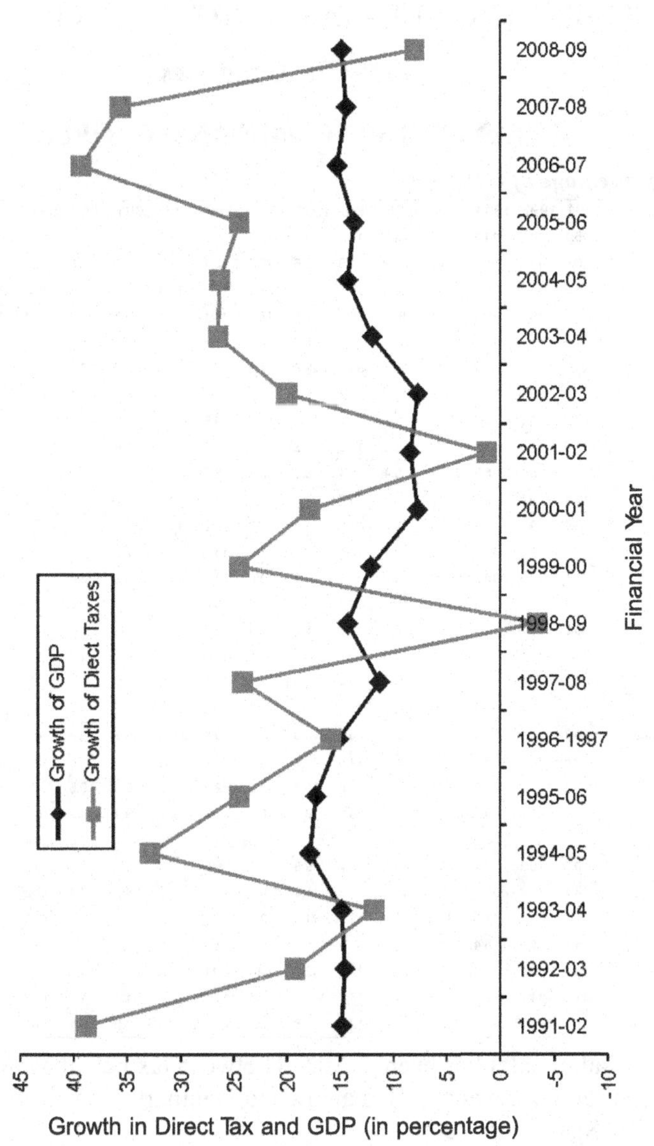

Table AT-9.2

(Source : Govt. of India, Ministry of Finance, Annual Report 2008-09)

PUBLIC FINANCE - TAXES - TOTAL TAX REVENUE

OECD Countries

TAXES ON INCOME AND PROFITS

As a percentage of GDP

	1991	1992	1993	1994	1995	1996	1997	1998	1999	2000	2001	2002	2003	2004	2005	2006	2007
Australia	15.1	14.7	14.6	15.2	15.9	16.6	16.5	17.7	18.3	18.1	16.7	17.2	17.3	18.2	18.2	18.1	..
Austria	10.6	11.1	11.3	10.3	10.8	11.8	12.6	12.8	12.4	12.1	13.9	12.9	12.7	12.5	11.9	12	12.6
Belgium	15.2	14.7	15.7	16	16.6	16.6	17	17.5	17.1	17.3	17.5	17.3	16.9	16.9	17.2	16.8	16.7
Canada	17.1	16.1	15.7	15.8	16.5	16.9	17.9	17.7	18.1	17.8	16.7	15.4	15.4	15.7	15.9	16.2	16.7
Czech Republic	..	..	10.3	9.7	9.4	8.1	8.7	8.1	8.3	8	8.6	9	9.5	9.5	9.1	9	8.7
Denmark [1]	27.7	28.2	29.1	30	30.1	30.2	29.8	29.4	29.6	29.8	28.7	28.5	28.8	29.6	31.1	29.5	29.3
Finland	17.2	16.2	15	16.4	16.5	18.2	17.7	18.1	17.8	20.3	18.2	18.1	17	16.8	16.8	16.6	16.9
France [1]	7.1	6.7	6.9	7	7	7.4	8.1	10.2	10.8	11.1	11.2	10.4	10	10.2	10.3	10.7	10.4
Germany	11.5	11.9	11.4	11	11.3	10.5	10.2	10.7	11.1	11.2	10.4	9.9	9.7	9.5	9.8	10.8	11.3
Greece	5.3	5.1	5.2	6	6.4	6.4	6.8	8.1	8.4	9.3	8	8	7.4	7.5	7.9	7.5	..
Hungary	12.4	9.8	9.5	9.1	8.6	8.7	8.3	8.4	8.9	9.2	9.7	10	9.3	8.9	8.8	9.1	10
Iceland	9.1	9.5	10.1	10.2	10.6	11.3	11.5	13	14.2	14.8	15.3	15.3	16	16.1	17.6	18.3	19
Ireland	12.9	13.2	13.7	14.1	12.7	13.2	13.1	12.9	13.1	13.2	12.2	11.1	11.3	11.9	11.7	12.7	12.5
Italy	13.8	15.2	15.6	14	14.2	14.5	15.3	13.6	14.4	14	14.3	13.4	12.9	12.9	12.9	14	14.8
Japan	14	12	11.5	10.3	10.3	10.2	10.1	9	8.4	9.4	9.1	8	7.9	8.4	9.3	9.9	10.6
Korea	5.8	5.8	5.7	5.9	6.2	6	5.5	6.4	5.3	6.8	6.4	6.2	7.1	6.9	7.5	7.9	9.1
Luxembourg	12.6	11.8	13.5	13.9	14.6	14.9	15.6	15.1	13.9	14.1	14.3	14.4	13.9	12.4	13	12.5	12.9
Mexico	4.7	5.2	5.5	5.2	4.1	4	4.6	4.7	5	5	5.2	5.2	5	4.7	4.8	5.2	5.7
Netherlands	15.1	14	14.7	12	10.9	11.1	10.7	10.3	10.2	10	10.1	10.2	9.4	9.2	10.8	10.7	11.1
New Zealand	20.7	21	21.1	22.3	22.4	20.7	20.9	19.4	19.4	20.2	19.5	20.5	20.4	21.6	23.6	22.8	22.3
Norway	14.8	13.2	13.3	14.2	14.3	14.8	15.7	15.7	16	19.2	19.3	18.8	18.5	20.1	21.4	22	20.7
Poland	7.6	11.2	12.3	11.3	11.1	10.6	10.4	10.2	9.9	9.7	9.5	9.6	6	5.9	6.4	7	..
Portugal	8	8.9	8.1	7.9	7.9	8.6	8.7	8.5	9.1	9.6	9.1	8.9	8.4	8.3	8.2	8.5	9.5
Slovak Republic	..	..	..	..	..	..	..	8.5	8.5	7	7	6.6	6.8	5.7	5.7	5.8	5.9
Spain [1]	10.2	10.1	9.8	9.3	9.4	9.2	9.8	9.4	9.6	9.8	9.7	10.1	9.8	9.9	10.6	11.4	12.6
Sweden	18.4	18	18.9	19.7	18.6	19.3	19.9	19.9	20.8	21.2	18.9	17.1	17.8	18.6	19.4	19.4	18.7
Switzerland	11.9	12.3	11.9	12.5	11.9	12.3	11.9	12.5	12	13.2	12.4	12.9	12.5	12.5	13	13.5	13.6
Turkey	5.4	5.4	5.4	4.9	4.8	5	5.7	7	7.3	7.1	7.5	6.1	6.1	5.3	5.3	5.3	5.6
United Kingdom	13.1	12.2	11.5	12	12.7	12.6	12.9	14	14	14.5	14.6	13.4	12.8	13	13.9	14.7	14.4
United States	11.9	11.8	12.1	12.3	12.8	13.5	14	14.4	14.6	15.1	14.1	11.7	11.2	11.4	12.7	13.5	13.9
OECD average	12.5	12.3	12.4	12.4	12.4	12.5	12.8	12.8	12.9	13.3	12.9	12.5	12.3	12.3	12.8	13	..

The capital transfer has been allocated between tax headings in proportion to the reported tax revenue. This applies to Denmark from 1990, France from 1992 and Spain from 2000.

OECD Factbook 2009: Economic, Environmental and Social Statistics - ISBN 92-64-05604-1 - © OECD 2009

Table AT-3.1

APPENDIX-2

RIGHTS AND DUTIES OF THE PERSON TO BE SEARCHED

Rights of the person to be searched

01. To see the warrant of authorization duly signed and sealed by the issuing authority.
02. To verify the identity of each member of the search party.
03 To have at least two respectable and independent residents of the locality as witnesses.
04. To have personal search of all members of the party before the start of the search and after conclusion of the search.
05. To insist on a personal search of females by another female only with strict regard to decency.
06. To have a copy of the *panchanama* togcthcr with all the annexures.
07. To put his own seals on the package containing the seized assets.
08. Woman having the occupancy of any apartment etc., to be searched has right to withdraw before the search party enters, if according to the customs she does not appear in public.
09. To call medical practitioner if he is not well.
10. To have his children permitted to go to school after examination of their bags.
11. To inspect the seals placed on various receptacles sealed in course of searches and subsequently re-opened by continuation of searches.
12. To have the facility of having meals etc., at the normal time.
13. To have a copy of any statement before it is used against him in an assessment or prosecution proceedings.
14. To have inspection of the books of accounts, etc., seized or to take extracts there from in the presence of any of the authorized officers or any other person empowered by him.
15. To make an application objecting to the approval given by the Commissioner of Income-tax for retention of books and documents beyond 180 days from the date of the seizure.

Party's Signature Witness 1.

Date:
Time: Witness 2.

Countersigned by
Authorised Officer

Note

A copy of this invariably be served on the person searched in the presence of witnesses by the authorized officer of the search party on entering the premises.

Duties of the person to be searched

01. To allow free and unhindered ingress into the premises.
02. To see the warrant of authorization and put signature on the same.
03. To identify all receptacles in which assets or books of account and documents are kept and to hand over keys to such receptacles to the Authorized Officer.
04. To identify and explain the ownership of the assets, books of the account and documents found in the premises.
05. To identify every individual in the premises and to explain their relationship to the person being searched. He should not mislead by impersonation. If he cheats by pretending to be some other person or knowingly substitutes one for another, it is an offence punishable u/s.416 of the Indian Penal Code.
06. Not to allow or encourage the entry of any unauthorized person into the premises.
07. Not to remove any article from its place without notice or knowledge of the authorized officer. If secretes or destroys documents with the intention of preventing the same from being produced or used as evidence before the Courts or public servant, he shall be punishable with imprisonment or fine or both in accordance with Section 204 of the Indian Penal Code.
08. To answer all queries truthfully and to the best of his knowledge. He should not allow any third party to either interfere or prompt while statement is being recorded by the Authorized Officer. In doing so, he should keep in mind that :
    i. If he refuses to answer a question on a subject relevant to the search operation he shall be punishable with imprisonment or fine or both, u/s.179 of the Indian Penal Code.
    ii. Being legally bound by an oath of affirmation to state the truth, if he makes a false statement, he shall be punishable with imprisonment or fine or both, u/s.181 of the Indian Penal Code.
    iii. Similarly, if he provides evidence which is false and which he knows or believes to be false, he is liable to be punished with imprisonment or fine or both, u/s. 191 of the Indian Penal Code.
09. To fix his signature on the recorded statement, inventories, *panchanama*.
10. To ensure that peace is maintained throughout the duration of the search, and to cooperate with the search party in all respects so that the search action is concluded at the earliest and in a peaceful manner.
11. Similar cooperation should be extended even after the search action is over, so as to enable the Authorized Officer to complete necessary follow-up investigations at the earliest.

Party's Signature — Witness 1.
Date:
Time: — Witness 2.

Authorised Officer

Note

A copy of this invariably be served on the person searched in the presence of witnesses by the authorized officer of the search party on entering the premises.

REFERENCES

Aaron, Henry J and Joel Slemrod (eds). (2004). *The Crisis in Tax Administration.* Washington DC: Brooking Institution Press.

Abel, T. (1977). "The Operation Called Verstehen", in Dallmayr F. and Mc Carthy T. (Eds.), *Understanding and Social Enquiry.* Notre Dame: University of Notre Dame Press.

Acharya, S. (1983). "Unaccounted Economy in India". A Critical Review of Some Recent Estimates, *Economic and Political Weekly* (Dec).

Acharya, Shankar N. (1985). *Aspects of the Black Economy in India,* Report of a study by NIPFP, Ministry of Finance, Government of India.

Adams, Charles. (1994). *For Good and Evil. The Impact of Taxes on the Course of Civilization,* Madison Books, pp. 530.

Adams, Charles. (1998). *Those dirty rotten taxes. The Tax revolts that built America,* NY: Free Press.

Adams, J.S. (1965). *Inequity in Social Exchange,* in L Berkowitz (ed), *Advances in Experimental Social Psychology*. New York: Academic Press. pp 167-299.

Ahmad, Ehtisham and Nicholas Stern. (1991). *The Theory and Practice of Tax Reform in Developing Countries.* Cambridge: Cambridge University Press.

Ajzen, I and Fishbein M. (1980). *Understanding Attitudes and Predicting Behavior.* Englewood Cliffs, NJ.: Prentice Hall.

Allingham, M. and Sandmo A. (1972). "Income Tax Evasion, a theoretical analysis", *Journal of Public Economics,* I. pp.323-338.

Alm J, Mc Callin N.J. (1990). Tax Avoidance and Tax Evasion as a Joint Portfolio Choice, *Public Finance,* 45, No.2. pp.193-200.

Alm, James. (1991). "A Perspective on the experimental analysis of taxpayer reporting", *The Accounting Review*. Vol 66. pp 577-593.

Alm, J.G.H. Mc Clelland and W.D. Schulze. (1992). Why do people pay taxes? *Journal of Public Economics* 48. pp.21-48.

Alm, J.I. Sanchez and A. De Juan. (1995). Economic and Non-economic factors in Tax Compliance, *Kyklos,* 48. p.3-18.

Alm, J.M.B. Cronshaw and M. Mckee. (1993). Tax Compliance with Endogenous Audit Selection Rules, *Kyklos,* 1. pp.27-45.

Alm, J. and B. Togler. (2004). 'Culture differences and Tax Morale in the United States and the Europe'. CREMA Working Paper No.14, Base, *Centre for Research in Economics, Management and the Arts*.

Alms, Jackson J.B. and M. Mckee. (1992). Deterrence and Beyond. Towards a kinder, gentler IRS in J Slemrod (ed), *Why People Pay Taxes*. Ann Arbor: University of Michigan Press. pp.311-329.

Altekar, A.S. (1962). *State and Government in Ancient India*, 4th Edn., Delhi: Motilal Banarsidas.

Amity, Shlaes. (1999). *The Greedy Hand. How Taxes Drive Americans Crazy and What to do about it*. New York: Random

Asher, Mukul. (1997). 'Reforming the Tax System in Indonesia' in Wayne Thirsk, ed. *Tax Reform in Developing Countries*. Washington: World Bank.

Asher, Mukul G AND Ramkishen S Rajan. (1999). '*Globalization and tax systems: Implications for developing countries with particular reference to South East Asia'*. Adelaide University, Centre for International Economic Studies, Discussion Paper 99/23.

Backhaus, Jurgen G. (2002). *Fiscal Sociology. What For?* [WWW] http://www.uni-berfurt.de/finanzwissenschaft/downl/valedictory_lecture.pdf. P 10.

Bagai, S.S. (1991). *Black Money in India*, Bombay, Bagai Tax Law Services (P) Ltd.

Bahl, R. and J. Martinez-Vazquez. (1992). *The Nexus of Tax Administration and Tax Policy in Jamaica and Guatemala*. In Casanegra de Jantscher and R. M. Bird (eds.), *Improving Tax Administration in Developing Countries*, IMF, Washington DC: p66-110.

Bailey DR. (1989). "How Widespread is Tax Cheating in America", *Indian Journal of Criminology*, 17. p.3-5.

Baldry, J.C. (1986). Tax Evasion is not a Gamble: A Report on Two Experiments, *Economic Letters*, 22, pp.333-5

Banerjee, Ramnath. (1922). *Fiscal Policy in India.,* Indian Reprint (1986). Delhi: Gian Publishing Company.

Bank, Steven A, Kirk J. Stark, and Joseph J. Thorndike. (2008). *War and Taxes*, Urban Institute Press.

Bartley, Hildreth and James A.Richardson (eds). (1998). *Handbook on Taxation.* New York: Basel

Basham, A.L. (1954). *The Wonder that was India*. London: P.S.

Bazart, Cecile and Michael Pickhardt. (2009). *Fighting Income Tax Evasion with Positive Rewards*. Experimental Evidence, Document de Recherche, Lameta.

Beck P.J, J S Davis and W. O Jung. (1991). Experimental evidence on Taxpayer Reporting Behaviour. *The Accounting Review*, 66. p.535-558.

Beck, P. J and W. Jung. (1989). *Taxpayers' reporting decisions and auditing under information assymmetry*. Vol 64(3). Pp. 468-87.

Becker, G.S. (1968). Crime and Punishment. An Economic Approach, *Journal of Political Economy*, 76. pp.169-217.

Beito, D.T. (1989). *Taxpayers in Revolt*. Chapel Hill. NC: University of North Carolina Press.

REFERENCES

Bell, R.R. (1981). *Worlds of Friendships*, Baverly Hills, C.A., Sage.

Benjamini, Y. and S.Maital. (1985). *Optimal Tax Evasion and Optimal Tax Evasion Policy*, quoted in Webley and Others (1991) *Tax Evasion. An Experimental Approach*, Cambridge University Press: Cambridge.

Berger, P. and T. Luckmann. (1967). *The Social Construction of Reality*, London: Allen Lane.

Bhattacharya, Dilip K. (1999). On the economic rationale of estimating the hidden economy, *The Economy Journal*, 109/456, 348-359.

Bird, Richard M and Eric M. Zolt. (2003). *Introduction to Tax Policy Design and Development*, Paper for the course on Practical Issues of Tax Policy in Developing Countries, World Bank, April-May, p.4.

Bird, Richard M. (2003). *Administrative Dimension of Tax Reform*. Paper prepared for World Bank, April.

Birnbaum, M. (1973). The devil rides again. Correlation as an index of fit, *Psychological Bulletin,* 79. pp.239-242.

Blau, P. (1964). *Exchange and Power in Social Life*, New York: Wiley.

Block Water and Michael Walker. (1984). *Taxation. International Perspective*, Canada: The Fraser Institute.

Blumenthal, M and J. Slemrod. (1992). "The Compliance Cost of the U.S Individual Income Tax System. A Second Look After Tax Reform", *National Tax Journal, No.45.*

Blumenthal, M, Charles Christian and Joel Slemrod. (2001). Do normative appeals affect tax compliance ? 'Evidence from a controlled experiment in Minnesota', *National Tax Journal*, vol.54, pp 125-138

Blumer, H. (1969). *Symbolic Interactionism Perspective or Method?* Englewood Cliffs. NJ: Prentice Hall.

Blumer, H. (1975). Sociological Implications of the thought of G.H. Mead. In Jesser, C.J. *Social Theory Revisited*, Hinsdale: Dryden Press. p.325.

Bowles, Samuel and Herbert Gintis. (2000). *Reciprocity, Self-interest, and the Welfare State,* [WWW], http://folk.uio.no/hmehlum/NOPEC/vol26102.pdf.

Brennan Geoffrey and Buchanan James, M. (1980). *The Power to Tax. Analytical Foundations of a Fiscal Constitution*. Cambridge: Cambridge University Press.

Brooks Neil. (2000). *Taxation and Citizenship,* Paper presented to a 'Breakfast on the Hill' sponsored by the humanities and Social Science Federation, Canada, http://www.hssfc.ca/English/policyandadvocacy.

Brown, Karen B and Mary Louise Fellows (eds). (1996). *Taxing America*, New York: New York University Press.

Brownie, Elliot W. (2004). *Federal Taxation in America. A Short History*, Woodrow Wilson Center Press and Cambridge University Press.

Buchanan M. (1959). *Positive Economics, Welfare Economics and Political Economy: Selected Essays*. Chapel Hill: University of North Carolina Press. pp.105-124.

Buchanan M. (1977). *Freedom in Constitutional Contract. Perspectives of a Political Economist*. Texas: A&M University Press.

Bulmer Martin (Ed). (1978). *Social Policy Research*, London: Mac Millan.

Burke Peter. (1980). *Sociology and History*. London: George Allen & Unwin.

Burton, John. '*Underground Economy in Britain*', in Owen Lippert and Michael Walker (eds), *The Underground Economy. Global Evidence Of Its Size And Impact*, Canada ,The Fraser Institute Vancouver, British Columbia

Callon M. (1998). An essay on *framing and overflowing*: economic externalities revisited by sociology in John Law, *On Markets* http://www.vub.ac.be/SOCO/tesa/RENCOM/Callon%20(1998)%20on%20framing%20 and%20overflowing.pdf

Callon M and Law I. (1997). After the Individual in Society. Lessons on Collectivity from Science, Technology and Society, *Canadian Journal of Sociology*, 22(2). Pp.165-182.

Callon M. (1991). *Techno-economic networks and Irreversibility* in J Law, *A Sociology of Monsters* (ed.). London: Routledge. pp 132-164.

Caroll John, S. (1992). *How Taxpayers Think about Their Taxes*. Frames and Values, Joel Slemrod (Ed.). *Why People Pay Taxes*. Ann Arbor: The University of Michigan Press.

Caroll John, S. (1987). Compliance with the Law. A Decision Making Approach to Taxpaying', *Law and Human Behaviour* 11. pp.319-35.

Carter, Michael, R and Marco Castillo. (2002). *The Economic Impacts of Altruism, trust and Reciprocity. An Experimental Approach to social capital*, http://aem.cornell.edu/special_programs/AFSNRM/Pew/Papers/Carter/CarteMay2002 TeamMeetingPaper.pdf

Chandra Bipin. (1992). '*The Colonial Legacy*' in Bimal Jalan (Ed). *The Indian Economy*, Viking Penguin India, New Delhi,

Chelliah, R. (1969). *Fiscal Policy in Developing Countries*. London: George Allen and Unwin Ltd.

Chelliah, Raja J., Hessel J. Baas, and Margaret R. Kelly. (1975). "Tax Ratios and Tax Effort in Developing Countries." *IMF Staff Papers*.

Chopra, O.P. (1985). *Tax Ethics. Unaccounted Income or Black Money*. The Norm of the Day, New Delhi, Inter India.

Chu, Ke-young, Hamid Davoodi, and Sanjeev Gupta. (2000). 'Income Distribution and Tax and Government Spending Policies in Developing Countries', *IMF Working paper*, 00/62.

Chugh Ram, L. and Uppal, J. S. (1999). *Black Economy in India*, New Delhi, Tata McGraw-Hill.

REFERENCES

Ciadini, R B. '*Social Motivations to Comply, Norms, Values and Principles'*, in Roth, JA, Scholz, J T and Witte, AD (eds). *Taxpayer Compliance Social Science Perspectives*. (1989), Vol 2, Philadelphia, PA: University of Pennsylvania Press. pp 200-227

Citrin J. (1979). "Do People Want Something for Nothing: Public Opinion on Taxes and Government Spending", *National Tax Journal* (Supplement)32, June,pp113-130.

Clotfelter,C. (1983). "Tax evasion and tax rates: an analysis of individual returns". *The review of Economics and Statistics* (August), 363-373.

Cohn Bernard. (1997). *Colonialism and its Forms of Knowledge. The British India,* New Delhi, Oxford, (Reprint 2002) pp. 57-75.

Cowell Frank, A. (1990). *Cheating the Government: The Economics of Evasion,* Cambridge, The MIT Press.

Craib Ian. (1992). *Modern Social Theory From Parsons to Habemas*, Brighton, Harvester Wheatsheaf.

Craib Ian. (1997). *Classical Social Theory*, New York, Oxford University Press.

Cross, R. B. and G. K. Shaw. (1982). "The Evasion-Avoidance choice: A Suggested Approach". *National Tax Journal,* 34, pp. 489-491.

Cuccia, Andrew D. (1994). 'Economics of tax compliance', What do we know and where do we go?, *Journal of Accounting Literature*, 1994, Vol 13.

Cummings, RG, J Martinez-Vazquez, M Mckee and Togler. (2004). *Effects of culture on tax compliance*. A cross check of experimental and survey evidence, CREMA Working paper 13, Basel, Centre for Research in Economics and Management and the Arts.

Das-Gupta Arindam and Mookherjee Dilip. (1998). *Incentives and Institutional Reform in Tax Enforcement. An Analysis of Development Country Experience,* New Delhi: Oxford University Press.

Directorate of Inspection. (1985). '*Hundred Years of Income-tax Department 1886-1985*', Central Board of Direct Taxes, Department of Revenue, New Delhi

Doff, Gordon. (1971). *History and Social Theory*, New York: Double day.

Duarte, Joseph S. (1974). *The Income Tax is Obsolete*, NewYork:Aarlington House Pub.

Dubin, Jeffrey A and Louise L Wilde. (1988). 'An empirical analysis of federal income tax auditing and compliance', *National Tax Journal*, No.41, pp 61-74.

Duck, Steve and Daniel Perlman (Eds.). (1985). *Understanding Personal Relationship. An Inter-disciplinary Approach*, California, Sage.

Durkheim, Emile. (1893) and (1938). Quoted in Anthony Giddens (1971) *Capitalism and Modern Social Theory*. An Analysis of the Writings of Marx, Durkheim and Max Weber.

Eccles, Robert G. (1981). “The Quasi Firm in the Construction Industry”, *Journal of Economic Behaviour and Organization*, 2, 335-357.

Eicher Jeffrey D. (2001). Attitudes towards income taxes: Regional Vs National, *Tax Notes*, Vol.90, No.8, Feb 19.

Eisenstein, Louis. (1961). *The Ideologies of Taxation*, New York: The Ronald Press Company.

Eiser Richard. (1986). *Social Psychology. Attitudes, Cognition* and *Social Behaviour*, Cambridge University Press.

Erard Brian. (1992). *The Influence of Tax Audits on Reporting Behaviour in Joel Slemrod, Why People Pay Taxes.* Ann Arbor: The University of Michigan Press.

Etzioni, A. (1986). Tax Evasion and Perceptions of Tax Fairness. A Research Note, *Journal of Applied Behavioural Science*, 22, pp.177-85.

Etzioni, A. (1988). *The Moral Dimension.* New York: Free Press.

Falk, Armin and Urs Fischbacher. (2001). *A Theory of reciprocity.* CESifo working paper, No.457.

Falkinger J. 'Tax Evasion and Equity. A Theoretical Analysis', *Public Finance*, 1988, Vol.43, 388-395.

Falkinger, J and Watter, H. (1991). 'Rewards versus Penalties, On a New Policy on Tax Evasion' *Public Finance Quarterly*, 19. pp 67-79.

Fehr, Ernst and Klaus M Schmidt. (2000). “Fairness, Incentives and Contractual Choices”, *European Economic Review*, 44 (4-6):1057-68.

Fehr, Ernst and Simon Gachter. (2000). “Fairness and Retaliation, The Economics of Reciprocity”, *Journal of Economic Perspectives*, No.14. pp 159-181.

Feige, E.L. (1990). "Defining and Estimating Underground and Informal Economiesm, The New Institutional Economics Approach. *In World Development*, vol. 18, no. 7 (July).

Feinstein, Jonathan S. (1990). 'Detection Controlled Estimation'. *Journal of Law and Economics*, Vol 33. pp 233-76.

Feinstein, Jonathan S. (1999). 'Approaches for estimating non-compliance: Examples from federal taxation in the United States', *The Economic Journal*, Vol.109, pp 360-369.

Festinger, L. (1957). *A Theory of Cognitive Dissonance*, Evanston, III.: Row, Peterson.

Fischer, C.M., Wartick, M. and Mark, M.M. (1992). 'Detection probability and taxpayer compliance. A Literature Review', *Journal of Accounting Literature*, Vol.11, pp 1-46.

Frey, Bruno S and Stephan Meier. (2004). Pro-social behaviour, Reciprocity or Both?, *Journal of Economic Behaviour and Organization*, No.54, pp 65-68

REFERENCES

Friedland, N. and Others. (1978). "A Simulation Study of Income Tax Evasion", *Journal of Public Economics*, 10, 107-116.

Friedland, N. (1982). "A note on Tax Evasion as a Function of the Quality of Information about the Magnitude and Creditability of Threatened Fines", Some Preliminary Research. *Journal of Applied Psychology*, 12, pp.54-99.

Friedland, N., S Maital and A Rutenberg. (1978). 'A Simulation study of Income Tax evasion', *Journal of Public Economics*.10:107-116.

Frisby, D. (1992). *Simmel and Since: Essays on Georg Simmel's Social Theory,* London, Routledge.

Furnham Andrian and Lewis Alan. (1986). *Economic Mind. The Social Psychology of Economic Behaviour*. Sussex: Harvester Press.

Galeotti, G and Marrelli M (eds). (1992). *Design and Reform of Taxation Policy*, Dordrecht: Kluwer Academic Publishers.

Garret, G and D Mitchell. (2001). 'Globalization, Government Spending and Taxation in the OECD', *European Journal of Political Research* 39(2): 145-177.

Genschel, Phillip. (2005). Globalization and the transformation of the tax state, *European Review*, 13: 53-71.

Ghoshal, U.N. (1976). *Contributions to the History of the Hindu Revenue Systems* mentioned V.A. Smith and P. Spear (1988) *Oxford History of India*, London, Oxford.

Giddens, A. (1990). *The Consequences of Modernity*, Oxford, Polity Press.

Giese, S. and A. Hoffmann. (2000). *Tax Evasion and Risky Investments in an Intertemporal Context*. An Experimental Study, *Discussion Paper, No.30.* Berlin: Humbold-Universitat zu.

Glaser, B. and Strauss, A. (1968). *The Discovery of Grounded Theory*, London, Weidenfeld & Nicholson.

Glaser, Barney, G. and Strauss Anselm. (1967). *The Discovery of the Grounded Theory. Strategies of Qualitative Research*, Chicago, Aldine.

Goffman E. (1971). *Frame Analysis. An Essay on the organization of experience.* Chicago: North Eastern University Press.

Goldscheid Rudolph. (1925). *A Sociological Approach to the Problems of Public Finance in Richard.* A. Musgrave and Alan, T. Peacock (Eds.) (1967), Classics in Public Finance, London, Mac Millan.

Goldschield, Rudolf. (1919). 'Quoted in Jurgen G Backaus(2001) Fiscal Sociology' What for? *American Journal of Economics and Sociology*, 2002, vol. 61, issue 1, p.10.

Goode, W. and Hatt, P. (1952). *Methods in Social Research*, New York: McGraw-Hill.

Gottfredson, Michael R and Travis Hirschi. (1990). *A General Theory of Crime*, Stanford: Stanford University Press

Gouldner, A. (1960). The Norm of Reciprocity: A Preliminary Statement, *American Sociological Review*, 25: 161-178.

Government of India. (1971). *Report of the Direct Taxes Enquiry Committee* (N. N. Wanchoo) Ministry of Finance.

Government of India. (1985). *Aspects of Black Economy in India*, Report of the National Institute of Public Finance and Policy, New Delhi.

Graetz,M J and L.L Wilde. (1985). "The economy of tax compliance. Facts and Fantasy", *National Tax Journal* 38, 355.

Granovetter, M. (1985). Economic Action and Social Structure. The Problem of Embeddedness', *American Journal of Sociology*, 91, 481-510.

Granovetter, M and Swedberg, R (eds). (1992). *The Sociology of Economic Life.* Boulder: Westview Press

Granovetter, M. (1985). "Economic action and Social structure. The Problem of Embeddedness", *American Journal of Sociology*,91(3): 481-510.

Grapperhaus Ferdinand, H. M. (1998). *Tax Tales from the Second Millennium: 1938-1998*, Netherlands: IBFD.

Groenland, A.G. and Van Veldhoven, G.M. (1983). "Tax evasion Behaviour. A Psychological Approach", *Journal of Economic Psychology,* 3, 129-44.

Gruber Jonathan and Emmanuel Saez. (2000). *The Elasticity of Taxable Income.* Evidence and Implications (NBER Working Paper No. 7512), http://www.nber.org/digest/jul00/w7512.html

Gupta Poonam and Sanjeev Gupta. (1983). *Black Economy: A Review of Methodologies* in Monga G.S. and V.J. Sanctis, *The Unsanctioned Economy in India*, Bombay: Himalaya.

Gupta, H. R. (1981). *Search and Seizure:Law and Practice*, Delhi, Legal Study Circle.

Hans Gerth and C. Wright Mills. (Eds.). (1958). *From Max Weber: Essays in Sociology*, New York: Oxford University Press.

Hansard (1860) 'Statement of Sir C.E. Trevelyan of the circumstances connected with his recall from India', quoted in http://en.wikipedia.org/wikei/sir_charlestrevelyan.

Hansen, Susan B. (1983). *The Politics of Taxation*, New York: Praeger

Harberger, Arnold C. (1989). '*Lessons of tax reform from the experiences of Uruguay*, Indonesia, and Chile', in Malcom Gillis. ed.(1989) Tax Reform in Developing Countries. Durham NC: Duke University Press.

Harriss, Lowell C. (1972). *Innovations in Tax Policy and other Essays*, Connecticut:John C Lincoln Institution.

Hasseldine John, D. and Kaplan Steven, E. (1992). *The Effect of Different Sanction Communications on Hypothetical Taxpayer Compliance.* Policy Implications from New Zealand, Public Finance Vol 47(1), pp. 45-60.

REFERENCES

Healey Joseph, R. (1999). *Statistics: A Toolfor Social Research*. New York: Wadsworth Publishing Company.

Hessing, D. J. and Elffers, H. (1987). *Economic Man or Social Man*?, in H Brandstatter and E. Kirchler (Eds.) Economic Psychology, Linz: Trauner. pp. 195-203.

Hessing, D.J. Henk Elffers, Henry Robben and Paul Webley. (1992). *Does Deterrence Deter*? Measuring the Effect of Deterrence on Tax Compliance in Field Studies and Experimental Studies.In Joel Slemrod (Ed.) *Why People Pay Taxes*. Ann Arbor: The University of Michigan Press.

Hettich, Walter and Winer Stanley, L. (1999). *Democratic Choice and Taxation. A Theoretical and Empirical Analysis*. Cambridge: University of Cambridge.

Hirschi, Travis and Michael R. Gottfredson. (2000). *Age and the Explanation of Crime*, in Crutchfield, Robert D., George S Bridges, Joseph G Weis, and Charis Kurbin, eds, *Crime Readings*, Thousand Oaks, Pine Forge Press: 138-142

Holmes, Oliver Wendell. (1995). *The collected works of Justice Holmes* (S Novick, ed). Chicago: Chicago Universiy Press

Hood, R. and Sparks, R. (1970). *Key Issues in Criminology*. New York: McGraw-Hill.

Indian Public Finance Statistics 2008-09, Government of India. http://finmin.nic.in/reports/index.html

Internal Revenue Service. (1984). *Taxpayer Attitudes Study*, Washington DC, Internal Revenue Service

Jackson, B. and Jones. (1985). "Salience of Tax Evasion Penalties versus detection risk". *Journal of the American Taxation Association*, Spring 7-17.

Jain Sugan, C. and Garg Rachana (Eds.). (1994). *Taxation and Tax Planning*, Jaipur, Arihant.

James Alm and Jorge Martinez-Vazquez. '*Institutions, Paradigms, and Tax Evasion in Developing and Transition Countries*', in Martinez-Vazquez and Alm, eds., *Public Finance in Developing and Transitional Countries* (Cheltenham, UK: Edward Elgar, 2003)

James Alm, Betty Jackson and Michael Mukee. (1992). *Deterrence and Beyond*. Towards a Kinder, Gentler IRS in Joel Slemrod, *Why People Pay Taxes*. Ann Arbor: The University of Michigan Press.

James, Simon and Christopher Nobes. (1994). *The Economics of Taxation*. New York: Prentice Hall.

Jary, David and Julia Jary. (1991). *Collins Dictionary of Sociology, Glasgow*, Harper - Collins.

Jayaswal, K.P. (1955). *Hindu Polity*, Bangalore: Bangalore Printing and Publishing Company, p.319.

Jenkins, Glenn P and Edwin N Forlemu. (1993). '*Enhancing Voluntary Compliance by Reducing Compliance Costs. A Taxpayer Service Approach*', Development

Discussion Paper No.448, Tax Research Series No.1. Cambridge: Harward University.

John, Hasseldine and Zhuhong Li. (1999). 'More Tax Evasion Research Required in New Millennium', *Crime, Law & Social Change*, Vol.31, p.91.

Johnston, David Cay (2003). *Perfectly legal. The Covert Campaign to Rig Our Tax System to the Benefit of the Super Rich and Cheat Every Body Else*: New York.

Kabra, K. N. (1982). *The Black Economy in India: Problems and Policies*, Delhi: Chanakya.

Kahn, R.L. and Antonucci, T.C. (1980). *Convoys over the life course*. Attachment, Rules and Social Support in P. Baltes and O. Brim (Eds.) *Life Span Development and Behaviour* (Vol. 3) Academic Press Net Work.

Kaldor, N. K. (1955) *An Expenditure Tax*, London, Allen & Unwin Ltd.

Kaldor, N. K. (1956). *Indian Tax Reform*: *Report of a Survey*, Ministry of Finance, Dept of Economic Affairs.

Kane, P.V. (1968). *History of Dharmasasthra*, Vol. I, Part I, Poona, Bhandarkar Oriental Research Institute.

Kantona,G. *Psychological Economics* , Amsterdam: Elsevier

Kapadia, S. J. (1975). *Search and Seizure under the Income Tax Act 1961*, Bombay, BCAS, Taxmann.

Kaplan, S.E. and Reckers, P.M.J. (1985). “A study of Tax Evasion Judgements”, *National Tax Journal*, 38: 97-102.

Kasper,W and M.E. Streit. (1999). *Institutional economics: Social Order and Social Policy*, Cheltenham, UK: Edward Elgar

Kelley, H.H. (1967). *Attributor Theory in Psychology* quoted in Webley and others (1991) *Tax Evasion: An Experimental Approach*. Cambridge: Cambridge University Press, p.18.

Kevin Avram. (1999). *The History of Taxation: inciting rebellion and civic discord*, http://www.enterstageright.com/archive/articles/0899taxrel.htm

Keynes. *Collected works*, XXI, P.245.

Kharabanda, S.R. (2000). *Search, Seizure and Survey* under Income Tax Law, Delhi.: Commercial Law Publishers (India) Pvt. Ltd., p.2.

Kinsey Karyl. (1984). '*Survey Data on Tax Compliance*: *A Compendium and Review*', Working Paper 8716, Chicago.: American Bar Association

Kinsey, Karyl.A. (1984). *Theories and Models of Tax Cheating*, Tax payer compliance working paper 84-2. Chicago, I.L.: American Bar Foundation.

Kinsey Karyl, A. (1992). *Deterrence and Alienation effect of IRS Enforcement* in Joel Slemrod (Ed.). *Why people Pay Taxes*. Ann Arbor.: University of Michigan Press.

REFERENCES

Kirchler, Erich Boris Maciejovsky, Friedrich Schneider. (2001). *'Every day representations of Tax Avoidance, Tax Evasion, and Tax Flight: Do Legal Differences Matter?* No.4, http://www.econ.jku.at/papers/2001/wp0104.pdf

Klepper, S and D. Nagin. (1989a). The Anatomy of Tax Evasion, *Journal of Law, Economics and Organization*, Vol 5(1). pp 1-24.

Klepper, S and Nagin D. (1989b). *The criminal deterrence literature:Implications for research on tax compliance*', in Taxpayer Compliance Vol.2: *Social Science Perspectives*, edited by Jeffrey A Roth and John T Scholz, Philadelphia: University of Philadelphia Press. pp 126-55.

Kumar, Arun. (1999). *The Black Economy in India*, New Delhi: Penguin.

Kumar, Narendra. (1987). *Taxing Reforms and Distribution of Revenue: A Study of Centre-State Financial Relations under Indian Constitution*, New Delhi, Deep and Deep.

Kurt J. Beron, Helen V. Tauchen and Ann Dryden Witte. (1992). The Effects of Audits and Socioeconomic Variables on Compliance in Joel Slemrod (Ed.) *Why People Pay Taxes*. Ann Arbor: The University of Michigan Press.

Laffer, Arther B and Jan P Seymour. (1979). *The Economics of Tax Revolt : A Reader*, New York: Harcourt Brace.

Lewis, Alan. (1982). *The Psychology of Taxation*, Martin Robertson, Oxford.

Lief, Muten. (1992). '*Income Tax Reform*' in Vito Tanzi, ed., Fiscal Policies in Economies in Transition (Washington), IMF, , P.187.

Listhaug, O and A. H. Miller. (1985). "Public Support for Tax Evasion: Self Interest or Symbolic Politics", *European Journal of Political Research*, 13,265-82.

Long Susan, B. (1992). *Commentary* in Joel Slemrod (Ed.) *Why People Pay Taxes*. Ann Arbor.: The University of Michigan Press.

Maciejovsky, B, E Kircher and H Schwarzenberger. (2001). *Mental accounting and the impact of tax penalty and audit frequency on the declaration of income*: An empirical analysis. Discussion paper No.16, quoted in Torgler, B (2000) Vertical and exchange equity in a tax morale experiment, Working Paper 3 , University of Basel.

Mahajan, V. D. (1978). *British Rule in India and After.* New Delhi, S. Chand & Co.

Malcolm Gillis. (1985). 'Micro- and Macro-economics of Tax Reform. Indonesia' *Journal of Development Economics*, 19:221-54.

Marshall Gordon. (1998). *Oxford Dictionary of Sociology*. Oxford.: Oxford University Press.

Maslove, Allan M. (1993). *Fairness in Taxation: Exploring the Principles.* Toronto: University of Toronto Press.

Mason, R. and L.D Calvin. (1978). A study of admitted tax evasion, *Law and Society Review*, 13, 73-89.

Mason, Robert and Lyle D Calvin. (1984). *National Tax Journal*, No.37, pp 489-96.

Massey, D.S. (2002). *A Brief History of Human Society*, The Origin and Role of Emotion in Social Life', *American Sociological Review*, Vol.67, pp 1-67.

Mathew, Sibichen K. (2000). Taxation in India : Social structural determinants in distinguishable periods in Indian History, South Indian History Congress, Madurai.

Mathew, Sibichen K. (2004). Tax evasion and health, in Philomena Mariadas (Ed.), *Health, Illness and Society in the new millennium,* New Delhi, Viva Books.

Mathew, Sibichen K. (2004). Tax Evasion and Tax Enforcement : A sociological study of Income Tax Raids in India, *unpublished PhD dissertation,* Bharathiar University.

Mathew, Sibichen K. (2008). Tax Compliance in India: The attitudes and perceptions of tax payers and their influence on tax behavior, Bangalore, Indian Institute of Management *Occasional paper series,* March 2008.

McGee, Robert W. (1994). Is Tax Evasion Unethical? *Kansas Law Review*, Winter Issue, pp 411-435.

McIntyre, Michael J, (1975) *Institutionalizing the process of tax reform: A comparative analysis,* Amsterdam, International Bureau of Fiscal Documentation.

Mead, G.H. (1934). *Mind, Self and Society*. Chicago : Chicago University Press, referred in Schwartz, Howard and Jerry Jacob Qualitative Sociology: *A Method to Madness*, New York Free Press.

Merton, R. (1949). *Social Theory and Social Structure*. Glencoe: Free Press.

Michael, J McIntyre and Oliver Oldman. (1975). *Institutionalizing the Process of Tax Reform*: A Comparative Analysis. Amsterdam: *International Bureau of Fiscal Documentation*.

Milliron, Valerie C and Daniel R Toy. (1988). 'Tax compliance: An investigation of key features' *The Journal of the American Taxation Association*, No.41, pp84-104

Minh Le, Tuan Blanca Moreno-Dodson and Jeep Rojchaichaninthorn. (2008). *Expanding Taxable Capacity and Reaching Revenue Potential: Cross-Country Analysis*, The World Bank Poverty Reduction and Economic Management Network Policy Research Working Paper 4559.

Mirus, Rolf and Roger S. Smith, (1997) *Canada's Underground Economy, Measurement and Implications*, in Owen Lippert and Michael Walker (eds), *The Underground Economy*: Global evidence of its size and impact, Canada, *The Fraser Institute Vancouver*, British Columbia

Mitchell, Daniel J. (2002). *The Correct Way to Measure the Revenue Impact of Changes in Tax Rates*, http://www.heritage.org/Research/Taxes/BG1544.cfm

Monga G.S. and V.J. Sanctis. (1983). *The Unsanctioned Economy in India*, Bombay: Himalaya

REFERENCES

Mukherji Partha Nath (Ed.). (2000). *Methodology in Social Research: Dilemmas and Perspectives*, New Delhi, Sage, pp. 13-86.

Musgrave, Richard. (1980). *An Essay on Fiscal Sociology*, in H. Aron and M. Boskins (Eds), *The Economics of Taxation*. Washington DC: Brookings Institution.

Musgrave Richard. (1996). *Public Finance in a Democratic Society*: Vol III, The Foundations of Taxation and Expenditure, USA: Edward Elgar p.3.

Musgrave, Richard and Alan Peacock. (Eds). (1957). *Classics in the Theory of Public Finance*. New York: Mac Millan.

Musgrave, Richard. (1997). 'Reconsidering the fiscal role of Government'. *The American Economic Review*, 87(2): p.158.

Narayanan, S. (1983). *Honey for Caesar: Loopholes in Tax Avoidance and Evasion*, Delhi: Taxmann.

National Tax Research Center (1987). '*Confronting the Problems of Tax Avoidance and Evasion: Selected Countries in Asia and the Pacific*'. Project of the Study Group on Asian Tax Administration and Research, Philippines, Department of Finance

Nikolaieff George. (1968). A *Taxation and the Economy*. New York: The H W Wilson Company.

Niyogi, J. P. (1929). *The Evolution of the Indian Income Tax*. London: P. S. King & Sons Ltd.

Ockenfels, A and J Weimann. (1999). "Types and patterns: An Experimental East-West German Comparison of Co-operation and Solidarity", *Journal of Public Economics*,71, 275-287

Owen, Lippert and Michael Walker (eds), *The Underground Economy: Global Evidence Of Its Size And Impact, Canada*, The Fraser Institute Vancouver, British Columbia.

Page, B I. (1983). *Who gets what form of government*? Berkeley, CA: University of California Press. pp.22-40.

Panda, Jagannath and P Venkateshwar. (1991). *Corporate Taxation in India*. Jaipur: Pointer.

Paris, Roland. (2001). *Global Taxation and the Transformation of the State*, Research paper, *Annual convention of the American Political Science Association*, Sanfrancisco, August 30-September 2.

Parsons, T. and Shils, E. (1951). *Towards a General Theory of Action*. Cambridge: Harvard University Press.

Parsons, Talcott. (1964). *The theory of Social and Economic Organisation*, Talcott Parsons (Ed.): New York, Free Press.

Pechman, Joseph A. (1986). *The Rich, the Poor and the Taxes they pay*. Colorado: Westview

Pen, J. (1987). *Expanding budgets in a stagnating economy*:The experience of the

1970s. In C.S. Maier (ed.), Changing Boundaries of the Political. Cambridge: Cambridge University press.

Peters Guy, B. (1986). "Upon My Honour:The Causes and Extent of Tax Evasion", *Journal of Public Policy,* 6,3.

Peters Guy, B. (1991). *The Politics of Taxation: A Comparative Perspective.* Cambridge: Blackwell.

Phillip Sawicki. (1983). *Income Tax Compliance: A Report of the ABA Section of Taxation*, Philadelphia, American Bar Association.

Pillarisetti, Ram, J. (2003). 'World Income Distribution and Tax Reform: What Tax Systems Do Low-Income Countries Need?' *Development Policy Review*, 2003, 21(3):301-317.

Polanyi K. (1944). *The Great Transformation*, Boston: Beacon Press.

Pollack, Sheldon D. (1996). *The Failure of the US Tax Policy.* Pennsylvania State: University Press.

Pollack, Sheldon D. (2003). *Refinancing America: The Republican Anti tax Agenda,* State University of New York Press.

Pommerehne,WW, Hert A and Frey BS. (1994). Tax Morale, Tax Evasion, and the Choice of Policy Instruments in Different Political Systems, *Public Finance*, 49 suppt, pp52-59

Porcano T M. (1988). Correlates of tax evasion. *Journal of Economic Psychology*, 9, pp.47-67

Porcano, T. and C Price. (1993). The Effects of Social Stigmatization on Tax Evasion', *Advances in Taxation*, Vol.5, pp197-217

Poterba, James. (1987). 'Tax evasion and capital gains taxation'. *American Economic Review*, No.77,pp.234-39.

Pragar, Madhav Shankar (1920) *'The Indian Income tax: its history, theory and practice',* Ph.D Thesis submitted to the Columbia University http://www.archieve.org/details/indianincometax i00paga

Prest, A. R. (1979). *The Taxable Capacity of a Country. Taxation and Economic Development.* London School of Economics and Political Science: London, UK

Raj, A. K. (1987). *The Historic Evolution of Corporate Tax in India*, Calcutta, Firma KLM Pvt. Ltd.

Ramsey F.P. (1927). A Contribution to the Theory of Taxation, *Economic Journal*, Vol. 37, No 145, pp.47-61.

Randles, Sally. (2001). *'On Economic Sociology, Competition and Markets'*, Discussion paper 53, The University of Manchester and UMIST, Centre for Research on Innovation and competition.

Raychaudhari, Tapan and Irfan Habib. (1982). *The Cambridge Economic History of*

REFERENCES

India, Vol I, C1200-C 1750, Cambridge.

Reckers Philip M J, Debra L Sanders and Stephen J Roark. (1994). The Influence of Ethical Attitudes on Taxpayer Compliance, *National Tax Journal*, Vol.47, No.4, pp 825-36.

Report of the Joint Economic Committee, US Congress, Gorbachev's Economic Plans, vol. 1, Washington, DC, 1987, pp. 213-229.

Report of the Joint Economic Committee, Washington, Congress of the United States, April, 1986, http://www.house.gov/jec/fiscal/tx-grwth/reagtxct/reagtxct.htm.

Report of the Raja J. Chelliah Committee. (1991). 6.140, New Delhi, Govt. of India.

Report of the Transparency International(UK), 'Corruption and the funding of UK Political Parties', October 2006.

Report of the Wanchoo Committee 2.9 (1971) New Delhi, Govt. of India.

Richardson, M and A J Sawyer. A Taxonomy of the tax compliance literature: Further findings, problems and prospects' (2001) Vol 16, *Australian Tax Forum,* pp 137-320.

Robson, Alex. (2005). *The Costs of Taxation*, Perspectives on Tax Reform (8), Canberra, CIS Policy Monograph 68. p.ix.

Roording J. (1996). The Punishment of the Tax Fraud, *Criminal Law Review*, April, pp240-9.

Rose Richard and Terence Karran. (1987). *Taxation by Political Inertia.* London: Allen and Unwin.

Roth, J A , Scholz, J T and Witte A D (eds). (1989). *Taxpayer Compliance: An Agenda for Research*, Vol.1. Philadelphia PA: University of Pennsylvania Press.

Rudra, N. (2002). Globalization and the decline of the Welfare States in Less-Developed Countries, *International Organization* 56(2): 411-445.

Rush Brook, Williams, L.F. (1985). *India in 1917-18, Socio - Political and Economic Developments,* Vol. I, Delhi, Anmol p. 69 (Reprint).

Sabine, B. E. V. (1966). *A History of Income Tax.* London: Allen & Unwin.

Sandford, Cedric ed. (1993). *Successful Tax Reform: Lessons from an Analysis of Tax Reform in Six Countries*, Washington: IMF.

Sandford, C.T. (1973). *Hidden Costs of Taxation*, Institute of Fiscal Studies

Sawicki Phillip. (1983). *Income Tax Compliance: A Report of the ABA Section of Taxation*, Philadelphia , American Bar Association

Scheider Friedrich, Kausik Chaudhuri and Sumana Chatterjee. (2003). *The Size and Development of the Indian Shadow Economy and a comparison with other 18 Asian countries: An empirical investigation*, Working Paper No. 0302, Department of Economics, Johannes.:Kepler University, Cinz

Schmolders, G. (1970). Quoted in Benno Torgler. (2002). *Vertical and exchange Equity in a Tax Morale Experiment*, WWZ-Discussion paper 02/02, Basel:WWZ, WWW.unibas.ch/wwz/wipo/portraits/torgler.htm

Schumpeter, Joseph Alois. (1953). '*Aufsatze zur soziologie*' English translation by W F

Stolper and Richard A Musgrave in *International Economic papers*, Vol.IV, London: Macmillan. (1954).

Schumpeter, Joseph, Alois. (1954). *History of Economic Analysis*, Oxford.: Oxford University Press.

Schumpeter, Joseph Alois. (1976). *Capitalism, Socialism and Democracy*, London: Unwin University Press.

Schwartz Howard and Jacobs Jerry. (1979). *Qualitative Sociology. A Method to Madness*, New York.: The Free Press.

Schwartz, R.D. and S Orleans. (1967). On Legal Sanctions. *University of Chicago Law Review*, 34, pp.282-300.

Sears, D.O. and J Citrin. (1985). *Tax Revolt, Something for nothing in California.* Enlarged ed. Cambridge, MA: Harward University Press.

Sheffrin, Steven, M. and Robert K. Triest. (1992). *Can Brute Deterrence Backfire*? Perceptions and Attitudes in Tax Payer Compliance in Joel Slemrod (ed) *why people pay taxes?* Ann Arbour: The University of Michigan Press.

Shireen, Moosvi. (1987). *The Economy of the Mughal Empire, C 1595: A Statistical Study*, Delhi.

Shu, Wei. (1992). Income Tax Evasion and Enforcement. A Purely Theoretical Analysis of Chinese Income Tax System, *Public Finance* Vol. 47(2). pp.287-302.

Simmel, Georg. (1900). *Philosopie des Geldes Leipzig* referred in Anthony Giddens (1971). *Capitalism and Modern Social Theory. An Analysis of the Writings of Marx, Durkheim and Weber*. Cambridge.: Cambridge University Press.

Singer Milton. (1996). *The Indian Joint Family in Modern Industry in Singer, Milton and Bernard S Cohn Structure and Change in Indian Society*, New Delhi, Rawat (Indian Reprint).

Singh, K.S. (Ed.). (1997). *People of India: Tamil Nadu*, New Delhi, Anthropological Survey of India.

Slemrod Joel (Ed.). (1992). *Why People Pay Taxes*? *Tax Compliance and Enforcement*. Ann Arbor, Michigan.: The University of Michigan Press.

Slemrod Joel and Bakija John. (1996). *Taxing Ourselves. A Citizen's Guide to the Great Debate Over Tax Reform*. Cambridge.: The MIT Press.

Slemrod, Joel. (Winter 1990). "Optimal Taxation and Optimal Tax Systems". *Journal of Economic Perspectives* 4 15778.

Slemrod,Joel. (1985). "An empirical test for tax evasion", *Review of Economics and Statistics*, No.67, pp 232-38.

REFERENCES

Smelser, N.J and R Swedberg (eds.). (1994). *The Handbook of Economic Sociology*, Princeton, N.J.: Princeton University Press.

Smith, H.J. and T R. Tyler. (1996) "Justice and Power", *European Journal of Social Psychology*, Vol 26, pp 171-200.

Smith, Adam. (1776). *The Wealth of Nations*, Book V, Chapter II, Part II, P.310 edited by E. Cannan, Methuen. (1950).

Smith, K.W. and K.A. Kinsey (1987). "Understanding Taxpaying Behaviour", *A Conceptual framework with Implications for Research Law and Society Review* 21:639-63.

Smith, Kent, W. (1990). 'Integrating three perspectives on tax compliance-A sequential model', *Criminal Justice and Behaviour*, No.17, 350-69.

Smith, Kent, W. (1992). *Reciprocity and Fairness*. Positive Incentives for Tax Compliance. In Joel Slemrod (Ed.) *Why People Pay Taxes,* The University of Michigan Press.

Smith, Kent, W. and K.A Kinsey. (1987). "Understanding Tax Payer Behaviour" A Conceptual Framework with Implications for Research, *Law and Society Review*, 21, pp. 639-663.

Smith, V.A. and P. Spear. (1988). *The Oxford History of India*, 4th Edn. London: Oxford, p.111.

Sobel, Lester A. (1979). *The Great American Tax Revolt*, New York: Facts on File.

Song, Young-dahl and Tinsley E. Yarbrough. (1978). "Tax Ethics and Tax Payer Attitudes", A Survey, *Public Administration Review*, 38 No.5, pp 442-52.

Spicer, M W. (1986). 'Civilization at a Discount: The Problem of Tax Evasion', *National Tax Journal*, No.39

Spicer, M W and J E Thomas. (1982). "Audit Probabilities and the tax evasion decision", An experimental approach, *Journal of Economic psychology*, 2:241-245

Starr, Tim. (2001). The Myth of the Social Contract, No Treason: *A Journal of Liberty*, www.no-treason.com.

Stein, Herbert (ed). (1988). *Tax Policy in the twenty first century*, New York: John Wiley and Sons.

Stigler, George J. *The Theory of Economic Regulation. Bell J. Econ.* (Spring 1971). 2, 3:21.

Stones Julious. (1966). *Social Dimensions of Law and Justice*, Bombay, Tripathi.

Stotsky, Janet G. and Asegedech WoldeMariam. (1997). "Tax Effort in Sub-Saharan Africa." IMF Working Paper. The International Monetary Fund: Washington, DC.

Stratton, S. (2004 February 9). 'Taxpayer advocate Addresses disclosure, withholding' Tax Notes 714.

Subramanian, N. (1988). *Search, Seizure, Summons, Survey and Settlement Commission,* New Delhi, Snowhite, p.151.

Suman, H. (1974). *Direct Taxation and Economic Growth in India*, New Delhi, Sterling.

Sury, M. M. (1997). *The Indian Tax System*, Delhi, Indian Tax Institute.

Sutherland, E. H. (1940). "White Collar Criminality". *American Sociological Review*, 5:pp.1-12.

Sutherland, E. H. (1949). *White Collar Crime.* New York: Holt, Rinehart & Winston.

Swedberg, R. (1989). 'Joseph A Schumpeter and the tradition of Economic Sociology', *Journal of Institutional and Theoretical Economics*, 145(3) Sept 508-24.

Swedberg, R. (1990). *Economics and Sociology: Redefining the boundaries; conversations with economists and sociologists*, Princeton NJ: Princeton University Press

Swedberg, R. (1991a). *Joseph A Schumpeter, His Life and Work.* Cambridge: Polity Press

Swedberg, R. (1991b). ' Major traditions in Economic Sociology', *Annual Review of Sociology*, 17, 251-76.

Swedberg, R. (1998). *Max Weber and the idea of economic sociology*, Princeton, N.J: Princeton University Press.

Tan L M. "Taxpayers' Perception of the Fairness in Tax System" A Preliminary Study (1998), Vol 4, *New Zealand Journal of Taxation Law and Policy*, pp 59-71.

Tanzi, Vito. (1987). *Quantitative Characteristics of the Tax Systems of Developing Countries*, in David Newbery and Nicolas Stern, eds., The Theory of Taxation for Developing Countries, World Bank, Oxford University Press

Tanzi Vito. (1998). 'The impact of Economic Globalization on Taxation'. International Bureau of Fiscal Documentation Bulletin, August/September, pp 338-43.

Tanzi Vito. (1998). "Corruption Around the World". *IMF Staff Papers*. Washington, D.C.: International Monetary Fund.

Tanzi Vito. (2000). 'Governance, Corruption and Public Finance:An Overview' in Schiavo Campo, S (Ed.), *Governance, Corruption and Public Finance*, www.adb.org-kimpraswil.go.id.

Tanzi Vito. (2000). 'Globalization, Technological Developments and the Work of Fiscal Termites'. IMF Working Paper, November.

Taylor, Natalie. (2003). 'Understanding taxpayer attitudes through understanding taxpayer identities', in V Braithwaite (ed) *Taxing Democracy: Understanding tax avoidance and evasion*, London, Ashgate, pp 71-92

Thapar, Romila. (1963). *Asoka and the Decline of Mauryas*: Delhi

Thirsk, Wayne. (1990). 'Recent Experience with Tax Reform in Developing Countries', *Ricerche Economiche*, April-September.

REFERENCES

Tittle, Charles. (1980). *Sanctions and Social Deviance:The Question of Deterrence.* New York:Praeger.

Tomasic R and Pentony B. (1990). 'Defining Acceptable Tax Conduct', Discussion Paper (No.2), Centre for National Corporate Law Research, University of Canberra.

Tomkins, C., Packman,C., Russel, S and Colville, I. (2001). Managing Tax Regimes. A call for research, *Public Administration*, Vol. 79(3), pp. 751-58.

Torgler B. (2001). Is tax evasion never justifiable? *Journal of Public Finance and Public Choice*, 19, 143-168.

Torgler B, C A Schaltegger, and M. Schaffner. (2003). Is forgiveness divine? 'A Cross-cultural comparison of tax amnesties', *Swiss Journal of Economics and Statistics*, 139,375-396.

Torgler B. (2005). *Tax Morale in Latin America*, http://ideas.repec.org/a/kap/pubcho/v122y2005i1p133-157.html

Torgler B. (2003). *Does culture matter*? Tax morale in an East-West German comparison, *Finanz Archiv* 59, 504-528.

Trivedi, Umashankar V, Mohammed Shehata, and Bernadette Lynn. (2003). 'Impact of Personal and Situational factors on taxpayer compliance'. An experimental analysis, *Journal of Business Ethics*, Vol 47, No.3, pp 175-197.

Turner Jonathan, H. (1987). Reprinted (2002). *The Structure of Sociological Theory*, Jaipur, Ravath.

Vatter, Harold G and John Walker F (eds). (1996). *History of US Economy since World War II*, New York, ME Sharpe.

Vihanto Martti. (2003). "Tax Evasion and the Psychology of Social Contract", *Journal of Socio-Economics*, 32,2, pp111-125.

Vogel,J. (1974). "Taxation and Public Opinion in Sweden", An Interpretation of Recent Survey Data, *National Tax Journal*, 27, pp 499-513.

Wagner, Richard E. (1999). *States and the Crafting of Souls: Mind, Society, and Fiscal Sociology*, http:/mason.gmu/~rwagner/erfurt fiscal sociology1.pdf.

Wallschtzky, I.G. (1984). "Possible causes of tax evasion". *Journal of Economic Psychology*, 5, 371-384.

Warneryd, K E, and Walerud B. (1982). "Taxes and economic behaviour", Some interview data on tax cheating in Sweden. *Journal of Economic Psychology*, 2, pp. 187-211.

Warsham, R.G. (Spring 1996). "The Effect of Tax Authority Behaviour on Tax Compliance: A Procedural Justice Approach", *Journal of the American Taxation Association*, Vol.18, No.2, 19-39.

Weber, M. (1968). *Economy and Society. An Interpretative Sociology*, ed. by Roth, G and Wittich, C., Berkeley: University of California Press.

Weber, M. (1922). Referred in H Gerth and C Wright Mills (1958). *From Max Weber Essays in Sociology*, New York, Oxford.

Webley Paul, Robben Henry, Elffers Henk, and Dick Hessing. (1991). *Tax Evasion. An Experimental Approach*, Cambridge.: Cambridge University Press.

Webley, P. (1987). 'Audit Probabilities and Tax Evasion in a Business Simulation', *Economic Letters*, 25:pp.267-270.

Webley, P. and Halstead, S. (1986). "Tax Evasion on the Micro: Significant Simulations or Expedient Experiments", *Journal of Interdisciplinary Economics* I,pp.87-100.

Webley, P. (1985). 'Tax Evasion During a Small Business Simulation', in H Brandstatter and E Kirchler(eds.), *Economic Psychology,* Linz:Trauner:pp.233-242.

Wei, Shang-Jin. (1997). *Why is Corruption So Much More Taxing than Tax? Arbitrariness Kills*. Cambridge, Massachusetts: National Bureau of Economic Research.

Weigel R, D Hessing and H Elfers. (1987). 'Tax Evasion Research: A Critical Appraisal and Theoretical Model', *Journal of Economic Psychology*, Vol.8, pp 215-235

Wilensky, H.L. (1976). *'The New Corporatism: Centralization and the Welfare State'*, Beverly Hills, Sage.

Williams Rushbrook, L.F. (1985). *India in 1917-18, Socio-Political and Economic Developments*, Delhi, Anmol.

Winkler, Raymundo. The Size and Some Effects of the Underground Economy in Mexico, in Owen Lippert and Michael Walker (eds), The Underground Economy: Global evidence of its size and impact, Canada, The Fraser Institute Vancouver, British Columbia

Winnings, M C. (1993). "Ignorance is Bliss, Especially for the Tax Evader", *Journal of Criminal Law and Criminology*, 84(3), Fall, pp575-603.

Witte, A.D. and D.F. Woodbury. (1985). "The Effect of Tax Laws and Tax Administration on Tax Compliance: The case of the U.S. Individual Income Tax", *National Tax Journal* 38: 1-14.

Wolff, Kurt, H. (Ed). (1950). *The Sociology of Georg Simmel*, New York, Free Press.

World Bank. (1997). *'World Development Report 1997'*: The State in Changing World. Washington, DC: The World Bank Group.

World Bank. (1998). *'World Development Indicators 1998'*, Washington DC: World Bank

World Bank. (2005). *'Global Monitoring Report 2005: Millennium Development Goals'*, From Consensus to Momentum. 280. World Bank: Washington, DC.

Yancey, W. (1988). *Effect of Penalties on Under-reporting of taxable income*. Working Paper, Austin: University of Texas.

Zelizer, Julian E. (1988). *Taxing America*: Wiber D Mills, Congress and the State 1945-1975, Cambridge.

Index

INDEX

Excerpts from some feed backs (from among the many) on the first edition

'This is a wonderful book to be read by every citizen. A unique attempt'

(The Chartered Accountant)

'The lucid presentation with attractive text boxes, tables and cartoons make it readable even for a layman.'

(South Asian Journal of Management)

A scholarly work laced with humour (Taxindiaonline.com)

'This book will help in giving a clear understanding of the subject to the readers.'

His Excellency Hans Raj Bharadwaj
(Governor of Karnataka)

'A pioneering attempt in the area of tax compliance research. Insights emerged from this fiscal-sociological study have enormous policy implications.'

T S Krishnamurthy
(Former Chief Election Commissioner of India)

'Author's contribution is appreciable as he dealt with a complex subject having economic and social relevance.'

Sunil Mitra
(Revenue Secretary, Government of India)

'I bought a copy of the book on the day it was released. Believe me, I spent the entire night reading the book. I used to burn the midnight oil, only to read detective novels so far'

B J Chacko
(Former Member, Central Board of Direct Taxes, India)

'A monumental piece of work'

(G G Shukla, Director General of Income Tax, National Academy of Direct Taxes, India)

ABOUT THE AUTHOR

Dr Sibichen K Mathew belongs to the 1992 batch of the Indian Revenue Service and currently work as the Commissioner of Income Tax. He is a Certified Fraud Examiner (CFE). After securing First Rank and Gold Medal for Post Graduate Examination in Sociology from University of Kerala, he completed his MPhil in Social Systems and environmental movements from Jawaharlal Nehru University(JNU) and PhD in Fiscal Sociology from Bharathiar University. He was a college topper and university rank holder in LLB from Karnataka State Law University. He secured an A Grade in the two-year Post Graduation in Public Policy and Management from the Indian Institute of Management (IIM), Bangalore. He has completed a course on International Public Policy at Maxwell School of Public Policy, Syracuse University and a course of Corporate Taxation and Advocacy Skills at Duke University, United States. He was a recipient of gold medals from the National Police Academy and National Academy of Direct Taxes, India. He is a blogger and leadership trainer. His areas of interest include Corporate Governance, White Collar Crimes and Cyber Sociology. His latest book 'When the Boss is Wrong: Making and Unmaking of Leader within You' has been a best seller.

Website: www.sibichen.in E mail: sibi5555@gmail.com

ABOUT THE BOOK

Can a complex subject like tax compliance be handled in such a simple manner? Sibichen K Mathew is successful in presenting his in-depth study on what makes people pay taxes or what prevents them from paying in a very interesting style. The author takes us through the history, the economics and the politics of taxation to dissect the interconnected issues related to tax evasion and tax enforcement. He forcefully argues that the economic models are unable to fully explain the behaviour of taxpayers. For, if the tax laws are complex, the human mind is much more complex to yield to the economic models. His arguments are supported by data on attitudes, perceptions and experience of taxpayers, many of whom declare themselves to be tax evaders. The author also analyzes the sociological and economic causes and consequences of tax evasion and tax enforcement in the global context. He, rightly, argues that taxation has larger sociological and political dimensions. He has brought in an array of arguments to conclusively show that paying taxes is not only a matter of money. It is much more than that. A host of factors impinge on the decision to pay taxes. Therefore, he underscores the need for an interdisciplinary approach to taxation. The insights gained from these incisive analyses have enormous implications for policy makers as well as tax administrators all over the world.

Printed in the United States
By Bookmasters